SMALL COLLEGE GUIDE
TO FINANCIAL HEALTH

WEATHERING
TURBULENT TIMES

MICHAEL K. TOWNSLEY, PH.D.

NACUBO

Library of Congress Cataloging-in-Publication Data

Townsley, Michael K.
  Small college guide : weathering turbulent times / by Michael K. Townsley.
     p. cm.
  Includes bibliographical references and index.
  ISBN 978-1-56972-048-6
  1. Small colleges--United States--Finance. 2. Small colleges--United States--
Administration. I. Title.
  LB2342.T69 2009
  378.1'06--dc22

                          2009014690

NACUBO saved the following resources by using Rolland Enviro 100 paper (FSC certified 100% post-consumer fiber, certified EcoLogo, processed chlorine free, FSC recycled, and manufactured using biogas energy) and New Leaf Reincarnation Matte (designated Ancient Forest Friendly and manufactured with electricity that is offset with Green-e®certified renewable energy certificates, 100% recycled fiber and 50% post-consumer waste, and processed chlorine free: 37 fully grown trees, 22,227 gallons of water, 2,357 pounds of solid waste, 4,574 pounds of air emissions, 15 pounds of suspended particles in the water, and 5,402 cubic feet of natural gas. Calculations based on research by Environmental Defense and other members of the Paper Task Force.

Design by Colburnhouse

National Association of College and University Business Officers
Washington, DC
www.nacubo.org

Printed in the United States of America

CONTENTS

Tools on CD
    Composite Financial Index Worksheet (Excel)
    Credit Hour Matrix (Excel)
    Forecast Model (Word)
    Strategic Initiative Testing Instrument (Excel)
    Responsibility-Centered Management Matrix (Excel)

LIST OF FIGURES

LIST OF TABLES

LIST OF INTERVIEWS

Crouch, William. President, Georgetown College, Georgetown, Kentucky (Interviewed September 13, 2001, and August 13, 2008).

DeColfmacher, Robert. Board Member, Southern New Hampshire University and former Manager of Learning Tools, Dover, New Hampshire (Interviewed November 3, 2009).

Fisher, James L. President Emeritus of Towson University, Towson, Maryland (Interviewed September 5, 2001, in Baltimore, Maryland).

Miller, Scott I. President, Wesley College, Dover, Delaware (Interviewed August 5, 2001, and October 18, 2008).

Minter, John. President, John Minter and Associates (E-mail interviewed January 15, 2001, August 4, 2008, and October 30, 2008).

Nelson, John. Senior Vice President, Moody's Investors Services, New York, New York (Interviewed November 8, 2001, August 7, 2008, and August 25, 2008).

Owens, Kathleen. President, Gwynedd-Mercy College, Gwynedd, Gwynedd Valley, Pennsylvania (Interviewed September 8, 2008).

Stevens, John. President and Chief Operating Officer, Stevens Consulting, Grantham, New Hampshire (Interviewed September 11, 2001, September 18, 2001, and November 13, 2008).

Townsley, Debra. President, Nichols College, Dudley, Massachusetts (Interviewed July 3 and 4, 2008).

Varsalona, Jack P. President, Wilmington University, Wilmington, Delaware (Interviewed September 8, 2008).

Wirth, Gary. Vice President and Director of Admissions, Goldey-Beacom College, Wilmington, Delaware (Interviewed October 11, 2001).

ACKNOWLEDGMENTS

This book would not have been possible without help from my wife, Dr. Debra Townsley, Cynthia Brown, Elizabeth Laird, Paul Cotnoir, and Donna Klinger at NACUBO. Debra Townsley, who is president of Nichols College, made many suggestions that enriched my insight about systematic approaches to managing a private college effectively and the challenges facing private colleges over the next several years. In addition, she edited my text and offered changes that improved its clarity. Ms. Cindy Brown helped put the book and footnotes into their final format. Ms. Elizabeth Laird edited the bibliography so that it would comply with basic citation standards. Dr. Paul Cotnoir helped prepare several of the tables in the book. I have the deepest appreciation for the guidance that Donna Klinger has provided me during the writing of this book and work that I have done for other projects with NACUBO. I extend my gratitude to everyone who supported me as I wrote this book.

ABOUT THE AUTHOR

Michael K. Townsley, Ph.D., is special assistant for finance to the president at Becker College in Worcester, Massachusetts. He has also provided financial strategies and forecasts for many private institutions on the east coast through his work as a senior consultant with Stevens Strategy. Previously he was president of the Pennsylvania Institute of Technology and senior vice president for finance and administration at Wilmington College.

Dr. Townsley's published works include *The Small College Guide to Financial Health: Beating the Odds*, *Strategic Turnarounds: A Guidebook for Colleges and Universities*, and other works on financial management, strategic management, and major issues facing colleges and universities. He is a frequent speaker at national conferences on finance and management in higher education.

Dr. Townsley holds a Ph.D. from the University of Pennsylvania.

CHAPTER 1

INTRODUCTION

In 2002, the big issues facing independent colleges and universities were the stock market crashes of 2000 and 2001, tuition pricing, demographics, market competition, and institutional size. Guess what? These problems have not gone away, and now there are new problems facing private institutions: energy costs, new federal regulations, credit crunch, and endowment spending. Of course, this is not the first time that murmurs of *dismal consequences* confronting independent institutions have passed through the media, professional journals, association meetings, faculty senates, and board meetings.

Do these dismal consequences mean that economic and financial problems have reached a critical mass and that the pace of mergers and closings for independent colleges and universities will speed up? There is no surefire way of making that prediction now because at this moment most private institutions seem to be financially stable.

Financial markets deteriorated so quickly during the last half of 2008 and early 2009 that many private institutions were blindsided by calls to repay debt balances, frozen debt markets, sharp declines in interest rates on cash investments, loss of major gifts from reliable donors, and severe strains on liquidity as private investments lost significant value. During the tech bubble burst and the effects of 9/11/2001, markets also experienced sudden losses, but the direct impact on cash was not as dramatic as the financial market debacle of 2008–2009. Private institutions scrambled for money when they suddenly discovered that they could not draw down cash from Commonfund, or they were unable to sell into the market to provide cash for operations.

Independent colleges took two years to recover from the crash of 2001. Figure 1.1 suggests that it will take at least two years for most private institutions to recover from the latest crash; the recovery could take longer because the earlier crash was not nearly as intense nor as long. Colleges and universities may struggle for three or four years as they try to recover their footing.

Moody's Investors Service provides support for the conclusion that private institutions will face considerable pressure on their financial stability over the next five years. According to Moody's *Higher Education Outlook*, issued in January 2009, pressure will come from:

- Threats to tuition and financial aid because parents and students will select less expensive public institutions, which will force private institutions to increase financial aid awards to attract the same number of students that enrolled the prior

FIGURE 1.1—PRIVATE COLLEGES AND UNIVERSITIES REPORTING DEFICITS FOR THE FISCAL YEARS 2001–2007

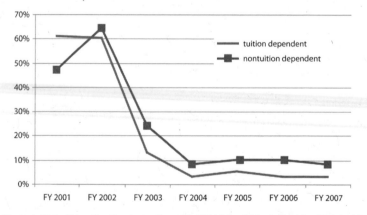

Source: "Strategic Higher Education Trends at a Glance" in JMA Higher Ed Stats. (Boulder, CO: John Minter and Associates, 2008), Management Ratios; Private Institutions, (Boulder, CO: John Minter and Associates, 2002).

year.[1] Less selective private colleges (these colleges tend to accept most applicants) are most vulnerable as students switch to public four-year colleges or community colleges.

- Loss of value in endowment funds have forced private colleges to postpone or cancel large capital projects planned to attract more students or new research funds. Investment losses have a direct impact on financial ratios (example debt to equity) that are required in debt covenants. Failure to maintain those ratios may mean that the college has to increase its reserves for debt thereby reducing funds for operations or they could be required to speed up their debt payback.[2]

- Loss of liquidity because endowments and gifts will generate less cash which will force colleges to cut expense budgets.[3]

- Debt at many major colleges was protected or insured by credit swaps which will require colleges to increase collateral to remain in compliance with credit agreements. Injecting new cash to support credit conditions is another factor that suctions cash from operations.[4]

- Volatility in credit markets will make it more difficult for colleges to refinance debt if they have to respond to a call provision, the debt has a balloon payment, or they have to rollover a debt package.[5]

Despite these five issues, Moody's believes that most colleges have the resources to withstand the threats that the chaotic debt market may pose to a private institution's financial stability.[6] They do expect that the keys to maintaining stability will depend on "operational management and governance."[7] Operational management will call for increased financial controls, difficult choices on debt versus program requirements, and slowing down the capital boom of the prior decade.[8] The current financial crisis calls for rapid decision making by colleges and universities, which they find to be difficult in the best of circumstances because they are consensus driven and decentralized.[9] Those institutions that can rapidly respond to change have the best chance of rebuilding their strength, according to Moody's.[10]

So, have private institutions reached a state where they are strong enough to withstand the gales of misfortune that might have sunk them several decades ago? There is no ready answer to this question. What this book does address is how to determine whether your institution has the financial and strategic resources to withstand major changes in the economics that drive institutional finances. The chapters, appendices, and CD-ROM tools provide a broad range of resources for estimating financial condition, reshaping strategy, designing turnarounds, and identifying the characteristics needed for presidents and chief management officers.

Independent colleges and universities do not have huge state bureaucracies or friends in the state legislature who will rescue them when times are tough. Survival of private institutions depends on strong leadership, mission- and market-driven strategies, and relentless assessment of a college's performance and position in the marketplace. The *Small College Guide to Financial Health: Weathering Turbulent Times* provides the reader with insights on how to deal with the uncertainties that can strengthen or severely weaken the financial and strategic stability of an independent institution. The book is organized to provide answers to questions about developing a strong and flexible independent college or university:

- The current state of finances for private colleges and universities—Chapter 2;

- The economics of markets, prices, and constraints that drive private institutions—Chapter 3;

- The financial structures found in most independent institutions—Chapter 4;

- The practices employed in a well-run business office—Chapter 5;

- Typical business models that are the framework for strategy, operations, and finance among private institutions—Chapter 6;

- The policies and procedures that presidents and chief administrative officers need to consider in managing their institution—Chapter 7;

- How to conduct strategic planning that will improve the performance of the institution—Chapter 8;

- The characteristics needed by a president to manage an independent institution successfully—Chapter 9;

- Warning signs of financial distress—Chapter 10;

- Case histories of several independent colleges that have failed—Chapter 11;

- Case histories of several independent colleges that conducted successful turnarounds and are now flourishing—Chapter 12;

- Major lessons from colleges that closed versus lessons from colleges that successfully rose above major threats to their existence—Chapter 13; and

- The set of principles that college presidents can apply to build and sustain strategic momentum—Chapter 14.

Customizable tools, forms, and templates on the CD will improve your understanding of financial analysis and guide the leadership of the college as you analyze your financial and strategic condition and formulate your strategic plans.

NOTES

1. Moody's Investors Service. *U.S. Higher Education Outlook.* (New York: Moody's Investors Service, January 2009), p. 1.
2. Ibid., pp. 3–5.
3. Ibid., p. 4.
4. Ibid., p. 6.
5. Ibid.
6. Ibid., p. 3–5.
7. Ibid., p. 7
8. Ibid.
9. Ibid.
10. Ibid.

CHAPTER 2

PRIVATE COLLEGES AND UNIVERSITIES: IN DANGER OR NOT?

Headlines are again proclaiming the demise of private colleges and universities. Do the media have a point, or is this merely fear mongering? Like all things in academia, there are no simple answers; but we need to understand the powerful dynamics that are reshaping the economy and that could restructure the market for higher education. The economic structure of independent colleges and universities does not necessarily place institutions in an inherently vulnerable position. However, they must become attuned to the threats embodied in frozen credit markets, rising tuition prices, falling home values, and mounting unemployment rates for parents and students.

How well a private institution is able to respond to the massive financial crisis of 2008–2009 depends on how well it is insulated from the vagaries of financial markets, the structure of its debt, its capacity to maintain enrollment, and whether the governance system will allow rapid changes in operational and strategic plans. As was mentioned in the preceding chapter, Moody's believes that most private colleges and universities will maintain their financial integrity if they are not trapped in a liquidity crisis unless they:

1. are unable to generate sufficient cash from investments or donations for operations;

FIGURE 2.1—COLLEGE COSTS AND DISPOSABLE PER CAPITA INCOME, 1998–1999 TO 2008–2009

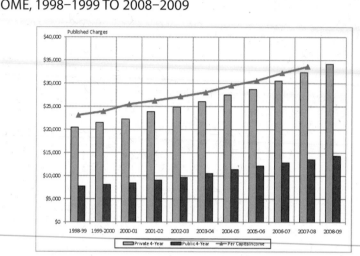

Reprinted with permission from Higher Education Landscape, *slide 84 (2009). New York: College Board.*

2. are prevented by market conditions from rolling over debt and forced to make a substantial and unexpected payback on loans;

3. find that enrollment has fallen so much that they face a massive deficit; or

4. have to make massive and unaffordable increases in financial aid packages to find new students and to keep the students that they have.

If there is a major vulnerability in higher education, it is the financial capacity of families and students to afford their education. Given that many families have paid for a college education from housing equity, investments, and private loans, the recent collapse in housing prices, the stock market, and credit markets has made a shambles of these means to pay for a college education. The tough news for families and for colleges is that families may have to rely on disposable* income if they want to send their children to college. It is tough news for independent colleges and universities because, as

*Disposable income is the money left after living expenses are deducted from pay.

Figure 2.1 shows, the gap between disposable income and private college costs is very small. How this minute gap between costs and income will affect the decision of a student to attend college, in particular an independent college, is not yet apparent.

Because the bedrock for most colleges is student tuition, presidents must figure out how to avoid pricing the college out of the market. In the past, competitive pricing was handled by fiddling with financial aid so that tuition prices were in line with peers (competitors, to the layperson). If students or their parents are unable to qualify for home equity loans, or cannot afford to further deplete their investment accounts, and are barred from private loans, then fiddling with financial aid is not enough. Colleges do not have much slack to increase financial aid because major increases in aid mean major reductions in cash flow to cover the fixed costs of operations. This invariably drives up the number of students needed to fund fixed and variable costs. Table 2.1 illustrates how average financial aid has changed relative to tuition, tuition revenue, and enrollment between 2002 and 2007. Except for small institutions, the average unfunded* financial aid award to students increased for the years 2002–2007. As a result, net tuition as a percentage of tuition declined except in the case of small institutions. It appears from these data that small colleges managed unfunded financial aid awards more closely than did medium or large institutions.

Table 2.1 on the next page points to a very large problem that could face colleges for the next decade. The problem is that despite increases in unfunded financial aid awards of nearly 9 percent, total enrollment shrank by a modest amount, which seems to be concentrated among small institutions. Enrollment at medium-sized and large institutions showed moderate, but definitely not explosive, growth. Will private colleges in regions where declining student markets combined with tighter credit requirements for loans be pushed in competitive price wars† just to keep enrollment static?

*Unfunded aid is the financial aid that is provided by the college but is not supported from endowment income or gifts.

†Competitive price wars could occur when colleges are forced to increase financial aid awards substantially; or, in the vernacular, they increase their tuition sales through large discounts.

TABLE 2.1—AVERAGES FOR TUITION RATE, FINANCIAL AID NET
TUITION, ENROLLMENT, AND NET TUITION REVENUE, 2002 AND 2007

INSTITUTIONS	SMALL	MEDIUM	LARGE	TOTAL
Average Tuition Rate				
2002	$7,739	$9,798	$9,930	$9,156
2007	$12,953	$12,289	$12,953	$12,732
Average Unfunded Financial Aid				
2002	$1,295	$2,808	$2,644	$2,249
2007	$2,039	$4,187	$4,043	$3,423
Unfunded Financial Aid as Percentage of Tuition				
2002	16.7%	28.7%	26.6%	24.6%
2007	15.7%	34.1%	31.2%	26.9%
Net Tuition Change				
2002	$6,444	$6,990	$7,286	$6,907
2007	$10,915	$8,102	$8,910	$9,309
Net Tuition as Percentage of Tuition				
2002	83.3%	71.3%	73.4%	75.4%
2007	84.3%	65.9%	68.8%	73.1%
Average Enrollment				
2002	423	1,341	4,868	2,512
2007	423	1,435	5,473	2,466
Growth Rate	−0.026%	1.4%	2.4%	−0.4%
Total Enrollment				
2002	252,816	419,839	2,497,291	3,169,946
2007	252,484	449,104	2,807,495	3,509,083
Growth Rate	−0.03%	1.40%	2.40%	−0.40%

Note: Total enrollment less than 1,000 students defines a small college; total enrollment equal to 1,000
and less than 2,000 students defines a medium-sized college; total enrollment equal to or greater than
2,000 students defines a large institution.

This chapter examines what is happening in the marketplace for private colleges and universities through four lenses: student markets,
student academic skills, operational costs, and financial condition of
independent institutions.

TABLE 2.2—PERCENTAGE CHANGE IN PUBLIC HIGH SCHOOL GRADUATES BY REGION FOR SELECTED YEARS 2004–2005 THROUGH 2017–2018

| Region | 2004–05 to 2011–12 | PROJECTIONS | |
		2011–12 to 2017–18	2004–05 to 2017–18
Northeast	0.4%	−5.3%	−4.9%
Midwest	0.9%	−1.2%	−0.3%
South	6.2%	10.7%	17.6%
West	8.9%	3.1%	12.3%
United States	4.5%	3.3%	7.9%

Reprinted with permission from U.S. Higher Education Outlook (2008). New York: Moody's Investors Service.

STUDENT MARKETS

Demographics, price, and academic skills are expected to have the greatest influence on student demand for private institutions. The previous section alludes to the impact that pricing may have on demand. This section delves more deeply into each factor.

Demographics

"Demographics" refer to the scale and population characteristics of the student market. Several striking changes will occur, as shown in Table 2.2: first, high school graduates through 2018 should increase in the South and West, while they will decline in the Northeast and Midwest; second, academic skills of first-year students will continue to be problematic; and third, high attrition rates will continue.

The chief feedstock for college tuition continues to be high school graduates, although adult students make a significant contribution to the bottom line. Table 2.2 indicates that the greatest regional change in high school graduates will occur in the Northeast, which has the largest number of private institutions in the country. Strong growth will take place in the South and West where public institutions tend to predominate. Moody's Investors Service is particularly "concerned that some regionally-dependent private universities are planning

TABLE 2.3—LARGEST DECLINES AND INCREASES BY REGION AND STATE: PUBLIC HIGH SCHOOL GRADUATES, 2004–2005 THROUGH 2017–2018

LARGEST DECLINES IN PUBLIC HIGH SCHOOL GRADUATES BY REGION

Northeast	2004–05 to 2011–12	2011–12 to 2017–18	2004–05 to 2017–18
Vermont	−13.5%	−12.1%	−23.9%
Rhode Island	−3.2%	−17.9%	-20.6%
Maine	−10.4%	−8.9%	−17.9%
Midwest			
North Dakota	−15.0%	−7.6%	−21.5%
South Dakota	−10.0%	−1.6%	−11.4%
Kansas	−7.6%	.2%	−5.5%
South			
Louisiana	−33.2%	−14.9%	−43.2%
Maryland	1.3%	−6.1%	−4.9%
West Virginia	−3.1%.	−7%	−3.7%
West			
Montana	−10.8%	−2.0%	−12.5%
Hawaii	−3.3%	−7.3%	−10.3%
Wyoming	−11.3%	1.4%	−10.1%

LARGEST INCREASES IN PUBLIC HIGH SCHOOL GRADUATES BY REGION

Northeast	2004–05 to 2011–12	2011–12 to 2017–18	2004–05 to 2017–18
New Jersey	9.4%.	5%	8.9%
Midwest			
Indiana	10.8%	4.2%	15.4%
Illinois	7.4%	−3.2%	4.0%
Iowa	1.7%	2.8%	4.6%
South			
Georgia	15.3%	17.7%	34.4%
Texas	11.8%	18.9%	32.9%
North Carolina	13.7%	12.8%	28.3%
West			
Nevada	37.7%	20.7%	66.1%
Arizona	34.4%	20.9%	62.5%
Utah	8.9%	26.3%	37.6%

Source: Hussar, W., & Bailey, T. (2008). Table 26: Actual and projected percentage changes in public high school graduates, by region and state: Selected years, 1999–2000 through 2017–2018. In National Center for Education Statistics, Projections of Education Statistics to 2017 *(36th ed.). Washington, DC: U.S. Department of Education, Institute of Education Sciences.*

unrealistically for dramatic growth in out-of-state enrollment [of high school graduates] and continued enrollment stability despite the demographic outlook for their catchment areas."[1] According to John Nelson of Moody's, private institutions in the South and West have made noticeable improvements in their marketing campaigns, which are designed to convince high school graduates that colleges in their region are as good as colleges located far to the north, where everything costs more and it is colder.[2]

Table 2.3 shows which states by region are expected to have the largest declines or increases in high school graduates through 2018. As is evident from this table, a region does not necessarily dictate which states have the largest increases or decreases in the number of high school graduates. The Northeast is an interesting case because only New Jersey is forecast to increase the number of high school graduates. Even though the states in the South should see growing student market pools, Louisiana is projected to have the largest decline in the country. The decline in Louisiana may be directly related to the population loss following Hurricane Katrina.

Many college presidents expect to be saved by recruiting minority students as a rich source of new students. However, the data suggest that the pool of Hispanic and African-American high school graduates is fairly stagnant and that current participation rates may not be contributing to a larger volume of new students going to colleges. (See Table 2.4 on the next page.) Furthermore, Hispanic and African-American students are less affluent and could see the higher cost of attending an independent college as a disincentive to enrollment.

Presidents will face a major challenge marketing their college if they are located in a state where the pool of high school graduates is forecast to shrink dramatically. Moody's points out that colleges in the Northeast and Midwest with in-state or regional markets that expect to pull students from outside their region such as the South or West will find that they are confronting very skillful marketers.[3] The old days of traveling south to tell students of the wonders of private colleges in the Northeast are quickly fading away. The disappearance

TABLE 2.4—HIGH SCHOOL GRADUATES, ENROLLMENTS IN COLLEGE, AND PARTICIPATION RATES, 2000–2006

	High School Completers				Enrolled in College				Participation Rates			
	Total	White	Black	Hispanic	Total	White	Black	Hispanic	Total	White	Black	Hispanic
2000	2,756	1,938	393	300	1,745	1,272	216	159	0.63	0.66	0.55	0.53
2001	2,549	1,834	381	241	1,574	1,178	210	124	0.62	0.64	0.55	0.52
2002	2,796	1,903	382	344	1,824	1,314	227	184	0.65	0.69	0.59	0.54
2003	2,677	1,832	327	314	1,711	1,213	188	184	0.64	0.66	0.57	0.59
2004	2,752	1,854	398	286	1,835	1,276	249	177	0.67	0.69	0.62	0.62
2005	2,675	1,799	345	390	1,834	1,317	192	211	0.69	0.73	0.56	0.54
2006	2,692	1,805	318	382	1,776	1,237	177	222	0.66	0.69	0.55	0.58

Source: U.S. Department of Education. (2007). Table 19: College enrollment and enrollment rates of recent high school completers, by race/ethnicity: 1960 through 2006. In Digest of Education Statistics. *Washington, DC: National Center for Education Statistics.*

of this practice will accelerate with the financial-crisis because parents will not be able to fund a college education at a high-priced college with low visibility on the reputation screen.

Affordability

Pricing will become critical to private institutions in the Northeast and Midwest as they compete for new students because, as Figure 2.2 illustrates, families and students are being pressed by the cost of going to college.

As noted earlier, colleges have customarily turned to tuition discounts to increase or maintain enrollments. However, declines in the high school market pool of a magnitude greater than 10 percent could obviate this strategy if lost income cuts too deeply into the revenue needed to cover operational expenses. Of course, this assumes that colleges follow a strategy allowing expenses to grow as fast as they have in the past. Between 2002 and 2007, expenses grew 5 percent at small, 7 percent at medium-sized, and 6 percent at large private institutions. Expenses increased 25 percent to 4 percent above inflation at private institutions.

FIGURE 2.2—TUITION COSTS ROSE FASTER THAN FAMILY INCOME, 1976–2006

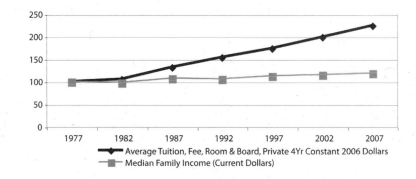

Average Tuition, Fee, Room & Board, Private 4Yr Constant 2006 Dollars
Median Family Income (Current Dollars)

Reprinted with permission from U.S. Higher Education Outlook (2008). *New York: Moody's Investors Service.*

Inflation between 2007 and 2008 jumped nearly 8 percent owing to increases in fuel, food, and other expenses.[4] If colleges follow past practice in fiscal year 2009, expenses would increase 2 percent to 4 percent above inflation, thereby increasing expenditure budgets between 10 percent and 12 percent. Tuition rates grew on average 1.5 percent above expenses between 2002 and 2007. If this pattern continues into FY 2009, tuition would spiral upward with increases ranging from 11 percent to 13.5 percent. These tuition rates could translate into dollar increases of $1,200 to $1,400 for small colleges, $1,400 to $1,700 for medium-sized colleges, and $1,500 to $1,800 for large institutions. Whether this is enough to drive students away from private colleges is not yet known, but there is evidence from the 1970s that double-digit increases in tuition rates pushed some prospective students from upper- or middle-income families into public institutions.[5] Moody's expects that economic conditions will result in a decline in federal and state aid forcing families to turn to private loans, which may no longer be available as a result of stricter credit requirements or where payoff costs may be too high for families or graduates to bear.[6]

FIGURE 2.3—NET PRICE TO INCOME BY INCOME GROUPS FOR PRIVATE INSTITUTIONS, 1992–2004

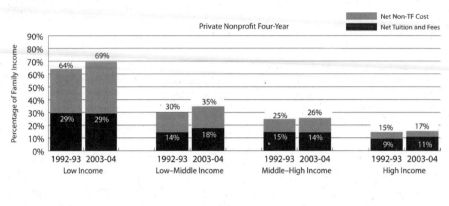

Source: Baum, S., & Ma, J. (2007). Trends in College Pricing (p. 19). Washington, DC: College Board.

Figure 2.3 indicates that as of 2007 net tuition price at private colleges places a tremendous burden on lower-income groups. More than likely, this burden grew in 2008 and will probably increase more in 2009. So, if private college presidents expect that a rich new vein of college students can be found among African-American or Hispanic groups, then they must deal with tuition prices. As any parent knows all too well, tuition is only part of the cost of attending college. Attending a private four-year college versus a public college can add another $12,000 to the cost of an education when room, board, transportation, and other expenses are added.[7] In fact, these added costs may only scratch the surface of costs of attendance because they ignore the opportunity cost of attendance where students could be earning money to pay for health care, their own refrigerator, television, game consoles, and other expensive incremental costs of a student attending college today.

The result is that for lower-income families it makes more sense to encourage students to attend community colleges or public four-year institutions where their net tuition is nearly 50 percent lower than at an independent institution, unless a student is exceptional

FIGURE 2.4—PERCENTAGE OF PRIVATE (NONFEDERAL) LOANS OVER 10 YEARS, 1997–2007

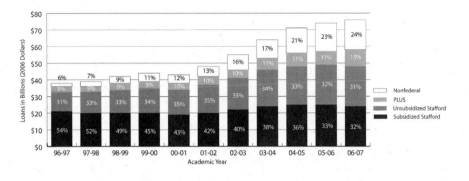

Reprinted with permission from Trends in Higher Education: Student Loans _(2007). New York: College Board._

academically, in which case the student may qualify for free tuition at an elite private institution.[8] If they attend community colleges, they also gain the savings from living at home and possibly working part- to full-time, which is common for many community college students.

The credit crisis of 2008 puts higher education in a place that presidents and boards never expected to see. They have lived under the assumption that higher education is immune from the downturns in the economy because enrollment is countercyclical; that is, as employment falls, college enrollments expand because more time is available for college. Workers advance their skills, and they could attend college while borrowing and arbitrage the interest costs with future earnings. A credit crunch throws this strategy and the countercyclical assumption out of whack. There is evidence that some banks and higher educational financial agencies either froze student loans or increased the credit requirements bar so high that many students could no longer borrow to go to college.[9] As Figure 2.4 indicates, private loans are paying for an ever-increasing share of the cost of attending college. The financial crisis is putting tremendous pressure on higher education institutions to raise tuition. The

FIGURE 2.5—HOUSEHOLD NET WORTH, 2001–2008

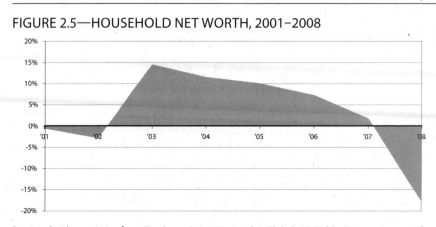

Reprinted with permission from Goodman, R. (2008). Moody's Global U.S. Public Finance: Impact of the Credit Crisis and a Weaker Economy on U.S. Higher Education (p. 4). New York: Moody's Investors Service.

problem parents in general and low-income parents in particular face is that the cost of attendance is forcing parents to use a growing proportion of their income for a college degree. Until very recently, parents have been able to fund the cost of attendance through equity loans on their homes or no collateral loans from private lenders. The home equity market has essentially disappeared and the government is taking over private lending for higher education. As parents are squeezed out of the market, and with tuition absorbing any slack in their income, they may find that their children are either forced out of the higher education market or must turn to less expensive and potentially lower quality schools. The evidence suggests that students are turning to public colleges and universities, many of which are capping enrollments and potentially leaving many students without access to higher education.

For many students and families, the problem is all too simple: if they cannot borrow to pay for tuition bills, going to college is out of the question. How the credit crisis plays out is still an unknown, but by Fall 2009, its effects, benign or pernicious, will become apparent. Figure 2.5 illustrates what has happened with household net worth, which is often the basis for home equity that had funded tuition for many students.

The high cost of attendance joined with a credit freeze represents a major storm brewing on the near horizon for private institutions over the next several years. Presidents of private colleges with a tenuous financial grasp on their existence may be tempted to retreat to the root cellar and hide from the storm of bad financial markets, demographic changes, and tight credit. These presidents, on resurfacing, may well find that whatever financial resources there were have blown away, leaving only the shreds of a once struggling but working institution.

Presidents at private colleges cannot wait until the full force of the storm hits. They must quickly press the board and college community to prepare and take action. They have to know how *vulnerable* their current students are to the credit crunch; they need to find a way internally or in consort with other private institutions or financial agencies to provide students with the *means to pay* for college; and last, but definitely not least, they must *deal with the high cost* of earning a degree at a private institution.

ACADEMIC SKILLS

Colleges and universities are seeing continuing declines in academic skills of students, skills that new students in the past were presumed to possess when they arrived on campus. Evidence from the College Board suggests that mathematics, reading, and writings scores have deteriorated over the last several years. How this plays out in the classroom can only be surmised, but it is probably fair to say that weak academic skills do not prepare students for the rigor of a college classroom. There is general sentiment that college students are just not performing as well as they have in the past. (See Figure 2.6 on the next page.)

The complaint that academic skills of incoming students are not up to academic standards expected by instructors is supported by findings that 29 percent of students in public four-year institutions are involved in academic remediation programs at an annual, national program cost of $500 million. If a student has taken three or four remedial classes, that student's chance of graduating *after eight years*

FIGURE 2.6—TEN-YEAR TRENDS IN READING, WRITING, AND MATH SAT SCORES, 1998–2008

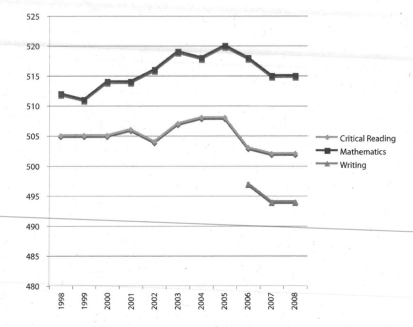

Reprinted with permission from Ten-Year Trend in Critical Reading, Mathematics, and Writing Mean Scores (2008). New York: College Board.

is only 19 percent.[10] Although the scale and cost of remediation at private institutions are not as high as the rate at public institutions, the National Center for Education Statistics found that 12 percent of entering students at private institutions were placed in remediation courses in 1995 and 2000.[11] Although the rate did not change in four years, there is still a cost for these remedial services that is borne by the institution and ultimately by tuition charged to the general student body. It would not be surprising that remediation rates are highest with nonselective privates, which means that the greatest remedial costs are borne by institutions with the least ability to cover these costs through endowments.

Clifford Adelman, a noted researcher formally with the U.S. Department of Education, dealt with the probability of graduation,

TABLE 2.5—PROBABILITY OF GRADUATING IN EIGHT YEARS FOR 1992 HIGH SCHOOL GRADUATES

(Population: All on-time 1992 high school graduates who continued to postsecondary education at any time)

Percent Completing Bachelor's Degree
Quintiles of Academic Resources Components

	Highest	Second	Third	Fourth	Lowest
Curriculum	81.7(1.50)	60.5(2.14)	35.5(1.93)	23.4(1.99)	8.7(1.37)
Class rank/GPA	78.8(1.47)	59.1(2.24)	40.3(2.11)	25.7(2.16)	13.0(1.94)
Senior test score	74.9(1.72)	53.9(1.92)	37.2(2.16)	26.7(2.41)	8.9(1.31)

Notes: Standard errors are in parentheses. Weighted N=1.6M
Source: National Center for Education Statistics: NELS: 88/2000 Postsecondary Transcript Files (NCES 2003_402 and Supplement)

Source: Adelman, C. (2006). Table 9: Percentage of on-time 1992 high school graduates who continued their education in any postsecondary institution who completed bachelor's degrees by December 2000, by quintile performance in the three component variables of Academic. In The Toolbox Revisited: Paths to Degree Completion From HighSchool to College *(p. 67). Washington, DC: U.S. Department of Education.*

which is dependent on academic skills. His data delve into the probability that an incoming student will graduate with a bachelor's degree in *eight years*. (See Table 2.5.) He found that college graduation rates for incoming high school graduates are subject to the rigor of their high school curriculum, their class rank based on grade point average, and their senior test scores. The probability of graduating in eight years is highest for incoming students situated in the highest academic quintile for their high school class, while high school graduates from the lowest academic quintile had the lowest probability of graduating in eight years. The respective probability for graduation in eight years ranges from 74.9 percent to 81 percent for the highest quintile and 8.9 percent to 25.7 percent for the two lowest quintiles.

Adelman's evidence does not differentiate graduation rates for high school graduates who chose either a public or a private institution of higher education. Even though his data were drawn from graduates of public high schools, a significant portion of those students attended private colleges. Recognizing the potential impediments to generalizing about high school graduates enrolled in private colleges, it is reasonable to assume that high school graduates from the highest academic quintile would have a higher graduation rate than high school graduates from the lower academic quintile. Therefore, his work suggests that as the selectivity of an independent college increases or declines, graduation rates would increase or decline accordingly. The implication is that less selective private colleges would have to invest more in remediation to retain their students. Regrettably, entering college students who did not do well in high school carry the highest risk of failure and also carry the highest financial burden from an investment that did not yield a degree or its commensurate lifetime earnings.

The quality of the academic skills that incoming students bring to college can positively or adversely affect academic programs and force colleges to make substantial investments to try and keep students in college until they graduate. High school graduates with high grade point averages will require little if any remediation, which means that a college can invest its resources in stronger academic programs. These students are valuable to private colleges because they enhance the academic experience, attract more high school graduates with solid academic records, finish their degree in four years, and become productive donors. On the other hand, new students who did not do well in high school will need more remediation, lack the skills to perform well in class, and more than likely will leave college before they graduate. As a result, nonselective or low-selective colleges are forced to constantly replace a large portion of their entering classes within a semester or a few years. When this happens, the academic reputation of the institution is degraded and the college loses a potential donor because students who take eight years to graduate will likely do so from another college.

Low graduation and high attrition rates represent a very expensive financial burden for students who graduated from high school at the lower end of the performance scale. Given that the average tuition at four-year private colleges was $25,143[12] in 2008, the cost of a degree is $100,572 with no further tuition increases (tuition excludes room, board, and other expenses). For the 30-year period

1977 to 2007, the average private college tuition increased $15,000 in inflation-adjusted dollars, while "average family income rose by only about $463 for the poorest 20 percent of families, $11,275 for the middle 20 percent, and $146,650 for the wealthiest 5 percent." Also, given that many families are paying about $35,000 a year for college, the probability of graduating from college with a degree becomes very important in the decision to attend an independent institution. In light of the preceding discussion on graduation, attrition, and tuition, the question for the student, for their family, and for the college is: does it make sense to invest tens of thousands of dollars in a private institution only to discover that the student is not ready for college and that the investment has gone down the drain?[13]

Assuming that parents and students make rational decisions about enrollment, it would seem that the probability of graduating and a six-digit tuition charge would weigh heavily in the decision to enroll in an independent college or university. This question can be stated simply: does it make sense to watch tens of thousands of dollars go down the drain because a child or student lacks the motivation to study or because the student does not have the academic skills to graduate? As tuition and other educational costs rise faster than inflation, and as the cost of a private institution continues to swiftly outpace family income, would it make more sense for students to choose a community college or public four-year college rather than a private college, especially if the student needs academic remediation?

OPERATIONAL COSTS

Operational costs, the expenses associated with running a college, drive tuition rates and the need for grants, gifts, and endowment income. If private colleges and universities are going to respond to the price and credit squeeze on parents and students, they need to do a better job of managing expenses. There is a tendency in the good years to run up expenses because investments, gifts, and grants produce large chunks of new revenue; but most institutions will take a chunk of the net income and add it to their financial reserves to improve their financial condition. When new revenue slows to

TABLE 2.6—NET INCOME INCLUDING AND EXCLUDING INVESTMENT RETURNS OF PRIVATE COLLEGES AND UNIVERSITIES, 2002 AND 2007

	SMALL	MEDIUM	LARGE	TOTAL
Net With Investment Returns				
FY 2002	−17.8%	−19.7%	−11.7%	−16.4%
FY 2007	12.3%	20.2%	19.9%	17.5%
Net Without Investment Returns				
FY 2002	−5.6%	−2.8%	0.3%	−2.7%
FY 2007	−4.9%	2.2%	3.6%	0.3%

a pittance, institutions must survive on the underlying operational nets flowing mainly from tuition. As shown in Table 2.6, net income including investments from FY 2002 was overwhelmed by a sharp downturn in the economy resulting from the bursting of the technology bubble and the economic damage from September 11, 2001. By FY 2007, all except medium-sized institutions were producing large increases in their net income that included investments. The massive crash resulting from the end of the housing bubble and the credit crises had not yet been felt by June 30, 2007. When investment returns are removed, net income ranges from an unsettling −4.9 percent for small institutions to a positive but feeble 3.6 percent for large private institutions.

Small margins from basic operations as suggested by net income excluding investment returns indicate that large nets can be quickly unmasked when markets fall. If economic downturns end quickly and are replaced by strong and sustained growth, then the unmasking of weak operational performance is easily ignored. However, if the downturn is long and deep or if downturns recur, then unmasking slim margins can be devastating to colleges or universities with meager financial reserves.

It helps that between FY 2002 and 2007 financial reserves increased at most private institutions regardless of size or tuition dependency because net income increased substantially. The only exception involved small institutions that were not tuition dependent. Their average annual deficit during this period was 5 percent of revenue.[14] This outcome is counterintuitive because most neutral observers would have expected that small, tuition-dependent institutions would run deficits. However, it makes sense that they do not because they do not have nontuition sources to support operations. As a result, small, tuition-dependent institutions must manage operations to generate positive net income and cash flow or else they would not survive.

What is to be done if institutions are to avoid the small net income trap embedded in their operating structure? The answer is simple and straightforward. Private institutions must develop better ways to manage budgets, control ongoing operational costs, and expand financial reserves. How can this be done (or is it too late to be done)? Presidents, working with governing boards, must lead the institution to better management practices or possibly face the consequences when the economy turns volatile. Table 2.7 on the next page offers several concrete suggestions.

FINANCIAL CONDITION OF INDEPENDENT COLLEGES AND UNIVERSITIES

If private institutions expect to survive the turmoil of uncertain economic times, the health of their financial condition is important to the institution, its students, donors, grantors, regulators, and financial agencies. Even before the economic crash in 2008, Moody's pointed out in its outlook for 2008 and its assessment of the impact of the credit crisis that challenges facing colleges and universities from demographics, regulations, operational efficiency, weaker economic conditions, and credit conditions were intensifying.[15] In October 2008, Moody's updated its report because economic conditions that

TABLE 2.7—OPERATIONAL CONTROLS

Collect data on operational costs for compensation and noncompensation items disaggregated by instruction, research, auxiliary services, athletics, and administration.

Compare costs to peers, competitors, and institutions with a strong reputation for controlling operational costs.

Set operational cost goals for compensation and major noncompensation budgets for each department in the college.

Design goals so that allocation decisions improve operational performance of the main instructional, research, auxiliary, or other departments offering a service for a price on the market. Operational cost limits for service and administrative departments should be closely managed to determine the productivity. The question is, do they improve delivery, simplification, coordination, and management of critical services offered to the market?

Analyze and review performance regularly during the year and prior to development of the budget.

Identify operational costs that are failing to meet goals and develop a plan to get those costs under control or prepare an explanation on how excess operational costs in a specific area benefit the financial condition of the institution.

Approve budgets and amendments to the budget subject to operational cost goals.

Hold administrators accountable for operational cost performance. Failure to perform should lead to close supervision of budgetary decisions and management of administrators who are unable to manage their budgets according to plan. Operational cost management should be included in annual administrative performance reviews.

were uncertain in January had turned sharply downward. Moody's now believes that "the potential impacts of the combined credit freeze and recession on some colleges and universities will be significant if current trends persist."[16] Before the effect from the economic crash in 2008 is taken into account, let's take a look at the financial condition of private institutions leading up to the crash.

TABLE 2.8—GROWTH RATES FOR REVENUE AND EXPENSES AT PRIVATE INSTITUTIONS OF HIGHER EDUCATION BY SIZE OF INSTITUTION, 2002–2007

	SMALL	MEDIUM	LARGE	TOTAL
Revenue	10.9%	11.9%	13.2%	12.0%
Expenses	4.9%	4.7%	6.7%	5.4%
Net Growth	5.9%	7.3%	6.5%	6.6%

Source: JMA Higher Ed Stats. (2008). Strategic Higher Education Trends at a Glance: F2 2002.csv and F2 2007.csv Financial Data. Boulder, CO: John Minter and Associates.

Five measures provide a rough picture of financial health: revenue and expense growth rates, net income and deficits, cash, debt, and investments. Although a better measure, the Composite Financial Index, exists to measure financial health, the data are not good enough to make a large-scale analysis. So, the analysis will use measures that represent conventional indicators of financial health.

Revenue and Expense Growth Rates

The revenue and expenses measure is based on the premise that growth rates should balance or favor revenue growth (Chapter 3 on economics discusses this issue further). Suffice it to say that when revenue grows faster than expenses, excess revenue builds financial reserves that can be employed in cash investments, endowments, or capital projects. Cash and endowments act as buffers against future events that may have an adverse impact on the college.

As Table 2.8 shows, revenue at small, medium, and large colleges or universities exceeded expense growth rates by 6 percent or more between FY 2002 and 2007. This suggests private institutions were able to set aside a substantial sum of money in financial reserves during this period. This places them in a good position to deal with the economic turbulence that began in 2008.

TABLE 2.9—PERCENTAGE OF PRIVATE INSTITUTIONS WITH DEFICITS BY SIZE OF INSTITUTION, 2002 AND 2007

	SMALL	MEDIUM	LARGE	TOTAL
Percentage of Group: Deficits With Investment Returns				
FY 2002	50.4%	58.5%	52.8%	52.9%
FY 2007	22.4%	6.4%	1.6%	11.4%
Percentage of Group: Deficits Without Investment Returns				
FY 2002	51.1%	54.9%	43.7%	49.3%
FY 2007	47.4%	36.1%	30.6%	38.9%

Source: JMA Higher Ed Stats. (2008). Strategic Higher Education Trends at a Glance: F2 2002.csv and F2 2007.csv Financial Data. Boulder, CO: John Minter and Associates.

Net Income and Deficits

Financial strength is not merely a matter of revenue growth for the average institution, as given in Table 2.8. Another critical indicator is whether an institution was able to avoid deficits. As Table 2.9 on deficits indicates, nearly half of the private institutions in the data set reported deficits at the end of the 2002 fiscal year. These figures are based on revenue that includes unrealized investment returns.* Year 2002 saw the culmination of the reaction of financial markets to the end of the technology bubble and the effects of September 11, 2001. By 2007, markets had strengthened and deficits declined significantly for all institutions except colleges enrolling fewer than 1,000 students. Twenty-four percent of small institutions still reported deficits. There is a tendency among small institutions to report chain deficits; that is, when an institution reports deficits several years in a row, then for one year it reports excess net revenue. There are many colleges where this happens five or six years out of a nine-year period.[17] They live in a precarious financial state where their existence is constantly at stake.

---

* If investments increase in value, the institution records an unrealized gain on its income report (statement of activities). If investments decline in value as they did in 2002, an unrealized loss is recorded. Unrealized gains are increases without sale of the investment to capture the value of the increase; while unrealized losses are decreases without sale of the investment that captures the value of the decline.

The second section of Table 2.9, deficits without investment returns, shows what happens when investment returns are removed from revenue (as discussed earlier in this chapter). The table clearly shows that many institutions depend on investments and other revenue sources to shore up financial performance. If these institutions pass through long periods when markets fail to provide a safety margin to cover their predisposition for deficits, then they will quickly burn off their financial reserves. Between FY 2002 and FY 2007, other revenue sources were able to generate sufficient income to cover operating deficits and throw off income for financial reserves. However, the market crash of 2008 will probably return many private institutions to their inherent deficit condition as investment gains are replaced with investment losses.

Although colleges report unrealized investment returns, cash is not changed because unrealized gains or losses are not real cash gains or losses. So, when the market turns down, cash is not reduced; and when the market turns up, cash reserves do not increase. The impact of unrealized returns on net income suggests that net is a necessary but insufficient measure of the financial health of an institution. The analysis will have to dig into the cash and investments to determine whether net income is actually strengthening the short-term financial health of the college. Unrealized gains or losses will have an impact over the longer term because unrealized gains mean that the college will be able to draw off more income for operations, while unrealized losses will reduce the draw for operations. Because most colleges follow a prudent rule of using a multiyear moving average for the value of investment funds, the scale of endowment draws will lag the actual reporting of unrealized gains or losses. This last injunction needs to be kept in mind when reading reports on the financial condition of a private college or university.

Cash

Cash is trump in finance, especially during major economic downturns or when the college is struggling to survive! Noncash financial measures are important, but cash and the liquidity of financial reserves determine the capability of colleges and universities to invest in

TABLE 2.10—OPERATING CASH FLOW MARGINS OF PRIVATE UNIVERSITIES, 2007

	2007
	Range from Low-Credit Rating to High-Credit Rating
Large Private Institutions	11.2% to 12.8%
Small Private Institutions	12.7% for low- and high-credit rating

Source: Fitzgerald, S. (2007). Private College and University Medians 2007. New York: Moody's Investors Service.

new opportunities and academic programs and to survive economic decline. The good news for small and large private colleges and universities is that their operating cash flow margins* are substantial, and there are also data that indicate that these margins were stable over five years.[18] (See Table 2.10.) Strong cash flow margins should have improved the cash reserve position for these institutions as they entered the financial crisis of the fall of 2008.

Even though the cash reserves of most private institutions should have withstood the credit crisis, some were caught unawares when Commonfund closed down its short- and medium-term money market funds.[19] Suddenly, chief financial officers had to scramble for cash to make payroll and pay bills when credit markets had stopped lending money except to those who did not need it. Even though the colleges will probably receive the full amount invested in Commonfund, banks were reluctant to come to the rescue because every loan had become a frightful experience.

Debt

Private institutions, unlike public universities, are totally reliant on their own resources to cover loan payments. Cash may be in a good position; but if a college is extravagant with debt and ignores risk, cash hordes will not save a college that is swamped with debt

*Operating cash flow margin is defined as unrestricted revenues subject to these conditions: limiting investment income to a 5 percent average of the previous three years' cash and investments; subtracting net assets released for construction and acquisition of fixed assets; subtracting operating expenses; adding back depreciation, interest, and other noncash expenses; and then dividing by adjusted revenue, which does not include the add-backs.

TABLE 2.11—LIABILITIES TO ASSETS RATIO BY SIZE OF INSTITUTION, 2002 AND 2007

	SMALL	MEDIUM	LARGE	TOTAL
FY 2002	28.4%	31.4%	34.6%	31.5%
FY 2007	28.8%	32.3%	33.7%	31.6%

Source: JMA Higher Ed Stats. (2008). Strategic Higher Education Trends at a Glance: F2 2002.csv and F2 2007.csv Financial Data. Boulder, CO: John Minter and Associates.

---

payments. Fortunately, the evidence suggests that most colleges re-strained any impulse to substantially increase debt during the period from FY 2002 to FY 2007 (see Table 2.11).[20] Restraint probably rested on their recent experience at the beginning of the decade when markets crashed and did not fully recover until late 2007. By early 2008, it was becoming apparent that financial markets and debt markets were weakening. By the fall of 2008, debt markets shut down, which would have foreclosed plans for projects dependent on large infusions of debt.

Private Investment Performance

Another major link in the financial condition of private institutions is performance of their endowment and investment funds. The evi-dence suggests that many investment funds produced returns that exceeded returns for general market indexes. (See Figure 2.7 on the next page.) These returns would build future debt capacity, reduce current debt loads, and enlarge financial reserves. Of course, this is not a major factor at tuition-dependent colleges because returns from their investment portfolios usually do not have a significant impact on the financial position of the institution.

Even though markets reported major declines through the fall of 2008, there is no evidence that markets will "erase all gains of the last five years" as noted in Figure 2.8 on the next page.[21] However, most private institutions have long investment horizons, which sug-gests that they can outwait momentary disruptions in the market until the market returns to a positive cycle.

FIGURE 2.7—INVESTMENT PERFORMANCE BETWEEN 1995 AND 2007

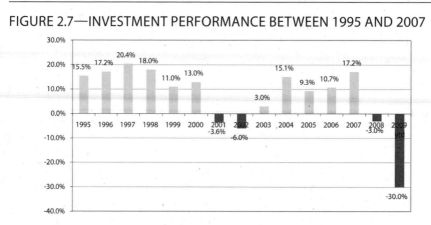

Reprinted with permission from U.S. Higher Education Outlook (2008). New York: Moody's Investors Service

FIGURE 2.8—INVESTMENT PORTFOLIO GAINS FROM 2003 TO 2007 WITH 2008 AND 2009 PROJECTIONS

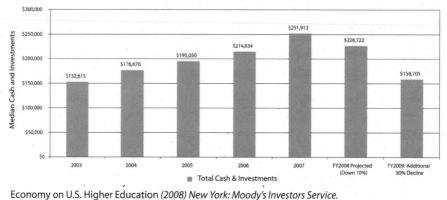

Economy on U.S. Higher Education (2008) New York: Moody's Investors Service.

Private institutions, such as Boston University, had to tighten their belts in response to the credit crunch and severe market declines.[22] It is likely that other private colleges and universities, as well as public institutions, had to develop contingency plans in response to the market. At least private institutions have some control over their destiny because they can look for new resources, whereas public institutions are subject to the cuts of their respective state governments.

TABLE 2.12—FACTORS THAT WILL INFLUENCE FINANCIAL HEALTH OF PRIVATE COLLEGES AND UNIVERSITIES

- Region where the institution is located
- Academic skills of the students entering the institution
- Effective programs to increase graduation rates, to reduce the time to graduate for the average student, and to reduce attrition rates
- Extent to which credit markets provide loans to entering students
- Financial reserves (cash and unrestricted investments) available to the institution
- Rate at which tuition increases
- Operating net income margins
- Avoidance of deficits, especially chronic deficits
- President's ability to manage costs
- Capacity of donors to provide gifts

SUMMARY

In general, many private institutions entered the unsettled economics of 2008 and 2009 in relatively strong financial positions. Yet the evidence shows that many operate with very slim margins, which are unmasked when investment returns decline. Those institutions with chronic deficits will find that their existence is put into question by the credit crises, changing demographics, and their inability to respond to tougher competition in their student markets. The factors described in Table 2.12 will determine the financial health of institutions over the next several years.

Despite the bleak picture painted by the economy of 2008, parents and potential students will still hold to the common belief that a college degree is worth its cost and that many lower-tiered or smaller private institutions care more about their students than do large public institutions.[23] Nevertheless, as pointed out here, demographics, academic skills, attrition, and affordability will impose tremendous burdens on financially weak colleges as they try to respond to growing or shrinking student pools or to the cost of accommodating students who are not fully prepared for the academic rigors of college.

NOTES

1.   Moody's Investors Services. *U.S. Higher Education Outlook* (New York: Moody's Investors Service, 2008), p. 7.
2.   Ibid.
3.   Ibid.
4.   U.S. Department of Labor. *Consumer Price Index.* (Bureau of Labor Statistics, 2008). Retrieved August 31, 2008, from http://ftp.bls.gov/pub/special.requests/cpi/cpiai.txt.
5.   McPherson, M. "The Demand for Higher Education." In *Public Policy and Private Higher Education,* edited by Breneman, D., & Finn, C., Jr. (Washington, DC: Brookings Institution, 1978), pp. 183–186.
6.   Moody's Investors Services. *U.S. Higher Education Outlook* (New York: Moody's Investors Service, 2008), p. 11.
7.   Baurn, S., & Ma, J. *Trends in College Pricing* (Washington, DC: College Board, 2007), p. 7.
8.   Ibid, p. 18.
9.   Wilson, R. "As Credit Crisis Freezes Colleges, Worries Mount," *Chronicle of Higher Education*, 2006. Retrieved August 31, 2008, from http://chronicle.com/.
10.   Strong American Schools. *Diploma to Nowhere* (Washington, DC: Strong American Schools, 2008)), pp. 3–4.
11.   Greene, B. "*Remedial Education at Degree Granting Post Secondary Institutions in Fall 2000*" (Washington, DC: National Center for Education Statistics, 2003), p. 33.
12.   Supiano, B. "Student Aid is Up, But College Costs Outpace Family Incomes," *Chronicle of Higher Education,* 2008. Retrieved October 29, 2008, from http://chronicle.com/free/2008/10/6171.n.htm?utm_source=at&utm_medium=en.
13.   Ibid.
14.   JMA Higher Ed Stats. "*Strategic Higher Education Trends at a Glance: F2 2002.csv and F2 2007.csv Financial Data.*" (Boulder, CO: John Minter and Associates, 2008).
15.   Moody's Investors Services. *U.S. Higher Education Outlook* (New York: Moody's Investors Service, 2008), pp. 1–6.
16.   Goodman, R. *Moody's global U.S. public finance: Impact of the credit crisis and a weaker economy on U.S. higher education* (New York: Moody's Investors Services, 2008), p. 1.
17.   Townsley, M. K. *The small college guide to financial health* (Washington, DC: NACUBO, 2002), p. 109.

18. Fitzgerald, S. *Private College and University Medians 2007*. (New York: Moody's Investors Services, 2007). Retrieved October 22, 2008, from http://www.nacubo.org/Images/Moody's%20HE%20 priv%20medians%20May07.pdf.

19. Field, K. "Bank Freeze Leaves Hundreds of Colleges Cut Off From Short Term Funds," *Chronicle of Higher Education*, 2008. Retrieved October 10, 2008, from http://chronicle.com/weekly/v55/ i07/07a02001.htm.

20. Moody's Investors Services. *U.S. Higher Education Outlook* (New York: Moody's Investors Service, 2008).

21. Goodman, R. *Moody's global U.S. public finance: Impact of the credit crisis and a weaker economy on U.S. higher education* (New York: Moody's Investors Services, 2008), p. 1. Goodman, R. (2008).

22. Wilson, R. "As Credit Crisis Freezes Colleges, Worries Mount," *Chronicle of Higher Education*, 2008. Retrieved August 31, 2008, from http://chronicle.com/.

23. Moser, K. "Worsening Economy Could Cause Trouble for Smaller Colleges." *Chronicle of Higher Education*, 2008. Retrieved September 5, 2008, from http://chronicle.com/weekly/v54/i45/45a01502. htm.

CHAPTER 3

THE ECONOMICS OF HIGHER EDUCATION: A BRIEF LESSON

Higher education institutions, despite vehement protestations to the contrary, are economic entities subject to the same marketplace forces that affect businesses and individuals. They have to take into account the impact of price, supply, and demand on short- and long-term decisions. If boards, presidents, and other key decision makers in an institution ignore these economic forces, they place their institution at risk. Only a small number of very wealthy institutions are effectively buffered from the daily vagaries of the marketplace. Even they must remain vigilant to changes in the market that could dramatically alter their position.

Key leaders must understand these economic forces or face the consequences of strategic decisions that strike out in the wrong direction. Economics, though the mathematics is arcane for the more complex parts of the theory, rests on commonsense formulations for its basic principles. Two basic principles explain the relationships of demand, supply, and price:

- As demand increases, price increases until supply is cleared from the market.

- As supply decreases, price increases until demand is cleared from the market.

Before these principles are used to tease out the impact of the market on a particular institution, it is necessary to recognize that higher education is a quirky marketplace distorted by the following conditions:

- the marketplace is not perfectly competitive,

- externalities alter market decisions,

- some of the benefit goes to others besides the students, and

- market imperfections (it is difficult to borrow funds without third party guarantees such as federally subsidized loans) prevent optimization of economic decisions by buyers and sellers.[1]

Perfect competition assumes that there are many buyers and sellers who are competing for goods or services in the marketplace. In this case, the purchase and sale of degrees define the marketplace for higher education. Externalities occur when the value from a purchase or the cost of production is diverted to other persons or entities. Market imperfections transpire when basic assumptions about the competitive market are not present; for example, complete information about the costs and risks associated with a purchase of a degree are not known by all parties.

QUIRKY ASPECTS OF THE MARKETPLACE

Economics assumes that markets operate efficiently under these conditions: perfect competition, product uniformity, small size and large numbers of firms, resource mobility, and perfect knowledge. Experience indicates that these assumptions are no more present in the market for higher education than they are in the broader market for goods and services. Keeping the meaning of these assumptions in mind can clarify how economic mechanisms work in the not-for-profit higher education market.

Perfect competition: If buyers and sellers enter the market with no impediments to their decisions, price will clear the market, resulting in no excess demand and no surplus supply. This proposition is governed by these conditions: product uniformity, small size and large numbers, resource mobility, and perfect knowledge.

Product uniformity: If a product or service is not uniform from firm to firm, then the firms are not competing on equal ground, which may result in market niches containing few competitors. For instance, a degree in criminal justice may vary by type of courses, hours of instruction, cost of instruction, and method of instruction, allowing an institution to create a market niche for a particular degree.

Small size and large numbers: When many small firms compete, no single firm can dictate price. This condition is compromised when several firms collude or a single firm dominates the market, such as happened when the Overlap Group, 23 prestigious private institutions, collaborated by setting financial aid for their applicants. The Department of Justice determined that this violated antitrust laws.[2]

Resource mobility: A market can adapt to changes in demand and supply when firms and labor can freely move within the market. Free movement in higher education is constrained by tenure, accreditation, licensing requirements, and product indivisibility (where colleges make it difficult for students to assemble a degree by taking courses from many colleges).

Perfect knowledge: This condition assumes that the seller and buyer fully recognize all costs and consequences associated with their transaction. Prospective students often misunderstand the true costs of their enrollment decisions and their future income potential. As a result, they may overpay for a degree that does not yield sufficient income to cover its cost.

Externalities

Externalities occur when graduates do not receive the full value from their investment in education because some of its value goes to society or the cost of producing the education is diverted to the public, for example, as the cost of pollution or the cost of poorly prepared graduates. The assumption is that cost externalities are minor for higher education. Following are several externalities where the benefit of a degree is diverted to society rather than to the graduate.[3,4,5]

- Graduates contribute to science through research and discovery.
- Fewer graduates than nongraduates participate in violent crime.
- Graduates tend to perceive people, regardless of their individual differences, more rationally and fairly than do nongraduates.
- Graduates produce goods and services, rather than depending on transfer payments from the government.
- The increased salaries and buying power of graduates contribute broadly to economic activity.

Several solutions are used to reduce the impact of these externalities on graduates. Ultimately, these solutions reduce the price of tuition, including paying subsidies to public institutions, adding tax incentives to spur donations, directing governmental grants to students, and providing access to tax-free bonds to colleges and universities for their capital expenditures.

Market Imperfections

When there is an underinvestment in education by potential students, a market imperfection occurs. Buyers and sellers may not optimize their economic decisions under this condition. David Mundel, a noted economist of higher education, identifies two market imperfections in higher education[6]:

Capital imperfections: Some students do not enroll because they cannot afford the cost of borrowing or because financial markets refuse to make loans. Financial institutions are reluctant to offer loans to students because the degree is an intangible that cannot be collateralized or because students often make adverse career choices that do not produce sufficient income to pay off a loan. Government resolves this impasse between banks and students by underwriting losses. However, as happened during the early part of 2008, when the government cuts subsidies on student loans, many banks stopped providing student loans or increased borrower credit ratings.

Investment risk: Students face another capital imperfection, investment risk, when they invest in a long-term degree program without a guarantee that they will graduate or that their career will produce the desired income. Many potential students, in particular poorer students, cannot accurately predict the future. They are unsure of whether they have the academic ability to complete a degree, and they are unable to estimate the potential income that a particular degree will produce. Because insurance does not exist to cover these risks, some potential students choose not to go to college.

Oligopolistic Markets

In economic theory, oligopolistic markets arise when a few firms (higher education institutions) control pricing within the market. Oligopolies come into being under these conditions: barriers to entry, economies of scale, critical factors of production, advertising, or collusion.

Barriers to entry: Starting a new college or entering a new academic or geographic market is expensive because of the cost of accreditation, licensing by state higher education authorities, new faculty, building or renting infrastructure, recruitment, provision of administrative and instructional support services, and establishing a reputation. Accreditation and state licenses are often the deal breakers because these agencies are reluctant to let new competitors threaten the stability of markets for existing institutions.

New nonprofits must have sufficient capital for operating costs until they accumulate cash reserves, find rich donors to cover deficits, and/or borrow funds personally guaranteed by trustees. The challenge of the first two options and the extreme unlikelihood of the third explain why new not-for-profit colleges struggle to achieve financial stability.

Economy of scale: This refers to the output (the number of students enrolled in a college) needed to achieve the average and marginal costs of production. Another way of looking at this concept is that economy of scale is reached when enrollment is at a level where the cost per student is at its lowest point. One way that colleges can reduce the cost of operations is by using gifts or drawdowns from the endowment fund to reduce the unit cost. However, this assumes that costs in excess of the gift are held constant or limited to some reasonable level of inflation. As is all too apparent from the rise in tuition, colleges rarely consider the need to minimize costs per unit. Studies suggest that the economy of scale for private colleges falls somewhere between 1,500 and 2,000 students.[7]

Factors of production: In higher education, factors of production include faculty, classrooms, distance education delivery systems, and supporting technology. Well-established institutions can take control of the factors of production in their markets. Some examples include paying top dollar for the best instructors, using tenure to increase the opportunity cost for faculty who want to leave, or "buying" the best students through top-dollar scholarships.

Advertising: The creation of market niches may be abetted through advertising, which allows some institutions to act as small monopolies or oligopolies. The purpose of advertising is to foster the notion that one college is so superior and unique that an applicant choosing another institution is making a serious error detrimental to his or her future well-being.

Many colleges use the same ad themes, which essentially say that one college is the same or as good as another. There is nothing original anymore about phrases like these: student-oriented, career-focused, fast-paced, small, friendly, practical, here to serve, or dozens if not hundreds of similar phrases. In some ways, it appears that colleges receive a bag of commonly used words, and then they mix them around on a table until they come up with an ad.

Collusion: When several colleges meet to set standards for applicants and guidelines for financial aid, they risk landing on the slippery slope of collusion to establish an oligopolistic market as was the case with the 23 colleges in the Overlap Group.

Although higher education is not oligopolistic in general, some markets are oligopolistic. A classic oligopoly case involved the previously mentioned Overlap Group, a set of 23 prestigious private universities that collaborated on setting financial aid awards for prospective students.[8] In 1991, the Department of Justice claimed that the group violated antitrust laws by setting market prices for tuition. The group reached an agreement that year with the Justice Department to cease the setting of student financial aid awards.

ECONOMIC MODEL OF PRIVATE COLLEGES AND UNIVERSITIES

The preceding discussion on quirky and oligopolistic markets sets the foundation for a general economic model of private institutions. This model is constructed around a six-piece economic framework: goal optimization, resource allocations, production functions, market structure, financial constraint, and financial equilibrium.[*][9,10]

Goal optimization is the driving force behind economic decisions. The main proposition is that an organization maximizes something of value by trying to get the largest amount of value that it can from the services or products that are offered in the market. The set of decisions supporting goal optimization involves the allocation of

*The model presented in this section is based on the work of David Hopkins and William Massy's *Planning Models for Colleges and Universities*, and Gordon Winston's *Subsidies, Hierarchy and Peers: The Awkward Economics of Higher Education*.

resources, the organization of resources into a production function to produce products or services, recognition that the products or services must respond to market needs, and a set of internal financial constraints that limit the scope of what an organization can do. Constraints force the organization to adapt its decisions to limits imposed by its production function, its position in the market, and its financial resources.

If we can accept the idea that colleges are economic entities offering a service in a competitive market, then it is useful to see how an economic perspective explains allocation decisions, financial stability, and financial strategies. The basic economic premise for a higher education institution is that it attempts to maximize something of value. While business firms maximize profit, nonprofit colleges are by definition not charged with making a profit. The government protects them from the profit motive by granting tax-free status for their activities.* As a result, they have the opportunity to maximize something else, such as academic quality, research, community service, or other values important to the board. As will be shown in the next section, that something else does not necessarily involve a single goal or even a typical economic goal such as money. Most colleges are trying to achieve multiple goals. This is why colleges are not simply business firms offering a different line of business with government protection from taxes.

Goal Optimization

Howard Bowen contends that although colleges do not maximize profit, they do maximize revenue and spend all of it on academic excellence, prestige, and influence; thereby, they also maximize "ever-increasing expenditures."[11]

Although Bowen's model is appealing, Hopkins and Massy offer a richer explanation of the economic forces that shape decisions in higher education. Their model treats the governing board as having

---

* Colleges cannot avoid taxes under all circumstances. For instance, they may owe taxes on income generated from unrelated business activities. Tax liabilities may be incurred when a large amount of bookstore revenue comes from noninstructional revenue. The best example involves the sales of clothing and fan gear for popular sports teams. Local governments are also pressing nonprofit colleges to make payments in lieu of taxes (PILOTs) for sewage, water, policing, and other local services.

paramount decision-making authority in the institution. The government charges the board of trustees with overseeing the financial assets of the institution and using those assets for the public good. This charge presumes that the college acts as a not-for-profit entity and, as such, is not liable for income taxes at any level of government. However, the board must assure the government that the college does produce a valuable *public benefit* without simultaneously rendering private benefits to the trustees or key members of the institution. A public benefit is college degrees that students use to advance their social or income position or to improve the general welfare of society through government service or research. A private benefit is hiring unqualified board members, directing contracts to firms held by board members or their families, or paying exorbitant salaries and benefits to key administrators.

The governing board determines a set of core values for the institution that should achieve desirable social goals (i.e., public benefits).[12] As Hopkins and Massy see it, colleges maximize their core values rather than monetary profit, and core values are maximized by allocating resource activity, stocks, or price.[13] Activity, stocks, and price are described more as follows:

- *Activity:* Activity is an action conducted over some time period, usually described in physical or behavioral terms, which may be either tangible or intangible and which may be described as flows that employ stocks and price to achieve an outcome.[14] Tangible activities include factors such as students, credit hours, degrees, skills, research articles, and faculty.[15] Intangible activities include factors such as student academic potential, class performance, quality of research, faculty effort, and quality of library resources.[16]

- *Stock:* Stock variables are described in physical or human capital terms and are fixed in time.[17] Stocks typically include balance sheet categories, such as cash, receivables, investments (endowments), debt, and net worth, but stocks can also comprise the number, capability, and quality of human capital employed by the institution.[18] The value of stocks is that they are converted into activities; and conversely, activities can be converted into stocks. An important decision boards must make is the "spending-savings" question.[19] They must decide how much stock to turn into activities. For example, boards must determine an acceptable endowment payout rate to be used for current operations (activities). They must also determine how surplus revenue will be used to increase the size of the endowment fund, to build cash, to construct buildings, or to buy equipment.

- *Price:* Monetary value that is assigned to inputs such as labor, materials, and capital and to outputs such as degrees, athletic events, or continuing education credits is the price. Price is subject to demand and supply for inputs and outputs.[20] Many institutions discount price (tuition) to gain control over the "quality and/or quantity of admissions."[21] However, some institutions discount price not to gain control over quality and quantity but to match real price levels for their segment of the market. In this case, an institution raises its tuition to match the tuition of similar colleges within its competitive market.

The board must allocate the institution's activities and stocks and set prices before it can maximize its core values. For example, the board may choose to maximize teaching as a core value by adding star instructors, choosing students from the top of their high school classes, or building a new biomedical research lab. Doing any one of these activities to support a core value will require the board to make allocation decisions by setting a higher salary for the new faculty star, establishing a higher tuition discount for the top high school graduates in their application pool, or converting stock such as cash into fixed assets for the new lab.

Resource Allocation

Resource allocation is the assumption that management directs the allocation of resources, money, time, and energy within an organization to the achievement of a single goal. In business, that goal is profit. Higher education does not work within this assumption because the typical college does not have a unified management system and neither does it have a single goal to focus its resource allocation decisions. Management of most colleges or universities has multiple factions among and within the board, administration, and faculty, each having its own interest in which goal(s) should be pursued. This tearing of the fabric of management sees the president playing the role of mediator, trying to get some sort of a decision made while pacifying those who would prefer that the president be only a messenger.

A president's problem in allocating resources in some rational manner is diminished by the reality that there is no consensus on what the mission or goals of the institution are or should be. Some board members may see the institution in classic academic terms, while another faction sees it as an instrument to prepare students for the job market. Faculty may agree with one faction or the other and may even have their own interest in what the institution should be. Some members of the faculty may wish it to have a rigorous course of study in liberal arts and sciences; others may want the institution to develop students for professional graduate programs; and still others believe that research and science are the highest calling and that students are nuisances or handmaidens to research. What is significant is that the several factions compete for the internal allocation of scarce resources. In some ways, it appears that some powerful blocs within the college do not accept the concept of scarce resources and believe that the duty of the president and the administration is to deliver dollars for the benefit of the faculty.

This fractious interplay of powerful forces within institutions results in resource allocation decisions that simply move around money on the budget game board. The expert game players get more money, and the disinterested receive the same amount year to year. The notions of marginal cost curves, cost optimality, and productivity are not even in play when resource allocation decisions are made in the budget process.

Private institutions have lived with the luxury that even during bad economic periods money continues to flow through enrollment increases. However, economic and demographic forces, a major, long-term recession, a reduction in high school graduates, and changes in the mix of academic skills could end the luxury of depending solely on revenue to cover ever-increasing expenses. These economic and demographic conditions could force private institutions to take resource allocation decisions more seriously and focus on simplification of the cost structure to bring it in line with revenue rather than the other way around.

Production Function

The production function specifies how a college uses its resource inputs to generate outputs such as degrees, research, and service. The production function normally sets out the amount of labor (time and cost), the amount of capital (assets such as buildings, equipment, or land), and the amount of product or service produced from its investment in labor or capital. The effectiveness of the production function is limited by the characteristics of the colleges (students, faculty, instructional methods, and facilities). Because these characteristics are relatively immutable over the short term, they inhibit a board's decisions to reallocate resources, change priorities, or go in new directions.

The production function in higher education defies easy description because colleges are multiproduct firms, the technology used to produce (for example, an educated student) is not understood, and the production methods (labor and capital) vary across instructional programs, within instructional programs, and between instruction and research. Finally, there is a confounding aspect of instruction because the student is both an input (intellectual capabilities) and an output (acquiring new knowledge).

Each output produced by an institution of higher education has its own production function. For example, there are separate functions for each degree, certification program, research project, or community service. Each function has its own unique set of activities and stocks that have to be allocated for the production of a particular output. Most institutions have a thick catalog of academic programs leading to a degree (such as business, criminal justice, nursing, information technology, political science, physics, chemistry, mathematics, literature, education). The list could run for pages and not fully exhaust the outputs for even a small college. Over the past decade, the academic programs have grown by leaps and bounds as colleges have offered more majors hoping to snare the next student.

Market Structure

Private colleges and universities must purchase inputs and sell outputs in the marketplace where their price is set by the interplay between demand and supply. Pricing of inputs varies across segments of the labor market for faculty, administrative staff, and support staff. Input prices depend on the market structure, which encompasses the type of colleges competing for inputs (students and labor) and the control those institutions have over price of those inputs.

The evidence suggests that there is a gradation of market segments for pricing of student quality that depends on institutional wealth as measured by tuition dependency (tuition/total revenue). The segment for institutions with a low rate of tuition dependency (i.e., the wealthiest) offers the most generous financial awards so that these institutions can enroll high school graduates with the best academic credentials. The bottom segment (i.e., the poorest colleges) with the highest rate of tuition dependency offers meager financial awards and will take any student who comes to the door. Between the wealthiest and poorest market segments there are many fine gradations as colleges fight over students with financial aid awards limited by their wealth. Similar segmentations of the market can be drawn for labor input with the wealthiest segment buying the best faculty talent and the bottom segment taking whatever is left.

The interplay of buyer and seller is interesting for both labor and new students. Faculty or high school graduates with the best credentials have greater pricing value and more independence in selecting an institution than do faculty or high school graduates who have minimum credentials. In the latter case, the college can dictate wages and financial aid because there are usually fewer choices for those faculty and students.

Institutional wealth and market pricing of inputs drive the production function. Wealthy colleges use large amounts of high-quality activity inputs for faculty, classroom services, or student services and substantial amounts of stock inputs, such as endowment income, that is converted to activity expenses. In contrast, the least wealthy colleges make small investments in quality inputs, and the only stock input is the use of classroom assets because endowment income is either nonexistent or negligible.

Financial Constraint

Colleges deal perpetually with financial constraints on revenue, expenses, asset values, and liabilities. As Bowen notes, expenses are bounded by revenue, which assumes that all private colleges and universities are also restricted to zero net profit (the nonprofit constraint). Of course, the zero net profit is not a condition that must be met each year. An institution must produce a profit (or as it is called in the not-for-profit industry, an increase in net assets) so that it has sufficient financial reserves to withstand the shocks of unexpected changes in the economy or so that it can respond rationally to changes in the market. If financial operations only yield zero profit, an institution will never add to its financial reserves, putting it at risk in the event of unknown future events. If the institution produces only deficits, its financial reserves, given that it has reserves, will slowly erode with time, leaving it vulnerable to dissolution.

Financial Equilibrium

Activities, stocks, price, production function, market structure, and financial constraints describe a dynamic economic model that identifies the essential elements that influence input allocations and output decisions that maximize an institution's core values. The options that any single institution has in making input and output decisions depend on its ability to buy activities, convert stocks to activities, and produce output that is valued in the market given its production function, market structure, and financial constraints.

If the purpose of the model is to maximize the core values of an institution, Hopkins and Massey posit that this can happen only when the institution reaches a state of long-range financial equilibrium (i.e., when the long-term growth rates for revenue and expenses are in balance), given its own economic model. (Note: their economic model is available in Appendix I, Massey and Hopkins's Economic Model.)[22] This occurs when the underlying economic forces of demand, supply, prices, and production can sustain the long-run financial equilibrium of the institution. Reaching and maintaining equilibrium are accomplished through careful monitoring of key factors, such as the rates of growth and the real dollar growth in revenue and expenses.

Because of sheer size, large wealthy private institutions tend to achieve and maintain financial equilibrium more readily than do smaller less wealthy colleges. As such, the former can easily compensate for any imprecision of allocation decisions made by governing boards based on recommendations of presidents, who may be far removed from the daily operations of their institution. In contrast, small colleges have maintained (sometimes just barely) their financial equilibrium in the *absence* of sufficient reserves through superior management control by boards, presidents, and faculty who have the wit and agility to respond to and improvise more quickly in the face of economic uncertainty.

HOW DOES ECONOMICS ANSWER THESE TYPICAL QUESTIONS?

The preceding discussion on the basic economic elements of private colleges and universities can address several questions about the interplay of economics with higher education institutions.

How Do Markets Change Colleges?

If a college is at equilibrium, changes in the market have the potential to upset the production function that placed the college at equilibrium. Major changes in demand, supply, and market pricing of degrees, financial aid, faculty, utilities, debt, and all the resources needed to operate a college flow back to the allocation decisions that underlie the production function.

Short-term market bumps are resolvable through short-term reallocations, which are canceled after the bump has passed. When the changes are significant, the board, president, and key decision leaders must rework the resource allocations and redesign academic output to drive the college back to equilibrium.

Examples of several of these big changes are abundant. Huge increases in fuel costs, limitations on loans for students, tougher rules for new capital debt, vast changes in the size and make-up of applicant pools as demographics upset the old recruiting assumptions, retirement of Baby Boomers from the faculty, new technology that alters delivery of courses, and many other changes too numerous to mention show how colleges are driven from financial equilibrium.

Then, there are the impecunious colleges where even trivial changes in pricing, demand, or supply will upset the state of equilibrium. A small market bump can propel weak colleges to the very brink of extinction. These colleges live every play in a survival mode, where the president's pluck and wit are often the difference between survival and failure.

How Does Competition Force Colleges to Change?

Colleges have traditionally competed in fairly stable markets where the market is defined in terms of geography, applicant pools, and the other institutions in the competitive set. However, the traditionally stable and predictable market has changed dramatically in the past two decades. Colleges have moved out of their traditional market nests for a variety of reasons. More students are needed to provide more revenue to cover higher costs; stronger academic performance by applicants is sought to upgrade the reputation of the college; or top-level faculty is needed to encourage high-quality applicants to apply or to increase grant revenue. Whatever the reason, institutions are moving into new markets and pushing slower-moving colleges to look farther afield for new markets. Market crowding is also caused by new entrants into the market, with for-profit colleges being the primary example.

As more colleges compete for the same resources, they change the relationships among supply, demand, and prices that have characterized markets for students, athletes, faculty, and other critical resources unique to higher education. As new and more competitors crowd into the market, competition becomes harsher and more aggressive, and prices and costs go up dramatically. Several examples exist of competition for students that leads to larger financial aid packages, which are often not underwritten by endowment funds, and of competition for student athletes that has nearly created a professional atmosphere of bargaining and selling sports talent. Additionally, replacing retiring Baby Boom faculty from a smaller pool of doctorates may compel colleges to hire less qualified faculty or offer more lucrative pay packages.

Institutions that must enter intensely competitive markets will find that supply and buyer relationships are unstable and that the price for inputs and outputs is changing in ways that are not under management control. As noted earlier, long-term price changes destabilize the economic model that supports its state of equilibrium. The turmoil fostered by unfettered competition is expected to continue into the future, which will place the economics of institutions into a constant state of flux as they try to reach equilibrium.

Why Does Tuition Keep Going Up and Never Goes Down?

In a word, *productivity* is why there is steady upward pressure on tuition. Productivity is the ratio of outputs to inputs. If total revenue is given as the output (obviously this is not the real output, it is a typical measure of output) and instructional and administrative expenses are given as the inputs, it is possible to see why tuition keeps going higher.

For most colleges, even the poorest, tuition revenue is a major source but not the only source of revenue to cover expenses. Apart from unusual cases, the contribution of other sources of revenue is small, so the main burden of covering expenses is borne by tuition and enrollment.

Productivity is notoriously stagnant or declining in higher education because expense inputs grow at a rate faster than tuition revenue does. Also, colleges are stuck with a labor-intensive model of delivering education. Cost savings are stymied by the difficulty of improving classroom productivity and by the double whammy that cost savings are not a high priority in most colleges. The reason cost savings are given short shrift in higher education is that the bottom line is not the main focus of operations. Rather, the focus is clouded by the attempt to deliver on a group of core values where priorities and goals are constantly modified subject to the interests of the board, president, faculty, and other power players in the institution.

Even the new technology of delivering classes online has not substantially changed the old instructional rule of one instructor in front of a class of students. The reason that technology has not cut into the cost of instructional inputs is that colleges have not been able to invest in developing sophisticated interactive models of technology-driven education.

So, if we return to the productivity model of revenue to expenses, and assume that the primary revenue source is tuition, and assume that costs continue to grow faster than tuition revenue does, we can now explain why tuition keeps spiraling higher. The components of tuition revenue are tuition rates and enrollment. If enrollment does not increase, then tuition rates must go up to cover rising expenses. If enrollment does grow, then tuition rates are modified, but there is evidence that enrollment needs to grow at a double-digit rate to keep tuition rates constant. This rate of growth in enrollment is a rare condition in higher education. Therefore, tuition rates tend to go up and not down.

Why Do Colleges Not Control Costs?

The answer to this question was given in the discussion in the preceding section titled "Why Does Tuition Keep Going Up and Never Goes Down?" Just a quick summary of that discussion will suffice. Cost savings are not a high priority because profit or changes in net assets (use of this phrase is a sure way to obscure the need for profit) is not governed by the iron discipline of the market. Colleges and universities are pressed to produce on their core values, which are notoriously difficult to define. Even if they could be defined with precision, this would have no impact on cost savings because it is not a core value.

SUMMARY

Although economics can be a dreary science, it provides important insight into the factors that influence the financial condition of colleges and universities. Markets are becoming more challenging because we are passing through a dynamic period in how education is delivered, how costs are changing, and what students and society want higher education to produce. An institution's financial health depends not just on the quality of its programs and services, but also on the qualities of its students and their potential to perform well. Boards, presidents, faculty, and key decision makers must have a well-honed appreciation of the markets that drive their institution if they want to foster vibrancy.

REFERENCES

1. Bowen, H. R. (1990). "What Determines the Costs of Higher Education?" In *ASHE reader on finance in higher education,* edited by L. L. Leslie & R. E. Anderson (Needham Heights: Ginn Press, 1990), p. 253.

2. Jashik, S. "Ivy League Agrees to End Collaboration on Financial Aid," *Chronicle of Higher Education*, 1991. Retrieved July 17, 2008, from http://chronicle.com/che-data/articles.dir/articles-37.dir/issue-37.dir/37a00101.htm.

3. Feldman, K. A., & Newcomb, T. M. *The Impact of College on Students* Vol. 1. (San Francisco: Jossey-Bass, 1976).

4. Astin, A. *What Matters in College?* (San Francisco: Jossey-Bass, 1994).

5. Mundel, D. (1973). "Whose Education Should Society Support?" In *Does College Matter?* edited by L. C. Solmon & P. J. Taubman (New York: Academic Press, pp. 313–314).

6. Ibid.

7. Getz, M., & Siegfried, J. J. "Costs and Productivity in American Colleges and Universities." In *Economic Challenges in Higher Education*, edited by C. T. Clotfelter, R. G. Ehrenberg, M. Getz, & J. J. Siegfried (Chicago: University of Chicago Press, 1991).

8. Jashik, S. "Ivy League Agrees to End Collaboration on Financial Aid," *Chronicle of Higher Education*, 1991. Retrieved July 17, 2008, from http://chronicle.com/che-data/articles.dir/articles-37.dir/issue-37.dir/37a00101.htm.

9. Hopkins, D. S. P., & Massy, W. F. *Planning Models for Colleges and Universities*. (Stanford, CA: Stanford University Press, 1981).

10. Winston, G. C. "Subsidies, Hierarchy and Peers: The Awkward Economics of Higher Education," *Journal of Economic Perspectives*, 13(1), 13–16, 1999.

11. Bowen, H. R. *The Costs of Higher Education* (San Francisco: Jossey-Bass, 1981), pp. 19–20.

12. Hopkins, D. S. P., & Massy, W. F. *Planning Models for Colleges and Universities*. (Stanford, CA: Stanford University Press, 1981), p. 80.

13. Ibid, pp. 8, 83.

14. Ibid, p. 75.

15. Ibid, p. 76.

16. Ibid.

17. Ibid.

18. Ibid.

19. Ibid, p. 77.

20. Ibid.

21. Winston, G. C. "Subsidies, Hierarchy and Peers: The Awkward Economics of Higher Education," *Journal of Economic Perspectives*, 13(1), 17, 1999.

22. Hopkins, D. S. P., & Massy, W. F. *Planning Models for Colleges and Universities*. (Stanford, CA: Stanford University Press, 1981), p. 77.

CHAPTER 4

FINANCIAL STRUCTURE

It is not easy for men to rise whose qualities are thwarted by poverty.
—Juvenal, *Satires*

Never spend your money before you have it. —Thomas Jefferson

The highest use of capital is not to make more money, but to make money do more for the betterment of life. —Henry Ford

Juvenal speaks to a singular value served by higher education, which is to support the rise of individuals, but that is not possible if higher education in general or institutions in particular lack the money. Jefferson's admonition describes a condition that many private institutions are unable to follow given the common practice among some independent institutions of operating with a deficit. The first lesson that most presidents must learn is how to provide a credible education with money that is on the way but never quite there. Ford's quote is the hope of all boards and presidents who undertake to coax reluctant donors to employ their money to better the life of others and not themselves.

For most private colleges, however, money is the necessary evil that must be plucked from the students' pockets because it does not always come from the generosity of well-meaning donors. Money from either students or donors calls for prudent stewardship so that the money is not lost to frivolous or unwise decisions or fails to provide the education sorely desired by students and their parents or by donors to serve a greater good.

The issue here is how a college manages its finances so that the board is assured that it is acting as prudent stewards of the institution's assets held in trust for future use in operations. The avenue for understanding this issue is the financial structure of an institution, which manages the flow of funds through the institution. This chapter considers how the financial structure works, the main revenue flows into the system and expenditures of those funds, pricing strategies, the preservation of funds through capital investments, and the financial management of the system to keep it in a state of equilibrium.

HOW THE FINANCIAL STRUCTURE WORKS

The financial structure for nonprofit higher education institutions is complicated by its nature as a nonprofit. This status does not negate the production of excess revenue, that is, profit; rather, nonprofit colleges cannot distribute their profits for personal gain. The transfer of excess funds for personal use and self-dealing through contracts to family members or hidden business associates is prohibited by tax law. Tax regulations penalize the organization with the possible loss of nonprofit status. Severe tax penalties are also charged to those individuals who benefit from the proscribed practice. Unlike publicly owned companies, nonprofits do not have a duty to maximize profit; however, they may optimize some other set of values.

Being nonprofit denotes that they are not governed by the iron discipline of the marketplace to maximize profits. Because profits are of small import, minimizing costs is not vital to financial planning until there is a revenue crisis. Constrained from profit maximization and ignoring cost minimization lead to Bowen's proposition cited earlier that colleges maximize revenue and spend it.[1] Revenue becomes the engine that determines the expenditure bounds of the institution. Although net income is happenstance and nice to have, it is deemed trivial to financial strategy and misunderstood as to its importance to the financial structure and financial equilibrium. Net income can act as an essential building block for cash reserves, a buffer against short-term exigency, investments as a lever for future growth, reserves for long-term uncertainty, or a trade-off for debt when rates are high.

Private institutions are saddled with the difficult task of rationally allocating scarce resources because they are governed by a multitude of goals—instruction, research, and community service—that are not clearly stated and are not ranked in order of importance. Consequently, resource allocation decisions are rife with conflict. Cohen and March note with some acerbity that decision making in higher education is best described as organized anarchy, where goals are ambiguous and decisions are the product of chance events.[2]

Exclusion from the equity market leaves nonprofit colleges with donor or debt markets to fund capital growth. Unlike for-profits, where capital formation supports future profit maximization, private colleges seem to lack a clear vision of the purpose of capital formation to strengthen the financial integrity of the institution and improve the value of its services. In some cases, such as residence halls, the funds go to improve future income; in other cases to advance the reputation of the institution such as with libraries, classrooms, and laboratories; and in others to please athletic boosters, for example, with a new stadium. Then, there is the burnishing of the image of intellectual superiority, which is useful in finding top flight students and big buck donors by creating Babylonian displays of architecture. These decisions are not inherently wrong or morally abstruse, but many presidents push for them without thought to their immediate or long-term impact on the financial equilibrium of the institution, the marketability of instructional programs, or the productivity of operations. There is substantial evidence that faddish architectural extravaganzas carry with them monstrous operational, maintenance, and repair costs as they age.[3]

Nonprofits, although they benefit from their tax-free status, find that being limited to donor and debt markets results in heavy costs and limits their opportunities. Harvesting gifts from donors necessitates huge expenditures for development offices and officers that act as babysitters for the wealthy, perennial nags for the annual funds, and unwanted guests at the death watch of moneyed alumni. Large contributions rarely come without strings that tell the college how the gift must be spent. Most times the conditions are benevolent; however, sometimes—especially with older gifts—the gifts are highly restricted, such as scholarships only for people from a certain place, with a particular last name, or from a specific ethnic or religious group. The problem with endowed gifts (restricted in perpetuity for a particular purpose) is that mores, fashions, and laws change. What does the college do with gifts that may have dated limits or embarrassing conditions?

When big dollar projects are funded by debt instruments, the college is necessarily bound by limitations (covenants) imposed by the lender. Covenants can impose restrictions by setting limits on future loans, the amount of cash reserves, and/or the necessity of avoiding deficits and may establish other indicators of financial health. The debt market is very demanding, and when there is a debt crunch, only colleges with the strongest financials will get money. Financially struggling colleges can be denied money desperately needed to dig out of their financial hole.

Because colleges are not run under the white hot heat of equity markets, they often pay no heed to basic financial practices. However, boards and presidents should still test every project rigorously to see whether it makes financial sense. This involves tedious but essential computations of financial value, trade-offs between projects and financial methods, risk analysis, and forecasts of future earnings or expenses. When presidents sidestep these practices, they put their institution at risk because they may not even know how predictable but untested events could affect the project and the college's finances.

Although the preceding issues deal with big financial issues, small matters obfuscate financial planning and can turn the financial structure into a murky swamp. These issues arise from higher education accounting and reporting systems that fail to clearly distinguish the revenues and costs that drive an institution. This can turn planning into a loopy exercise of guess and hope, with little reality behind the plans, if the data are invalid.

One place where fuzzy data are evident is in the audit where tuition and fee revenue is not classified as revenue produced from associate, undergraduate, masters, or doctoral degree programs. Because tuition and fees are mixed together, it is impossible to figure out the sources of revenue increases or if fee increases and not tuition are the source of tuition and fee revenue. This information is important for planning to be pertinent. Of course, institutional planners have more detailed data, but local records may be a hash if they are not regularly reconciled to ensure accuracy.

Similar cost problems may ensue when instructional costs are lumped together in reports without clear distinctions for programs, degrees, instruction, research, compensation, materials, or debt. For example, expenses reported in the audit turn into mush when depreciation and plant costs are allocated in instruction, academic support, student services, institutional support, or auxiliary departments, without the report specifying the departments that comprise each function. Though designed to ensure consistency, GAAP*and FASB† rules are sufficiently vague enough that colleges can move pay or other expenses from one function to another. The result is that one can seldom tell what the expense report is saying, which makes it useless in understanding the institution's financial structure. This causes major mistakes in forecasting and analysis, which lead to errors in understanding the present and preparing for the future.

Many board members from business see an enrollment decline and expect that the college expenses will fall proportionately. They incorrectly assume that operational expenses in higher education (like their businesses) are split between variable and fixed costs. This assumption does not work in higher education because instructional costs move in step-wise fashion and are not directly related to changes in enrollment. Reasons for this disconnect include faculty tenure or its variations such as multiyear contracts, the size of classrooms, and the lag between contracting for faculty before the semester begins and discovery that enrollment is down after the semester starts. In some ways, managing class schedules is similar to putting an airliner in the

---

*GAAP stands for generally accepted accounting principles.

†FASB is the Financial Accounting Standards Board.

air. Once the minimum enrollment is met and there are empty seats, the class still goes. It almost suggests that the Priceline* model of auctioning empty seats might work. However, empty seats in classrooms are usually limited to the set of students within geographic reach of the college, which appears to be about 20 miles. Also, if the college is a residential institution, it is too late to enroll more students at the start of a new semester. Enrolling new students after a semester starts is only possible at commuter colleges or in continuing education programs. If potential students do not need the class, then the seat remains empty. There are also issues of how bidding by colleges to fill individual classes would fit into earning a degree with a specific major, or how bidding would affect either institutional or governmental financial aid awards.

As the preceding discussion suggests, institutions exist as idiosyncratic oddities filled with peculiarities that are difficult to fathom until someone is immersed in them for a long period. This is not an excuse but a difficult and painful reality faced by the public, board members, parents, students, and new employees. It usually takes a fiscal year cycle before new accountants, faculty, or administrators learn the real politics and operational factors that drive the financial structure. This long learning cycle explains why any changes in key financial employees or accounting systems have long lead times before accurate reports are available and financial policies are enforced.

The next sections take you inside the financial system to explain money flows through the system, pricing strategies, capital investment, and financial equilibrium. Keep in mind that the following commentary discusses the financial system for the average private, nonprofit college or university. Individual institutions are very creative in how they set up and work with their own financial structures.

Fund Flows

The flow of funds through the financial structure depends on the type of funds (tuition, grants, gifts, debt, or other sources) entering the institution; the allocation and expenditures of those funds for labor

*Priceline refers to the travel discount Internet site.

or noncapital goods or services; or conversion of those funds into reserves such as short- or long-term investments, or capital goods. The board is responsible for governing the major allocations and overseeing their use. The president's job is to carry out the decisions of the board and to monitor performance given their decisions. Finally, the chief financial officer must record and report performance.

Accounting rules based on the principles set forth by the Financial Accounting Standards Board (FASB) determine the often complex financial structure that is common to most private higher education institutions. Two major factors complicate accounting in higher education. The first factor is restricted funds, which are limited in use. The second factor is the endowment fund, which is a repository of capital that is preserved for future use. The result of these two factors is that accounting in higher education is characterized by an ungainly *fund accounting system* that FASB has tried to simplify. Nevertheless, most financial offices have found it prudent to keep fund accounting so that they have precise records showing compliance with regulations or contractual conditions of restricted funds and endowments.

However, fund accounting is confusing; and the confusion will not go away no matter how hard FASB or anyone tries! It splits the financial structure into subfunds that record, regulate, and monitor the funds entering or held by the institution according to their use restrictions. Each fund is a separate financial structure with its own accounting, budget, and reporting system. Audit regulations require that audited financial statements combine the funds into a single fund report. However, financial reports include the separate funds in the statement of activities (income statement) and the statement of financial position (balance sheet). The need for fund accounting becomes apparent in the latter statement because net assets (similar but not the same as equity) are reported for each major type of fund held by the college. The typical funds include the following:

- *Unrestricted funds:* Unrestricted funds are funds that do not have restrictions (conditions on how they are used). Examples of unrestricted funds are tuition and fees, residence and food service income, gifts that have no conditions, and interest income.

- *Restricted funds:* Restricted funds are funds with specific restrictions on how and when the funds are to be used. Examples include government funds (financial aid, grants, bonds, or loans), gifts for use in a specified construction project, scholarships, athletics, research, endowment income that has restrictions on use, and debt that is limited to a specific purpose.

- *Temporarily restricted funds:* Temporarily restricted funds are to be used within a specified time period. One of the time restrictions is when revenue is received for construction and is to be allocated annually to cover depreciation on the project.

These definitions do not fully cover the complexity of the financial structure. For instance, if $1 million is budgeted annually to operations from endowment funds, that amount may include money taken from dozens or even hundreds of different restricted accounts. Each withdrawal and each use is recorded independently to assure donors and auditors that the dollars are spent as specified in the conditions of the original gift. This level of accounting is comparable but not as simple as the accounting that banks must do with checking and saving accounts.

Fund accounting forces the financial structure into an array of funds like a giant railway switchyard with each track representing a particular subfund that eventually feeds into the main line. The components of the financial structure typically include revenue, expenses, net income, assets, liabilities, net assets, allocation decisions, financial controls, and performance reports. What follows is how funds are entered, used, and retained in the structure:

Entry of funds: Because nonprofits cannot sell equity, the two main entry points are revenue or debt:

- Revenue can enter through unrestricted and restricted portals. Tuition and fees, residence and food service (room and board) fees, and short-term cash investment interest come as unrestricted, whereas other forms of revenue such as gifts, grants, and government funds pass through the restricted portal.

- Funds from short-term debt such as credit lines and funds from long-term debt are also designated as restricted.

Use of funds: Unrestricted revenue and some restricted revenue such as government grants or financial aid are expended within a fiscal year. Restricted funds that entered in prior years and that are now held by the institution are drawn from the particular fund account and assigned to a specifically restricted expenditure. Funds subject to restrictions and allocation decisions are used for standard expenditures, such as compensation, supplies, equipment, contracted services, or interest payments.

Retained funds: Net income from operations or income received during the fiscal year from gifts, grants, or income from endowment investments is retained funds. The net income is placed in a particular fund account, such as unrestricted, restricted, or temporarily restricted funds. The money from these funds is usually held in short- or long-term asset accounts, for example, cash, investments, endowments (usually managed as an investment portfolio), or property.

Allocation decisions: The governing board is responsible for allocation decisions, which are usually expressed through the annual budget. The board also has the authority to clarify the restriction on funds where the restrictions are ambiguous; however, clarification of restrictions is usually done with the assistance of the donor or the courts, if the donor is unavailable or deceased. If the original restriction is no longer possible (for example, a college changes its athletics programs to NCAA Division III and can no longer award athletic scholarships), the institution must also request a change in restriction from the donor or the courts if the donor is unavailable or deceased.

Revenue and Cash Flows

Tuition dependency (the ratio of tuition revenue to total revenue) is a convenient way of classifying the revenue flows into private institutions. Colleges or universities that rely on tuition for 60 percent or more of their revenue are classified as tuition dependent, whereas those that receive less that 60 percent of their revenue from students are classified as nontuition dependent. Revenue for the latter institutions generally comes from gifts, grants, or draws from endowment funds.

The long-term financial reserves of an institution are often subject to its tuition dependency classification. Tuition-dependent institutions are more likely to have smaller financial reserves than do low tuition-dependent institutions because they have large endowments. The proportion (endowment draw) taken from the investment fund for current operations is subject to legal constraints. The draw provides the main source of revenue for the latter institutions. These funds act as a generator of current operating income and as a buffer against unexpected financial events that could threaten the financial stability of institutions that are tuition dependent with reserves that are in short supply.

Institutions with high rates of tuition dependency are not necessarily small institutions. The evidence suggests tuition dependency tends to be higher in smaller institutions. Yet this is not a firm rule because some large private universities are very tuition dependent and some small colleges are not tuition dependent.[4] This phenomenon suggests that private institutions with little or no endowment funds must count on tuition revenue to stay even or ahead of the inflationary pressure inherent in their expense structure. High tuition dependency is deadly when enrollment growth slows to a crawl because it will not provide enough revenue or cash for expenses.

Tuition and Fee Revenue

Nearly 35 percent of private institutions could be classified as tuition dependent. The vast majority of private institutions discount tuition revenue with noncash institutional financial aid packages so that they can remain price competitive with other institutions. These aid packages have a considerable effect on the conversion of revenue into cash because the reduction in aid is not supported by cash from governmental aid or endowment funds. When tuition and fees are discounted by institutional aid, accounting reports show the result as net tuition and fees.* The reason for showing the net result is to acknowledge that the discount acts like a sale and that the college does not gain the full-cash value from its tuition and fees.

As tuition discounts approach 50 percent, tuition-dependent colleges face cash shortages because the cash from tuition is inadequate to support operational expenses.[5] Also, high tuition discount rates are found at colleges that give loans to students who cannot pay the balance of their bills, even with these large discounts. In the housing industry, these loans are described as ninja loans—no income, no job, and no assets. These colleges are now at risk that the loan will not be repaid and that they will be in a larger cash hole. Some institutions manage their billing portfolio with proficiency and keep delinquent loans to less than 2 percent of billings. The billing office does this through an aggressive campaign of tracking every payment and immediately contacting students who are not keeping current with their bills. The late bill payers may be dropped from any future courses and even sent to court if delinquency lasts more than 45 days. Other colleges are lackadaisical about collecting late payments. Their billing office may use a simple balance forward that is rarely monitored until the auditors begin to raise questions about the true level of delinquencies and force the college to substantially increase its uncollectable reserve. Some institutions, when they begin to take an active interest in their unpaid balances, discover that they have inadvertently granted an "unpaid bill scholarship" for many of their graduates. Clearly, this situation will devastate the financial condition of the institution.

Nontuition Revenue Flows

Nontuition revenue flows come from gifts, grants, endowment income, investment income, and other governmental and private

*Accounting formula for net tuition and fees: Tuition and Fees − Institutional Aid = Net Tuition.

sources. In most cases, the scale of these flows is tied to the reputation of the college or university. Economics would suggest that a bargain is reached between the reputation of the institution and the donor's desire to be connected to the prestigious image of an institution. *Reputation* here refers to a long and cherished tradition with a lineage of graduates who have accumulated great wealth, to major research conducted by star researchers with Nobel Prize winners thrown in the mix for good measure, to faculty recognized nationally for their publications and expert presentations, or to dreams that the gift will yield a seat on the board, which is nice to have on the résumé. Whatever the reason for giving the gift, nontuition-dependent institutions will find that their main revenue flows have to expand constantly to keep pace with expenses required to nurture and enhance their reputation. Marketing reputation to capture large gifts and grants is as challenging as what tuition-dependent institutions face in finding more students.

Nontuition-dependent colleges, unlike tuition-dependent institutions, rarely face the immediate threat of deficits wreaking havoc with their financial condition. However, economic conditions do arise and combine to reduce gifts, grants, and endowment principal. The latter is an issue because the "prudent steward rule" keeps endowment draws at a level commonly between 4 percent and 5 percent so that principal is not diminished by inflation or excessive draws.[6]

During the great bull market of the 1990s, endowment income grew by a spectacular 180 percent as endowment values skyrocketed, which under the prudent steward rule was a license to increase endowment draws by the same proportion.[7] Not only did endowments grow at a spectacular rate, but donors were more generous. Many private colleges during this period thought that they had escaped their former tuition-dependent status because their small endowments increased beyond expectations and large donors willingly thrust huge gifts into their hands. This golden age ended with a resounding crash with the puncture of the technology bubble in early 2000 and the catastrophic events of September 11th. A market crash of the magnitude that occurred in 2000 and 2001 quickly wiped out the excess capital gains that many donors used as the basis for their gifts to private institutions (these gifts offset a good chunk of the taxes owed during the run-up to the crash). Big gifts vanished and some endowments returned to the reduced values that they saw prior to the bull market. Presidents at many of the *nouveau riche* colleges found that their financial safety cushions were gone following the collapse in the value of their endowments and the loss of the big donor gifts.

Even colleges with reliable endowment and gift income found themselves hammered in the relentless bear market of the new century. "The market in 2001 [was] brutal," says William M. Rose, treasurer of Case Western Reserve University. Its endowment dropped about $115 million in value (after the collapse).[8] Beginning its plunge in September 2000, Standard & Poor's 500 Index fell 25 percent by the spring of 2001.[9] At the same time, the NASDAQ Index, home to various technology companies, took a breathtaking 60.8 percent dive from its high.[10] Endowments heavily invested in the technologies suffered as a result. The market downturn that started with the credit crunch of 2007 is further evidence that endowments are volatile and that only the superwealthy private universities have the wherewithal to buy the advice needed to keep endowments at double-digit pace while the general market turns down or stagnates.

Revenue and Unrealized Income

"Unrealized income" is gains and losses in investments that are not realized (i.e., the investment has not been sold but the gain or loss at the time of measuring value is recognized as a result of accounting rules).* Table 4.1 on the next page shows what happens when unrealized gains and losses are included or excluded from net income according to tuition dependency (the table uses net income/revenue).

Table 4.1 shows that unrealized gains or losses obscure the apparent operating state of the institution by several magnitudes. This distortion can make planning tricky, owing to the volatility

---

*These unrealized changes can distort the true state of operations of the institution, even though they do suggest that institutions with substantial investments will eventually feel the impact as money is drawn from the investment. The impact occurs because institutions use a multiyear average of total investment value as the basis for determining the draw (average value times the draw). This causes the impact on value and draws to lag the real value of the market.

TABLE 4.1—NET INCOME TO REVENUE BY FTE ENROLLMENT AND TUITION DEPENDENCY, 1998–2001

	1998	1999	2000	2001
Include Unrealized Gains and Losses				
Enrollment > 2000	35.2%	25.6%	28.7%	–3.2%
Enrollment < 2000 and > 1000	35.6%	24.6%	35.9%	–13.7%
Enrollment < 1000	25.5%	16.3%	15.4%	–3.1%
Tuition Dependency > 60%	6.4%	4.7%	14.3%	–6.9%
Tuition Dependency < 60%	34.6%	24.5%	32.7%	–9.1%
Exclude Unrealized Gains and Losses				
Enrollment > 2000	6.2%	5.3%	2.2%	2.0%
Enrollment < 2000 and > 1000	2.7%	3.0%	4.3%	0.3%
Enrollment < 1000	2.8%	5.9%	3.5%	1.5%
Tuition Dependency > 60%	–0.1%	0.4%	–3.3%	–2.7%
Tuition Dependency < 60%	3.9%	4.6%	4.6%	1.1%

Note: FTE stands for full-time-equivalent enrollment. This number is constructed by equating part-time students to full-time students and summing. Usually, an FTE student takes 10 courses during a fall and spring semester academic year.

Source: JMA Higher Ed Stats. (2002). Management ratios: Private institutions, xls: 1997–2000. Boulder, CO: John Minter and Associates.

of financial markets. If budget plans or financial strategies do not remove the effect of unrealized gains from the analysis, it could obscure long-term operational losses.[11] Neither tuition-dependent nor nontuition-dependent colleges should ignore this circumstance. Budget planners should remove the impact of the unrealized income to identify the true operating state of the institution. This will ensure that plans are made relevant to the activities of the institution and not in reference to unpredictable changes in the market valuation of investment funds. After the operational budget or financial forecasts are prepared, then "what ifs" on unrealized income can be introduced to determine the impact. In the short term, unrealized gains or losses have no real effect on cash flows, which should be the immediate concern. Long-term unrealized income will reduce or increase cash flows, as noted earlier.

Cash Flow

Cash is the preferred measure for estimating the financial condition of the institution because revenue is not useful until it becomes cash. Cash is what makes payroll, pays the bills, and covers debt service payments. Payments are not made with pure tuition revenue or receivables. Accrual accounting rules can show positive net income, but cash may have disappeared if students or third-party payees such as employers or government agencies do not pay their bills on time or do not pay their bills at all.

A credit squeeze like the kind experienced at the end of the real estate bust is tough on cash flow for tuition-dependent colleges. Students who used loans from private sources to pay for the balance of their bills were cut short when loans were no longer available. What compounded the problem is that the remaining loan agencies tightened their credit standards by increasing the credit ratings required of borrowers. In addition, they upped interest rates to offset potential losses. The main impact appears to have fallen on low-income students whose families do not have the funds or credit wherewithal to get a private loan. These students either are forced to leave college or to attend a less expensive state institution.

PRICING STRATEGIES

Relationship Between Tuition Discounts and Tuition Revenue

Table 4.2 on the next page illustrates what happens when tuition discount rate tops out at 45 percent. As Table 4.2 shows, net tuition revenue declines as the tuition discount rate increases. The marginal rate of change nearly doubles when the discount rate increases from 35 percent to 45 percent and net tuition revenue declines for each rate. Of course, this table does not take into account the inelasticity

TABLE 4.2—IMPACT OF DIFFERENT TUITION DISCOUNT RATES ON NET TUITION REVENUE, 2005–2008

	2005	2006	2007	2008
Posted Tuition	$27,000	$27,000	$27,000	$27,000
Financial Aid Discount Rate	25%	30%	35%	45%
Net Tuition	$20,250	$18,900	$17,550	$14,850
Enrollment	1,500	1,500	1,500	1,500
Net Tuition Revenue	$30,375,000	$28,350,000	$26,325,000	$22,275,000
Marginal Change		–$2,025,000	–$2,025,000	–$4,050,000
Marginal Rate of Change		–6.7%	–7.1%	–15.4%

of tuition prices where increases in price do not necessarily lead to commensurate losses in tuition revenue. Colleges need to analyze the effect carefully when they increase the tuition discount rate so that they avoid the unintended result that tuition revenue drops off precipitously and unexpectedly.

Pricing

Pricing strategy manages the relationship between posted price (advertised tuition rate), unfunded financial aid, and net tuition revenue. This relationship undergirds tuition revenue flow at nearly every institution, be it rich or poor. Tuition pricing strategies become counterproductive if they are applied willy-nilly and are not accompanied by a monitoring plan that tracks the effect on enrollment and net tuition revenue. Several years ago, a set of tuition-dependent colleges substantially increased their unfunded aid, rather than enrolling more students; enrollment fell and net tuition tanked.[12] Their pricing strategy was a miserable failure. They had a plan but not a strategy. A strategy assumes that the consequences both good and bad are understood and that contingencies exist to limit damage. For these colleges, the strategy carried uncertain risks that could have been disastrous to their long-term viability.

Financial aid, like other things sold in the market, has to be revised, adjusted, or abandoned when the market changes. Here are several financial aid strategies that many private institutions have employed to increase enrollment:

- *Financial aid grid:* The grid is a sophisticated approach to financial aid that lays out award amounts related to the type of student sought by the college. Typically, the grid displays some sort of academic goal in terms of student achievement, or high school rank, or a composite score in the columns, and the average award is displayed in the rows. The cells contain the expected number of awards. By multiplying the value in the cell with the average award, the college can estimate the total value of the tuition discount for that cell. As a rule, awards increase with the scale of the academic measure.

  The grid also acts as a monitoring instrument that tracks the number of awards for each cell to make sure that financial aid is meeting its enrollment and academic goals. Table 4.3 is a grid showing the financial aid goals. (Two

TABLE 4.3—SAMPLE FINANCIAL AID GRID

High School Rank	Top 10%	11% to 20%	21% to 30%	31% to 40%	41% to 50%	51% to 70%	Totals
Awards							
70% of tuition	50						50
60% of tuition		75					75
50% of tuition			150				150
40% of tuition				200			200
30% of tuition					400		400
25% of tuition						500	500
Total Awards	50	75	150	200	400	500	1,375

more grids displaying the grid and its impact on net tuition rates and net tuition revenue are included in Appendix F, Financial Aid Grids for Net Tuition Rates and Net Tuition Revenue.) Note that high school rank is stopped at the 70 percent level because evidence suggests that students with lower ranks have a very low probability (33 percent) of graduating within eight years.[13]

- *Price–quality financial aid strategy:* Many private colleges employ a pricing strategy that targets the assumption by students and parents that higher tuition rates indicate better academic quality. Two groups of private institutions use this strategy. The first group includes highly respected institutions such as Harvard, University of Pennsylvania, Duke, and Gettysburg. They use their endowment draws to fund large financial aid awards to attract the best students. The second group of colleges raises tuition rates to a level charged by colleges with stronger academic reputations. Their goal is to gain enough revenue to stave off another year of reporting an operating deficit.

- *Financial aid trolling strategies:* Some colleges are trollers offering anything to get a student so that the college can survive another semester or another year. These colleges throw financial aid at potential students, confusing the difference between revenue and cash. They achieve nothing by using this strategy because they slowly consume their cash reserves.

ENDOWMENT INVESTMENTS

The principal goal of endowment investments is to protect the value of the endowment so that future students can acquire the benefits of the institution; this is commonly known as the "intergenerational equity rule."[14,15] This goal is served by a spending rule that maintains the relative value of the endowment fund given inflation and economic trends. To do this, the spending rule should not excessively deplete the value of the investments and neither should the rule be so conservative as to negate prudent and *reasonable distribution of resources to the current generation of students*. Typically, this has resulted in a spending rule between 3 and 5 percent of the total value of the endowment funds. Congress has expressed its concern that colleges and universities have used their spending rules to hoard money and not distribute it as financial aid, which has resulted in unnecessarily high debt burdens for students. This issue is being debated among institutions and continues to illicit disquiet in Congress. Several major independent institutions have restructured their spending rule to increase financial aid allocations. How this will play out under conditions of economic stress and greater demands for controlling tuition costs remains to be seen.

A prudent and reasonable distribution rule assumes that the investment portfolio has sufficient liquidity* so that the institution can draw cash to support its operations. During the recent financial debacle, several of the best-run endowment programs have discovered that a sizable portion of their alternative investments in their portfolio is illiquid. An illiquid investment could involve private real estate investments, hedge funds, or private ventures that are not traded publicly. As a result, they cannot price or sell the alternative investment. The value of the endowment portfolio is not known, which has a direct impact on managing the investments and determining the amount that can be spent. Overweighting a portfolio with alternative investments in which the market is restricted to a few investors places the college at great risk. Some institutions that encountered the perils of an illiquid investment were forced to go into the debt market at a time when it was nearly impossible to find reasonable rates or to borrow money. These institutions incurred two costs: the loss of real money and the lost opportunity to use cash spent on unplanned borrowing for other priorities.[16]

---

*Liquidity means that a tangible asset (building or land) or an intangible asset (certificate of deposit or stock) can be sold and turned into cash. Illiquidity happens when an asset cannot be turned into cash.

CAPITAL INVESTMENTS

Business firms use capital to invest in projects that will yield a greater return than their cost. Nonprofit institutions being restricted from equity markets only have access to tax-free debt markets or to tax deductible donations to fund capital projects. Debt and donations are just another way of acquiring enough capital to fund long-term projects. The problem with debt or donations, unlike equity, is that obligations expressed in the form of covenants or restrictions can limit what the institution can do with the money and how it operates.

Higher education does have capital projects that can yield income greater than its costs; examples include residence halls, food services facilities, athletic arenas, parking garages, and similar ventures. Before an income-producing capital project is initiated, the college should evaluate the validity of the underlying assumptions. *Net present value analysis* (see Appendix C, Financial Measures) is a classic method to evaluate whether the current value of future cash flows exceeds expected costs. The analysis computes the current value of future net cash flows based on the cash received and disbursed for each year of the useful life of the project.* There are two rules for selecting a project or a set of projects. *Rule 1* is to select the project that yields the largest net cash flow, and *Rule 2* is to rank order the projects and select every project until capital funds set aside for investment are exhausted.

Some projects do not yield excess income; rather, they increase operational expenses and debt service without any offsetting income flows. Samples of these projects include classrooms, student centers, administrative offices, student services buildings, information technology (this could generate savings, but ordinarily does not), gyms, and instructional laboratories, where grant-based research is not conducted.

Capital projects, whether they are income or non-income producing, call for a careful analysis by the administration under these conditions:

---

* For example, the institution is evaluating three projects yielding net cash as follows: project Alpha yielding $10,000; project Beta, $11,500; and project Omega, $9,500. The rank order of choice for the projects would be Beta, Alpha, and Omega. If the institution has $21,500, it could fund projects Alpha and Beta.

- Ensure that total debt for the institution is within the standards expected by leaders.*†

- Test cash flows against the possibility of shortfalls in the forecast. This is done by setting a statistical confidence interval for high and low estimates of the income and expense values.

- Make sure that projects are not "Field of Dreams" projects that are constructed on the untested assumption that new students or grant money will support the new building or new research program.

FINANCIAL EQUILIBRIUM

Equilibrium is simple to describe and hard to achieve. As noted in Chapter 3 on economics, equilibrium is achieved when long-term rates of growth are in balance. This does not mean that total revenue equals total expenses. Furthermore, balanced growth rates for revenue and expense growth rates are not necessary every year. It simply means that over the long term, for example, five years, if expenses are rising at a 5 percent annual rate, revenue should grow at the same rate or better.

Achieving balanced growth rates requires continuous monitoring of changes in revenue and expenses and the factors that drive them. It also puts a tremendous burden on the president because expenses have a powerful dynamic for growth. Higher education lacks the incentive to control growth to produce profits. Therefore, the focus of many administrators and the faculty is to push for expansion of their expense budgets without compensating improvements in productivity. William Massey and Robert Zemsky call this condition the "academic ratchet and administrative lattice."[17]

---

† NACUBO is an excellent source for financial ratios and ratio analysis.
§ Moody's Investors Service provides standards for various debt ratios. It also provides regular reports on financial ratios for private colleges and universities. Log in to the site at www.moodys.com to access the reports.

The academic ratchet posits that faculty steer work away from instruction toward "specialized concerns of faculty research, publication, professional service, and personal pursuits."[18] The faculty is left to its own devices to redefine at ever higher levels of expenditures the baseline for their work.[19] Student academic counseling is sloughed off to administrative counseling units; or instructional generalists teaching many different courses are replaced with specialists who teach only a few courses, some of which are truly arcane, and instructional preparation is replaced with work on articles and books. The result is that the cost of the faculty increases without a corresponding increase in productivity.

The administrative lattice, akin to empire building of days past, describes the expansion of administrative responsibilities and positions within colleges. Expert managers beget expert managers along with support services to execute their decisions so as to better serve their institution and self-interests. Moreover, consensus decision making, formerly reserved for the faculty, is now spread to administrative units, a transfer that has had several less than salutary effects on cost.[20] Consensus makes decisions cumbersome, contentious, and time-consuming. When one decision is reached, a forward momentum generates other costly decisions that cannot be reversed because so many parts of the institution have affirmed them. Moreover, consensus obscures responsibility and enhances risk aversion to change because the parties to the decision often have a vested interest in the status quo.

Oliver Williamson, who wrote a seminal work on economic imperatives within organizations, suggests that colleges, because they operate in the absence of measurable goals, will see internal transactions governed by opportunistic self-interested decisions.[21] This happens as experts and specialized cadres take over decision making in an organization. The organization loses the ability to establish goals without the review and approval of those same experts. The experts gain power, independence, and the opportunity to exploit decisions to their advantage. When productivity is based on unmonitored self-interest opportunism, as occurs in colleges, administrative and faculty costs will necessarily rise because decisions stem not from institutional goals but from personal ones.

FIGURE 4.1—FTE CHART: FOR-PROFIT SLOPE FOR EXPENSES AND ENROLLMENT

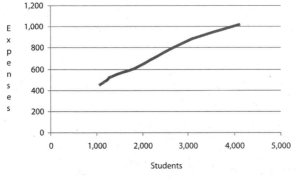

FIGURE 4.2—FTE CHART: NONPROFIT SLOPE FOR EXPENSES AND ENROLLMENT

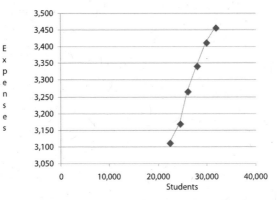

Reprinted with permission from U.S. Department of Education. (1999). Table 334: Current fund revenue of private nonprofit institutions of higher education by source: 1980–81 through 1995–96. In Digest of Education Statistics. Washington, DC: National Center for Education Statistics.

Figure 4.1 compares growth rates for administrative (academic support, student services, and institutional expenses) with instructional expenses at for-profit colleges. Figure 4.2 makes the same comparison for nonprofit colleges. It can be fairly assumed in both cases that the greatest proportion of administrative and instructional expenses is for compensation.

The slope for nonprofit institutions is nearly five times greater than the slope for the profit-making colleges. These figures tend to support Zemsky's and Massey's condition of the "academic ratchet and administrative lattice," and they also appear to support Williamson's proposition that self-interested decision making is not productive. For-profit colleges are driven by the hard market realities that when costs eat into profit, equity prices will fall. They either pay attention to the operational costs or they will fail as competitive businesses. By pursuing multiple goals, nonprofit colleges do not have a clear mandate to control costs. As a result, the administration and faculty act independently, which leads to higher costs, and students and parents pay the price for this inefficiency! The financial dynamics of nonprofits make it difficult to manage their financial equilibrium. For instance, when nonprofits raise tuition to stay even with undisciplined cost increases, they avoid confronting their inefficiencies. In the long term, they will pay the consequences as operational inefficiency builds to a point where some sort of economic change forces a bloodletting that all private college presidents dread. Even these bloodletting exercises fail to achieve long-term efficiencies because they usually involve across-the-board cuts or cuts based on which administrator does the best job of gaming the decision-making process.

When goals are ambiguous and opposition seems to be a constant as they are at most colleges and universities, leadership turns to a political model to please as many constituencies as possible. The institution under this all-too-typical leadership model moves aimlessly and only luck keeps it in equilibrium because it is not in the interest of anyone to make hard financial decisions that will upset the political balance.

TESTING CHANGES IN THE FINANCIAL STRUCTURE

Successful management of the financial structure involves three stages: testing, installation, and performance tracking. Presidents of private institutions are under constant pressure to add new programs, expand capacity, and increase services. Whenever a new academic program or department is added to the institution, the financial structure is changed in unexpected ways if the changes are not carefully tested beforehand. Evaluating financial changes involves building a model, making any assumptions explicit, and testing the efficacy of the model. When the tests are completed, and the changes are deemed reasonable to initiate, then the operational plans should be based on the model. Success does not stop with testing and initiation of operational plans; success comes as operational performance is continuously tracked to determine whether actual performance matches expectations.

Expenses associated with new departments are simple to test because it is a matter of correctly estimating the costs and forecasting those costs over several years. However, expense forecasts never take into account the tendency suggested in the preceding section that department heads and subchiefs will aggrandize power by adding new positions and responsibilities.

Income-generating programs are more difficult to test because revenue flows are subject to events outside the direct control of the institution. The tests to determine whether or not to start the project should follow these steps:

1. Conduct a breakeven unit analysis to estimate the enrollment or other revenue-driving factor to reach breakeven. The purpose of this exercise is to assure the administration that the goals are realistic. (See Appendix C: Financial Measures for the method.)

2. Test the operational plan against a financial model of the college to determine its impact across all segments of the institution. The model should work with net cash flows because cash is the ultimate measure of performance; revenue is only a way station to cash.

3. Compute a confidence interval around the factors driving revenue projections; then, retest the financial model using the upper and lower bounds of the confidence interval.

4. Test cash flows using net present value analysis. (See Appendix C: Financial Measures.)

5.   If there are multiple projects and a set dollar value for invest-
     ments, select the projects in rank order of their net present
     value up to the investment limit.

6.   As a cautionary note, do not force the estimates to make the
     project work.

SUMMARY

The financial structure of the college is a set of entry points, cash
flows, and reserves that determines the financial condition of the
institution. The structure encompasses the revenue, expenses, assets,
and liabilities or, in other words, the basic accounting structure of
the institution. The important features of the structure are the set
of output and allocation decisions that will determine what flows
through the structure and whether the financial structure can reach
a state of equilibrium. Recall that financial equilibrium is present
when long-term revenue and expense growth rates are in balance.
Balance does not necessarily mean that this condition has to be met
every year. It does mean that when the growth rates are substantially
in favor of expenses, the college will reach a time when deficits are
commonplace, and the financial structure can no longer ensure fiscal health.

When there are changes to the structure, such as new revenue
generators, new expense departments, capital projects, and changes
in the investment portfolio for the endowment fund, the president
should require a careful evaluation of the financial impact on the
financial equilibrium. Evaluations should carefully and rigorously
test what happens if financial goals are or are not achieved. The tests
should use net cash flows to test outcomes because they are the real
measure of an institution's financial condition.

ENDNOTES

1.   Bowen, H. R. *The Costs of Higher Education* (San Francisco: Jossey-
     Bass, 1981), pp. 19–20.

2.   Cohen, M. D., & March, J. G. *Leadership and Ambiguity: The American College President*. (New York: McGraw-Hill, 1974).

3.   Townsley, M. K. "Leveraging Facilities for Competitive Advantage." In *Presidential Perspectives*, edited by M. Fennell & S. D. Miller (Philadelphia: Aramark Higher Education, 2007).

4.   Townsley, M. K. *The Small College Guide to Financial Health* (Washington, DC: NACUBO, 2002), p. 105.

5.   Lapovsky, L., & Hubbell. L. "An Uncertain Future," *Business Officer*, 29. http://www.nacubo.org/documents/bom/2001_02_future.pdf; 29. February 24, 2001.

6.   Adelman, C. *The Toolbox Revisited: Paths to Degree Completion From High School to College*. (Washington, DC: U.S. Department of Education, 2006).

7.   U.S. Department of Education. Table 334: Current fund revenue of private nonprofit institutions of higher education by source: 1980–81 through 1995–96. In *Digest of Education Statistics*. (Washington, DC: National Center for Education Statistics, 1999).

8.   Pulley, John L., & Borrego, Anne Marie. "Wealthiest Colleges Lost Billions in Endowment Value in Last Year," *Chronicle of Higher Education*, A-24. http://chronicle.com/weekly/v48/i08/08a02401.htm, October 19, 2001.

9.   Commodity Systems. S&P 500 Index: May 1999–May 2001 (2001). Retrieved June 12, 2008, from http://finance.yahoo.com/. NASDAQ.

10.   Ibid.

11.   Townsley, M. K. "Recognizing the Unrealized," *Business Officer*, 21. http://www.nacubo.org/x5632.xml, March 2005.

12.   JMA Higher Ed Stats. *Management Ratios: Private Institutions*, xls: 1997–2000. (Boulder, CO: John Minter and Associates, 2002).

13.   Reed, W. S. *Financial Responsibilities of Governing Boards* (Washington, DC: Association of Governing Boards and NACUBO, 2001), p. 3.

14.   Mehrling, P., Goldstein, P., & Sedlacek, P. Endowment Spending: Goals, Rates and Rules (2005). Retrieved February 19, 2009, from http://net.educause.edu/ir/library/pdf/ffp0516s.pdf.

15.   Salem, D. A. (2000). "Endowment Management." In *College and University Business Administration*, 6th ed., edited by C. M. Grills (Washington, DC: NACUBO, 2000), pp. 9–27.

16.   McKay, P. A., & Curran, R. "Smart Money Takes a Dive on Alternative Assets. *Wall Street Journal*, B1, January 18–19, 2009.

17. Zemsky, R. "The Lattice and the Ratchet," *Policy Perspectives*. (The Pew Higher Education Research Program, 1990), pp. 1–8.

18. Ibid, p. 5.

19. Massey, W. F. "A New Look at the Academic Department," *Distillations*. (The Pew Higher Education Research Program, 1990), p. 1.

20. Williamson, O. E. *Markets and Hierarchies*. (New York: The Free Press, 1975).

21. Ibid.

CHAPTER 5

FINANCIAL
PRACTICES

The finance office is misunderstood, ignored, and at times despised, but it is a significant player in managing the allocation decisions of an institution. The board, president, and all chief officers of the institution should have a working knowledge of the financial office. Even with this caveat about working knowledge, the business office staff are an obstinate lot because their obligations and work are constrained by outside regulations such as Federal Accounting Standards Board and Generally Accepted Accounting Principles, government laws and regulations, contractual and debt instrument conditions, and legal liability for signatures of federal reports. The conditions inherent in the preceding list limit the discretion of chief financial officers (CFOs).

There is another reason that CFOs are reluctant to take large risks: they are often held directly responsible to the board for budget performance. If they arbitrarily change the budget or are persuaded to make significant changes that benefit one part of the organization or a set of individuals, their job is on the line if problems occur. A prudent CFO asks for written confirmation from the president or the board for any action that lies outside the known bounds and conditions of the budget. Of course, demanding written authorization by the president to take action that seems on the surface to be intuitively justified is a nuisance, but it is in the interest of the board and president to have a CFO who is careful, knows the limits, and adheres to the conditions and regulations imposed on the college. Otherwise, the financial condition of the institution is in the hands of a reckless and out-of-control CFO, who can quickly put the college in financial jeopardy.

The balance of this chapter discusses budgeting, the basic business standards that should be expected in most business offices, the business practices that exemplify a good financial office, the qualifications of the business office personnel, typical reports from the business office, and board practices that ensure objectivity in allocation decisions and compliance with regulatory groups.

BUDGETS

Budgets are the plans for allocating financial resources to achieve the goals of the institution. Every institution has a process designed to elicit involvement from all sections and every nook and cranny of the college. The issue of interest here is not the purposes of the allocations or the processes that lead to allocation decisions; rather, it is the structure of budgets and the premise that determines the limits of the allocations.

Finance operates through three levels: operations, which includes the production of revenue, allocation of expenses, and the generation of net income; cash flow, which delineates the source and uses of cash that flows either from operations or from financial reserves; and financial reserves, which transfers cash to operations or receives cash from operations, converts long-term assets to cash for operations, or holds new long-term assets generated from operations or from liabilities. Ideally, budgets should forecast the end-of-year audited financial statements, which include the statement of activities, cash flow statement, and statement of financial position* for the college. These financial statements show how operational income is turned into cash, how cash is used for operations or investments, and how financial reserves are expanded through investment, converted to use in operations, or exhausted through depreciation.

* Laypersons call the statement of activities the income statement, and the statement of financial position is the balance sheet.

Obviously, it is in the college's interest to understand how plans will affect net income, cash, and the use of financial reserves. However, few colleges work through the problem of budgeting operations, cash, and capital budgets* simultaneously. Traditionally, most colleges develop an operations budget with their main worry being the production of some sort of net, even if it is $1. They become concerned with the way in which the budget influences the totality of the institution's financial position only at the end of the fiscal year when reports are made to the board and when the auditors prepare the financial statements. Some colleges do not even produce a summary financial statement. They depend on the auditors to close the books and produce the final statement. These colleges are often ignorant of their financial condition for the previous fiscal year until October or later. These colleges float into a year with little or no information on the validity of their budget assumptions.

Cash budgets are rarely prepared because the general assumption by many business offices is that one of, or a combination of, cash reserves, credit lines,† or cash from revenue will cover the periods when cash is short (usually during the summer). This assumption is not challenged by events until something unexpected occurs. One of those unexpected events happened in the fall of 2008, when Commonfund would not release short-term investments in full to colleges so that the institutions could cover their cash needs. The fall of 2008 also saw the credit market freeze to the point where many institutions found it difficult to expand or find credit lines.

Most institutions develop capital budgets on an ad hoc basis that occurs when they plan to construct or renovate a building or make major equipment purchases. Rarely do they consider capital budgets at the time that operational budgets are prepared even though it would make sense to see how operations, cash, and capital plans affect each other. The chief financial officer with the president and board should be able to produce a reasonable capital plan for the coming year.

---

*Capital budgets set out plans for major investments through the use of cash or debt, recorded as liabilities.

†Credit lines are short-term loans arranged in advance with banks to cover brief periods when internal cash is insufficient to cover cash needs. The bank usually sets conditions on these loans, such as amount, term of repayment, and interest rates.

The remainder of this section discusses the mechanics of operational, cash, and capital budgets. The chief financial officer has the main role in supervising the development of these budgets. As noted earlier, the process of budget development depends on policies of a particular institution. Although the chief financial officer is mainly responsible for coordinating budget development activity, the work is done collaboratively. In addition, the budget is not authorized until the president presents it to the board for approval.

Operating Budget

Many institutions work from Howard Becker's premise that colleges spend to the limits of their revenue. Developing budgets on the Becker premise means that the budget team is most interested in what it has available to spend, and then it figures out how much money needs to be raised to match expenditures. Usually, matching revenue to expenditures results in three ways of balancing the budget, depending on whether the institution is endowment-driven, a research university, or tuition-driven.

For endowment-driven colleges, endowment draws are estimated based on a three-year moving average, gift targets are set, and then tuition and enrollment are revised to make up the balance needed to match expenses. For research universities, grants, endowment draws, and gifts are the main revenue flows; after the flows from these sources are identified, tuition and enrollment are used to balance expenses. For tuition-driven institutions, the main revenue comes from the tuition revenue equation made up of tuition, price, and enrollment. Other sources of revenue are too small to have a significant impact on total revenue.

When revenues are budgeted to match expenses, several constraints determine the amount that can be spent. These constraints keep budgeting from becoming a simple-minded equation in which revenue, tuition, enrollment, gifts, and grants are increased until they equal the accretion of expenditures. The constraints limit what can be done with revenue and tuition increases so that private colleges do not go hog wild on expenses and so that students and parents can afford the price of attendance. Revenue increases are customarily restrained by these conventions:

- Tuition increases at the rate of inflation plus an additional 2 percent to 4 percent.

- Endowment draws are limited by the prudent fiduciary rule that the institution should draw only between 4 percent and 5 percent of endowment principal. The draw is usually made on a moving three-year average of principal so that the college neither gains the benefit nor incurs the loss from unexpected changes in market values of the underlying investments.

- Gift income is often determined several years in advance of receiving cash because most gifts are pledges of future cash donations.

- Grants are dependent on (1) the investment that the college places in research, (2) the known availability of grants, and (3) the relationship of grant writers and the key administrators of a foundation, business, or government agency. Inexperienced presidents go after grants that they have little chance of receiving and waste their time and the resources of the institution writing grants that have little chance of being funded.

- Fees and auxiliary income are a function of enrollment. So, if the college is careful in its planning, it will not expect that these areas will produce large sources of new revenue. There are two exceptions. First, sizable increases in fees, for instance, health services, have been used to moderate tuition increases. Second, new residence halls will generate an increase in revenue; however, much of the additional revenue will go for debt service for the debt instruments used to pay for construction.

- Other revenue is usually a minor proportion of total revenue that includes interest and other revenue that does not fit classifications for tuition, grants, gifts, or auxiliary revenue.

Although the mechanics of budgeting can seem arcane to the outsider, the basic equation is as simple as this: *Net Income = Total Revenue − Total Expenses*. The Howard Bowen principle says that the budgeting equation works like this: Expenses + Net Income = Revenue. The following formulas describe the major factors that are used to compute revenue and expenses:

- Total Revenue = Tuition Revenue + Fee Revenue + Endowment Draw + Grants + Gifts + Auxiliary Income + Other Revenue.

- Tuition Revenue = Tuition Rates × Enrollment.

- Fee Revenue = Fee Rates × Number of Students Charged the Fee. Different fees are charged for different purposes and not all students pay all fees. For instance, graduate students may not be charged an activity fee, or commuter students may not be charged a health fee, and some fees are charged based on the type of courses (for example, lab fees, theater fees, and travel fees).

- Endowment Draw = Three-Year Moving Average for Endowment Principal × Draw Rate.

- Grant Revenue = Amount of Grant Revenue Authorized to Cover Direct (direct expenses include compensation, materials, and other expenses directly related to the activity) and Indirect Expenses (indirect expenses are based on an approved rate of administrative and capital expenses and depreciation that support the project).

- Gift Revenue = Amount of Cash Expected From Prior Pledges or Expected From Annual Fund Drives, which is based on prior experience.

- Auxiliary Income = (Residence Hall Fee × Number of Residents) + Bookstore Net Sales + (Food Service Charges × Number of Students Using Food Services).

- Total Expenses = Compensation + Supplies + Equipment + Plant Costs + Debt Interest + Depreciation.

- Compensation = (Pay Rates by Category of Employee ×
  Number of Employees) × Factor for Benefits (benefits
  equal health, retirement, and whatever else the college may
  provide) and Taxes (taxes include social security, Medicare,
  and unemployment tax rates).

The budgeting formula can be expressed in another way so that
expenses do not completely drive revenue decisions. The alternative
method works through the following stages:

- The first stage estimates how much new tuition and fee
  revenue is available based on current enrollment that
  is modified for expected changes in enrollment. This is
  multiplied by planned changes to tuition and fee rates.

- The second stage adds known increases or decreases in
  grants, gifts, auxiliary revenue, and other income.

- The third stage estimates expenses that will be changed
  resulting from salary schedules, changes in benefit or
  tax rates, and changes in these areas: insurance, utilities,
  information services, and any other contract or expense
  that the college does not have the discretion to alter.

- The fourth stage sums revenue from stages 1 and 2 and
  deducts expenses from stage 3. The amount remaining from
  this arithmetic exercise is what the institution can use to
  fund new positions, a special salary increase, new student
  services, or any other budgetary expenditure that would
  serve institutional goals, delivery of academic services, and
  operational performance.

When a college follows this budgetary method, it has much
greater control over tuition rates and the rate of growth for expenditures.

Cash Budget

The cash budget should look similar to the audit cash flow statement,
which sets out how cash is produced, received, and used. There are

four main flows: net income; flows from operations, which contain adjustments to net income for noncash items such as depreciation and for changes in current assets and liabilities; flows from investments, which depict cash from the purchase or sale of investments; and flows from financing activities, which show cash generated from and repayments for debt obligations. The chief financial officer may also prepare a weekly cash flow budget, which indicates whether the college is on or off track in generating cash during the fiscal year.

Capital Budget

The capital budget presents for the coming fiscal year capital projects to be funded and how they will be funded. Institutional accounting policies set two conditions for a project to be categorized as a capital project: (1) the project must exceed a certain amount of cost, and (2) the value of the asset is not consumed in less than a year. Under these conditions, the project will be depreciated. If projects do not meet these conditions, the expenditure is classified as a current or operational expenditure that is not depreciated.

Internal cash reserves may be used to fund a capital project; typically, these expenditures are for renovations or equipment. In most cases, debt is the primary vehicle for funding a capital project (for example, the construction of a new building or the purchase of a new information technology system).

The board must approve formal debt instruments and should understand the conditions imposed by the financing agency, be it a bank or bondholders. Frequently, the conditions imposed by the debt instruments are covenants, which establish certain performance and reporting requirements. Covenants may state that the college must maintain a specified level of cash reserves, not incur deficits from operations, or not increase the amount of debt without review and approval of the debt holder. Failure to meet a covenant can lead to penalties that are spelled out in the debt instrument. The lowest level penalty is that the institution will have to file a report showing how it will come into compliance with the conditions stated in the covenant. In addition, the institution will have to file frequent reports showing how it is complying with the covenants. The highest and most devastating penalty is when the debt is called for failure to meet the conditions required by the covenants. A call on debt forces the institution to immediately find money to pay the balance owed on the debt. Refinancing the debt with another lending agency is very difficult if the debt has been called.

Budget Final Comments

Upon passage of the budget by the board, the budget moves from a forecast to an instrument of management by which it is used as a yardstick for performance, and it establishes a framework for decisions on resource control and allocations. As a performance yardstick, actual performance is measured against the bounds forecast by the budget. If revenue net of expenses exceeds the budget forecast during the fiscal year, the president must determine how the excess financial resources are to be allocated. Too often these decisions are whimsical in nature with little or no consideration of the strategic goals that resource allocations are supposed to achieve. If revenue net of expenditures falls below the budget, then the really tough job of presidential leadership comes into play. The issue is how to reallocate resources or more precisely cut resources to eliminate the shortfall and yet maintain momentum toward achievement of strategic goals. In either of these cases, excess or shortfall of net revenues, the president must always guide decisions so that resource allocations strengthen or at least do not diminish the strategic position of the college.

BUSINESS STANDARDS: GENERALLY ACCEPTED ACCOUNTING STANDARDS

Business standards are the principles and practices that govern a well-managed financial office. The Federal Accounting Standards Board (FASB) issues accounting standards for private higher education institutions. Its rulings over the last decade have substantially changed the way private institutions keep their records and prepare their financial statements.

The comment that financial statements conform to generally accepted accounting principles (GAAP) arises from the expectation

TABLE 5.1— GENERALLY ACCEPTED ACCOUNTING PRINCIPLES

ASSUMPTIONS

Business Entity—Assumes that the business is separate from its owners or other businesses. Revenues and expenses should be kept separate from personal expenses.

Going Concern—Assumes that the business will be in operation indefinitely. This validates the methods of asset capitalization, depreciation, and amortization. When liquidation is certain, this assumption is not applicable.

Monetary Units—Assumes a stable currency is going to be the unit of record. FASB accepts the nominal value of the U.S. dollar as the monetary unit of record unadjusted for inflation.

Time Periods—Implies that the economic activities of an enterprise can be divided into artificial time periods.

HIERARCHY OF ACCOUNTING QUALITIES

User Specific Factors—Information placed in financial reports should relate to the needs and accounting skills of the decision maker.

Relevance—Financial information should be relevant to decisions made and should use past and present information to predict future outcomes.

Timeliness—The information must be available to the decision makers before it loses its usefulness for a particular decision.

Reliability—Information is based on what it represents and the assurance that it represents that information in a fashion that makes it verifiable and neutral.

Verifiability—Information is based on consensus of independent measures. Faithful representation of information depends on agreement between accounting numbers and the events or resources being represented.

Neutrality—This depends on the data being represented, the reliability and verifiability of the represented event or resource. The reporting of data should not depend on a particular interest.

Comparability—Reports are useful when they can be compared to similar reports from other organizations.

Materiality—Disclosure is required if it has a significant effect on decisions and is reliable and verifiable.

Costs and Benefits—Disclosure is required if the perceived benefits exceed the costs.

Cost Principle—Companies are required to account and report on acquisitions based on original costs rather than fair market value for most assets and liabilities. This principle provides information that is reliable (removing opportunity to provide subjective and potentially biased market values), but not very relevant. Thus, there is a trend to use fair values. Most debts and securities are now reported at market values.

Revenue Principle—Companies are required to record revenue when it is (1) realized or realizable and (2) earned, not when cash is received. This way of accounting is called accrual basis accounting.

Matching Principle—Expenses have to be matched with revenues, as long as it is reasonable to do so. Expenses are recognized not when the work is performed or when a product is produced but when the work or the product actually makes its contribution to revenue. Only if no connection with revenue can be established may cost be charged as expenses to the current period (e.g., office salaries and other administrative expenses). This principle allows greater evaluation of actual profitability and performance (i.e., shows how much was spent to earn revenue). Depreciation and Cost of Goods Sold are good examples of application of this principle.

Disclosure Principle—The amount and kinds of information disclosed should be decided based on trade-off analyses as it costs more to prepare a larger amount of information. Information disclosed should be enough to make a judgment while keeping costs reasonable. Information is presented in the main body of financial statements, in the notes, or as supplementary information.

CONSTRAINTS

Objectivity Principle—The company financial statements provided by the accountants should be based on objective evidence.

Materiality Principle—The significance of an item should be considered when it is reported. An item is considered significant when it would affect the decision of a reasonable individual.

Consistency Principle—Accounting procedures should follow industry practices.

Prudent Principle—When choosing between two solutions, the one that will be least likely to overstate assets and income should be picked.

Note: Financial Accounting Standards Board (FASB) statements are the basis for the hierarchy of accounting qualities. Wikipedia provides a straightforward list of the basic concepts that are customarily recognized as part of GAAP. You can find additional information about GAAP concepts and statements on the FASB site at www.fasb.org/st/. See Statements of Financial Accounting Concepts.

Sources: Wikipedia. Generally accepted accounting principles (United States). Retrieved September 19, 2008, from http://en.wikipedia.org/wiki/Generally_Accepted_Accounting_Principles_%28USA%29; and Financial Accounting Standards Board. (2007). Statements of financial accounting concepts (pp. 30–33). Norwalk, CT.

that an audited set of financial statements is fair and the statements are presented consistently so that outsiders can understand them. Everyone in a key leadership role in the college should have a passing knowledge of GAAP so that he or she can appreciate what is expected from a financial office, its reports, and the institution's auditors. These principles, in addition to government regulations, clearly establish boundaries on what a chief financial officer can do. The GAAP schema is described in Table 5.1.

BUSINESS PRACTICES

Business practices are a necessary component of GAAP because they ensure that accounting records are prepared in a consistent and orderly manner. These practices call for a skilled team that has the knowledge, diligence, and ethical standards to carry out difficult and tedious tasks. The following practices represent significant components of a well-run business office, but they are not the only components characterizing such an office.

- *Post the books daily.* Postings must be done daily. If postings are not done daily, financial reports are delayed and inaccurate, resulting in information that does not represent the true financial condition of the institution until the auditors arrive to make the final postings and closing of the books. This is not good for making decisions.

- *Reconcile cash accounts.* Here is another instance where delay means inaccurate records. Cash accounts should be reconciled when cash statements are received. Many struggling colleges often fail to do this annually. Some get to the point that they create new checking accounts for restricted grants or gifts, hoping that these will not become muddled like the regular cash accounts. Of course, these accounts soon become a mess, too. Colleges that do not reconcile their cash accounts may not realize how short their cash position has become. They may even issue checks that bounce, resulting in penalties and embarrassment.

- *Pay the bills.* The only acceptable reason for not paying bills immediately is the standard management practice of taking advantage of bill due dates so that cash can remain invested and earning additional interest. Otherwise, bills should be paid quickly and within the discount period that some vendors establish for accelerating payments on their invoices. Too many officers use their desk drawers to manage bill payment when times are tough. This results in unpaid bills

---

* Dunn and Bradstreet rates timeliness of bill paying by businesses and not-for-profit organizations.

and a low Dunn and Bradstreet* rating. If late payments persist, the college may have to pay upon delivery, and it may find that it is cut out of the short-term credit market by banks.

- *Keep accurate payroll records.* Keeping accurate payroll records should be done so that tax reports and deposits are accurate, benefit deductions are correctly withheld and deposited, and employees receive the correct pay. Payroll records should be reconciled against benefit deductions, tax reports, and budget reports. Failing to do these reconciliations can result in tax penalties or health coverage that does not meet employees' expectations. Also, mistakes here can have a negative effect on retirement plans and income growth of employee retirement accounts.

- *Close the books monthly.* When books are not posted and closed at the end of the month, financial reports are delayed, not produced, or merely represent the best guess of the chief financial officer. Timely closings, like daily postings of the books, are imperative so that decision makers have access to the best and most timely financial information.

- *Reconcile enrollment against revenue.* Too many colleges ignore this basic step. They assume, without justification, that the financial records and the enrollment records are the same because enrollment in the registrar's system feeds receivables in the bursar's office. Experience indicates that this is a false assumption. The impact of this breakdown is incorrect billing, erroneous financial aid records, inaccurate financial reports, and lost cash.

- *Reconcile gifts, grants, endowment income, and draws.* This reconciliation practice avoids errors in recording the sources and uses of gifts and grants and the flow of income into and out of endowment funds. Nothing upsets a donor more than a failure to acknowledge or use a restricted gift properly. Foundation and governmental grants require accurate recording of income and expenses. In the latter case, sloppy recordkeeping and flawed reports can result in loss of funds or worse.

- *Create adequate cash controls.* Slack cash controls can result in the loss of control of the budget caused by unauthorized expenditures or even misappropriation of cash that an institution dearly needs to meet its financial obligations. The requirement of cash controls means that the person who receives or dispenses the cash does not also record it. The business office—unless it is so small that only a few people work in it—must have solid cash controls. Even small colleges can be mortified by a trusted employee who steals them blind. The scale of money that comes into a college is so large that sometimes supposedly reliable people are tempted to take a little for themselves. This is one reason for outside auditors to check against this possibility. However, even an audit can miss a sticky-fingered employee because audits randomly check only a few records. The assumption is that the random check will catch the villain, but random checks can also miss patterns of behavior.

- *Approve purchases or payroll made by the president or board members.* Governing boards often place the chief financial officer in an untenable position because the CFO is not provided with a secure and confidential means to report on violations by the president of ethical misdeeds or actions that may violate recognized legal constraints. If the chief business officer does the right thing and prevents the president from making a purchase, funneling money into a dubious business, or hiring relatives not sanctioned by the board, he or she can be fired and a million falsehoods used to explain the removal of the business officer. The board should set up a regular procedure for reviewing and approving cash disbursements and payrolls so that questions can be raised about obvious lapses in ethical or legal behavior. At the very least, the president's expenditures should be approved quarterly. The board should rotate this responsibility among members who are knowledgeable about financial practices to prevent collaboration. The work is tedious, thankless, and implies distrust, but it is necessary.

FINANCIAL OFFICE PERSONNEL QUALIFICATIONS

The only way to have a reliable and competent business office is to hire the best people. Stinting on pay fits the unfortunate epigram of "penny-wise, pound foolish." Good people cost money, so hire the best. Chief financial officers, except in the smallest institutions, do not have the time to be the chief accountant. So, make sure that the chief accountant or controller has a CPA. Also, anyone making critical entries on the books should have training in basic accounting practices and should understand how double-entry accounting works. There is nothing more dismaying than trying to explain to an unskilled clerk the accounting implications of posting errors. Remember, if they do not know what they are doing, they will make mistakes, and there is a good chance that they will make big mistakes.

BUSINESS OFFICE REPORTS

Rational decision making requires timely and accurate reports, whether financial, enrollment, or other statements! The fundamentals that support good decisions are based on skilled personnel, the practices used to record raw data summarized in the report, and the usefulness of the report. Accurate and timely reports provide insight into the condition of the college so that the president and board can respond appropriately to unfolding events and can prepare for the future. Here are several useful reports; most are obvious and standard in colleges with well-run financial offices:

- *Monthly, quarterly, academic period, and annual financial summaries:* These reports to the president should summarize performance and not be excessively burdened with detail. The president will decide what goes to the board. The reports should also include sections on major drivers in the institution, such as admissions, enrollment, financial aid, instructional costs, operational productivity, employee counts, gifts, grants, endowment returns, or any other factor critical to understanding the condition of the institution. The last section of the report should conclude with a summary of major strengths and weaknesses in operations.

- *Regular monthly budget reports:* The president will also determine who within the institution receives these reports. Generally, they are sent to anyone with budgetary responsibility. These reports should identify over expenditures, and policy should establish a time limit for corrective action. The president should receive a special report on any budgetary department that consistently over expends or where over expenditures are continuing to grow.

- *Regular budgetary net income reports:* Revenue-producing departments should receive a report that gives revenue, expenditures (major accounts), net income, and any nonfinancial drivers of revenue and expenses. The president and the cabinet should receive a copy of this report.

- *Special report for budget planning:* This report should give trends for the past several years for revenue and expenses with a multiyear forecast if growth rates remain the same. The forecast should include any known changes to occur in the coming year.

- *Responsibility-centered management report:* This report is prepared annually. It assigns revenue, direct expenses,[*] and allocated expenses[†] to revenue production. This report should go to the president, chief officers, and the particular board committee designated by the president.

---

[*]Direct expenses typically include compensation, materials, and other expenditures directly related to the operation of a particular department.
[†]Allocated expenses include administrative and service expenses that are allocated to a revenue-producing department based on a usage formula.

- *Multiyear forecast:* The forecast should establish a historical base for revenue and expenses. Then, forecasts should be prepared using revenue and expense drivers, known capital projects, major increases to expenditures, and any new project that will generate net income. The forecast should include an upper and lower risk boundary so that the president and chief officers can reach reasonable conclusions about the impact of a proposed project.

BOARD FINANCIAL OVERSIGHT

According to *Financial Responsibilities of Governing Boards*, published by AGB and NACUBO, board members are the "stewards of institutional assets."[1] They must "maintain equity between generations [of students]"[2] so that the strength of financial and physical assets carries on from current to future students. If assets cannot support future generations of students, then the board must consider transferring its assets to an institution that can fulfill its mission. Board members must insist on frequent financial updates from the president and key leaders as they endeavor to "monitor strategic planning" interactively.[3] Keeping abreast of economic and legal currents, board members must also "manage risk,"[4] sheltering their institution's physical assets from catastrophic financial losses and ensuring that actions taken on behalf of the college (whether by a board member, administrator, faculty member, or staff person) abide by contract rules and laws of state.

Through audits, conflict of interest policies, and reviews of financial transactions, "the board is responsible for ensuring that adequate financial controls are in place."[5,6] The board should hire a disinterested certified public accounting firm to audit the college's financial condition and management practices annually. To ensure that audit findings are not filtered through self-interested administrators, the board must contract directly with the auditors and demand that audit findings be prepared for the private consideration of its members.

The board must prevent conflicts of interests among the college, board members, administrators, their family members, and their private businesses. This policy is a reporting requirement of the IRS

Form 990 *Return from Organization Exempt from Income Tax (2008)*. This form expanded reporting requirements on employees with high levels of compensation and third parties receiving payments from the institution who have a relationship to a board member or to someone employed by the institution. The board, especially the auditing committee, should become familiar with the report and should see it before it is filed with the IRS. They should arrange a special meeting with the auditors to review the IRS form, and the auditors should explain current IRS rulings or regulations regarding the reporting requirements for Form 990.

Incidentally, board members and administrators should consider the tax consequences of employing family members. The IRS could interpret business transactions with, and/or employment of, family members who have not been properly presented for review and action by the board as a violation of tax rules prohibiting colleges from distributing benefits and excess funds for personal gain. Boards that overlook business dealings and employment practices could cost their college its nonprofit status. In some instances, the board and president may be held accountable by the IRS for the information reported on the form.

In addition to the significant reporting requirement required by the IRS, board members and administrators should at the very least identify business transactions that currently or potentially constitute conflicts of interest. Self-dealing can be limited through a policy that defines the conditions under which employees and their relations can conduct business with the institution. Only after several bids have been collected and arm's-length business agreements have been signed should transactions between the college and its leadership or their family members proceed.

The board and presidents must become more conversant in the risks that their college faces because private institutions tend to rely on their own resources to withstand the whiplash from economic, demographic, and regulatory changes. In the past, risks were parceled so that the college might face one of two major changes in risk in a short time period. Now there are more changes coming faster, giving independent institutions less time to respond and making greater demands on their limited resources. Over the next several years, colleges will need new strategies to deal with changes in enrollment patterns, academic preparedness of new students, competitive markets, private student loans, tuition rates, tuition discounts, government regulations, operational efficiency, cash flows, investment portfolios, returns on investments, and capital projects.

What does it mean to become conversant with risk? It means that the board and president must understand the risks inherent in the structure of the institution, the external factors that will increase those risks, and the implication of strategic changes for their risk structure. The board and president should regularly apprise themselves of conditions that create risk for the institution. These conditions include but are not necessarily limited to the following:

- Market risks
    - New student enrollment;
    - Tuition rates and discounts among competitors;
    - Academic skills of new students;
    - Private loans taken by new students; and
    - Parental income.
- Productivity
    - Retention rates;
    - Graduation rates;
    - Career potential of graduates;
    - Costs of instruction, administrations, and student services per student; and
    - Student performance outcomes.
- Capital investments
    - Debt, that is, principal, interest rates, and debt covenants;
    - Cash flow investment risks and performance; and
    - Long-term investment risks and performance.

Even though the board and president may be attuned to the numbers associated with these risks, they must take the time to understand their implications. A cursory report to the board by a lower-level administrator is not sufficient. The president should present the report and open discussion to the trustees, and the president should also hold a similar discussion with chief administrative officers. Within these forums insight into opportunities and the framework of a new strategy take shape. Risk assessment must become a regular feature of the institution if it expects to formulate a timely and valid response to the basic factors that drive the success of the institution.

Just because a college is a charity, the board should not grant it dispensation from rigorous financial and management standards. Board members must review financial reports and major financial transactions with critical eyes, scrutinizing business dealings involving key administrators. Expense reimbursements and purchase authorizations for administrators, up to and including the president, should not be made without due consideration. Clear lines of co-signer authority should be drawn to shield the college from charges of illicit spending and lack of financial oversight by the board.

Board members and administrators should annually submit a conflict of interest statement for board review, which contains the following information:

- List of board members or administrators whose family members are employed by the college. The list should include names, titles, duties, compensations, and familial relationships.

- List of business interests of board members, administrators, or their family members with the college. The list should include purchases, dates of agreement, relevant services or products, and company names.

DEBT MANAGEMENT

Debt management is not rocket science—if you follow your grandmother's rules of managing money, the college will be fine. The basic rule is simple: be very prudent when you borrow money. Make sure that you have tested every possible event that would upset your payback assumptions. Do not make up numbers because it will help sell the bond issue or the load proposal to the bank. You will have to live with the consequences of bad guesses; recall that Bradford College went after debt on bogus numbers and sank into oblivion. Of course, you should run all the appropriate debt ratios, prepare the statements; but in the end, colleges are low-risk institutions, so keep that in mind when you are forecasting the impact of debt.

EIGHT PRINCIPLES OF FINANCIAL MANAGEMENT

The chief principles of financial management are straightforward, and most people would recognize them immediately. These principles do not promise to transport a wounded college magically to a safe haven, but they will act as a shield protecting the institution against the normal wear and tear from external threats. There are many more rules that could be added, but these eight principles are basic to sound financial management.

Cash Principle

Cash is everything and there is never a time when there is enough cash. Revenue-producing programs or auxiliaries should generate cash to build reserves. Cash management is an integral part of the cash reserves. Follow this guideline with cash management: avoid rate chasing because too often the investment instruments underpinning the higher rates crash and burn. The best example is what happened in 2008 with auction market cash securities, which were used as high-yield, short-term investments. When the credit crunch hit the debt market, colleges that invested in these high-yield instruments discovered that they could not convert them back to cash. Another guideline follows from the preceding rate chasing guideline: do not put your cash investment eggs in one basket. Spread them around among safe investments and safe financial institutions.*

---

* This assumes that anyone can identify a safe financial institution after the 2008–09 financial crisis.

Expense Principle

Do not spend money you do not have; there is nothing brilliant here. Make sure that new expenses add to the productivity of the institution. Do not increase expenses to expand empires, to provide marginal services, or to overburden income-producing programs. In the short and long term, expense growth rates should be equal to or less than the growth rate for revenue. This is the expanded equilibrium principle of keeping expense and revenue rates balanced. When revenue rates grow faster than expenses do, the college can build its reserves.

Receivables Principle

If the college is tuition dependent, the president must keep track of the growth in uncollectable receivables. Uncollectable receivables can kill net tuition. Also, accounting games can be played with uncollectable receivables by not ignoring their impact especially when their rate of growth exceeds the growth rate in tuition. Disregarding uncollectable receivables means that expenses will be underreported because unpaid tuition bills should be written off, thereby increasing expenses.

Operational Productivity

Private colleges and universities must do a better job of managing their productivity because, as Moody's points out, "the ability to finance higher education from other, nongovernmental sources, may reach a limit that could begin to erode the pricing power and pricing flexibility of universities.... We believe that trends in the ratio of median family income relative to tuition costs and in the ratio of average student loan debt burden to average salary of a graduating student may be unsustainable."[7] In sum, higher education and private institutions in particular are pricing themselves out of the market.

The old days of budgetary incrementalism for managing expenses are nearing an end to be replaced by sophisticated management analysis of operational performance. The change must happen if private institutions expect to remain viable because pushing up tuition discounts will increase the risk that the college will need huge increases in enrollment to generate enough cash to survive.

Presidents will have to push colleges to assess and improve the operational costs of delivering and supporting their missions. This can be done by identifying the relevant costs, figuring out what is important and what is not, setting strict limits on what costs should be, and sticking to those limits. Too many administrators give little thought to how the college will pay for new expenses. Every dollar of new expense must be supported by new revenue. Either by increasing tuition rates, adding enrollment, finding new grants or gifts, or improving the financial performance of investments. Gifts, grants, and investment performance is beyond the immediate control of the institution, so tuition revenue has become the fallback to cover new expenses. As Moody's suggests, jacking up tuition rates may become counterproductive as new students turn to less expensive alternatives.[8]

Financial Sheet Management

In the past, higher education has sneered at the financial practices of chief executives in business, who are forced to manage operations and strategy to the expectations of the market that reviews business performance from the financial reports. Now this common business practice is on the edge of becoming pervasive in higher education as private institutions respond to GAAP* rules, accrediting requirements, lender expectations, and government regulatory reports. As a result, presidents and chief financial officers will have to work with other chief administrative officers so that financial reports show that the institution has reached certain performance targets. Tuition rates, tuition discounts, expenses, short- and long-term investments, and capital projects will have to be carefully managed or else the college will find that it is out of compliance with government standards or that lenders and accrediting agencies could conclude that the institution is not viable in the long run.[9]

---

* GAAP refers to the generally accepted accounting principles. Rules adopted over the past decade with the inclusion of cash flow reports will force colleges to pay more attention to the cash bottom line, which businesses take as a given.

Reserve Principle

The reserve principle rule goes hand in hand with the cash principle. Reserves are the buffer against the unknown and provide a private institution with the funds to invest in itself. The best circumstance is when cash reserves are large enough so that they can provide a low-risk funding pool for new projects or they can be transferred into long-term investments to grow the endowment fund. Reserves must grow at tuition-dependent private institutions because the government is not there to cover their mistakes. The board must protect its reserves, whether they are in the form of cash or long-term investments. The best rule matches the cash rule: be prudent in all things. Do not dump everything in the latest way to beat investment returns. For example, in the late 1990s, an investment manager put 90 percent of a small college's hard-earned investments into a Janus technology fund. The fund tanked with the bursting of the tech bubble. Now the college has only enough reserves to repaint the president's house.

Debt Management Principle

Use debt prudently and make sure that your payback estimates are based on solid figures and not hoped-for results that magically equal the amount needed to make the payback. The board should have an objective outsider test the assumptions on the debt payback plan.

Transparency Principle

Presidents need to insist on reporting systems that tie together the basic factors that shape the financial condition of the college. In other words, reports should clearly show the relationship between critical factors and revenue or expenses. These reports should cover the following:

- Student flows,[*] tuition, tuition discounts, instruction, and net from the respective revenue and expenses associated with student flows;

- Grants, expenses, indirect administrative charges, and the net from grant income;

* Student flows are admission yields, new students, attrition, and graduation rates.

- Auxiliary use, revenue, expenses and administrative charges, and net from auxiliary revenue;

- Investment portfolio mix, investment returns, and investment revenue;

- Operational performance for departments and schools that include the following:

  - Enrollment and demand for academic support, student services, and the cost of support and services;

  - Net revenue generated by income-producing departments;

  - Productivity for departments—instructional, academic, student services, and administrative;

  - Administrative personnel, compensation, and total expenses; and

  - Buildings and grounds—total square footage, preventative maintenance, breakdowns, personnel counts, compensation, and expenses.

- Information technology—enrollment, total employees, information technology use, and cost of these services; and

- Capital projects—planned usage, actual usage, and debt covenant performance.

Moody's Investors Service strongly recommends that financial reports should map back to external financial reports such as the audit.[10] This requires that the college go beyond showing summary revenue and expense reports to providing financial reports that include statements of activities, financial position, and cash flow. These reports must relate to prior periods and benchmarked goals.

SUMMARY

The practice of accounting and financial management can drown the uninitiated with detail, jargon, and obtuse rules. Yet just below the surface of this layer of confusing, common practices lays the truth about the financial state of the college. The commentary and principles cited here provide a good foundation for ensuring that the college does not go astray in managing its financial condition. Board members and presidents can get around the awe created by the professional speak of accountants and financial managers by insisting that they simplify what they are saying. The relevant question is: *What is the financial condition of the college?* When all else fails in making sense of the college's financial condition, ask these three questions:

1.   Do we have enough cash to operate this year without short-term borrowing?

2.   What are the short- and long-term growth rates for revenue and expenses?

3.   Are there any events on the horizon that could undermine the college's finances?

Board members should push back when administrators do not make sense or only create confusion. Insist that they give you accurate, up-to-date reports. If they cannot meet that simple requirement, get rid of them and find someone who can provide what you need.

ENDNOTES

1.   Reed, W. S. *Financial Responsibilities of Governing Boards* (Washington, DC: Association of Governing Boards and NACUBO, 2001), p. 5.
2.   Ibid.
3.   Ibid.
4.   Ibid.
5.   Ibid, p. 6.
6.   Ibid, p. 5.
7.   Moody's Investors Service. *U.S. Higher Education Outlook* (New York: Moody's Investors Service, 2008), pp. 11–12.
8.   Ibid, p. 13.
9.   Ibid pp. 17–19.
10.   Ibid, p. 16.

CHAPTER 6

BUSINESS MODELS

Business models explain how an organization operates and generates income.[*] The common elements of a business model are the buyers (students, in this case), pricing, production expenses, and financial structure. Private colleges and universities usually do not discuss their operations as business models or even conceive that they operate within the context of a business model. Nevertheless, it is important to consider different models because it provides a quick way of understanding what drives an institution, and many institutions looking for new ways of producing revenue need to appreciate the limitations of some models.

Moody's Investors Service neatly summarizes the business model for higher education:

Higher education has an "extremely resilient business model" with multiple sources of revenue and capital, inelastic demand,[†] and a seemingly unlimited willingness among parents and students to pay for higher education as a long-term investment in personal growth and career opportunity.... Those qualities insulate the education market from factors [that] can deteriorate other sectors, like health care.[1]

---

[*] Although there are other features of a business model such as infrastructure, strategic goals, procedures, and policy, this chapter is interested in only those elements that produce income.
[†] Inelastic demand means that although demand declines with higher prices, the decline is not large enough to offset higher revenue. In other words, higher prices result in higher revenue.

Obviously, the basic business model has helped private institutions survive the many vicissitudes in the economy and changes in student demographics over the past 40 years. As long as parents and students are willing to pay the higher price ticket for a degree from a private institution, private colleges and universities will survive and flourish. However, if the relationship between price and future payoff changes so that some sectors of the student market can no longer count on higher income to cover the cost of a private institution, then the willingness by some to attend private colleges may decline. There is already evidence that the link may be breaking between college degrees and higher pay for some disciplines.[2] If these trends continue, some business models that focus on degrees with a reduced potential for higher income relative to a high school diploma may no longer be viable.

This business model has worked since the late 1940s when soldiers went to college under the GI bill. They believed that a college education would improve their future and the future for their families. Enrollment reports for the fall of 2008 suggest that the model is under strain at least in private colleges. John Nelson, a managing director at Moody's, pointed out during an interview that if there is pricing strain on the model, parents and students will shift away from pricey independent colleges to less expensive community colleges and public four-year colleges.[3] There is evidence from the 1970s—when inflation jumped, tuition prices shot up, and the return on a degree slipped[4]—to support the proposition that students will switch their enrollment preferences from private colleges to public four-year institutions. Additionally, in the 1970s, community colleges did not have the market presences that they have now.

Another factor that could place a strain on the business model is the way that tuition revenue flows to colleges. For years, the flow, even with state and federal aid, came though student decisions. Tuition flow is a set of smaller streams such as government aid, government-subsidized loans, private loans, and student cash covering the balance. Neither the government nor private financial agencies have compelled students to make choices based on the best price or some benchmark for quality (except that the college had to be accredited). Student payment balances have been small enough that students have not been forced to consider price, except for the best and priciest private institutions, in their attendance decisions. Recently, though, the factor of price in student choice has changed at the priciest institutions where they have removed price as a consideration because most students receive large institutional tuition aid packages and because high academic standards limit who can apply. So, price does not play a major role in choice even at the most expensive schools today. This is unlike the hospital industry where a few third-party payees control the market and compel patient choice.

The recent credit crunch could change the dynamics in student choice, inducing them to consider price. As banks exit the student loan market or require high standards for a loan, the part of the revenue stream that undergirds student tuition payments could partially shut down. If this happens, and if the crunch remains in place for several years, students may take the option of switching their preferences from private colleges to public institutions. This could have a damaging impact on the business model and the viability of independent institutions that are financially fragile or heavily dependent on student tuition as the main source of revenue.

This chapter examines different models that typify most private colleges or universities, including tuition-driven, price–quality, residence hall, athletics revenue, endowment- and gift-driven, partnership, online, multinational, and market niches. There likely are more models, but this selection will show the variety of opportunities that are available to savvy presidents. Several models that are not common in the private sector are also assessed, for example, low price–high volume, minimum services, and combinations.

This chapter provides a brief description of each model and discusses various aspects of the models, such as the financial structure, enrollment and pricing strategies, cost of production, and/or critical features.

TUITION-DRIVEN MODELS

Tuition models are the classic financial model used by most private institutions to finance their operations. There are four forms of this model: traditional student model, two-plus-two model, off-site model, and coed model. In the traditional student model, students come to the institution for all four years or until graduating. In the two-plus-two model, students transfer from a community college after they receive their associate's degree or after their second year, and they complete their degree at a four-year institution. In the off-site model, an institution has another location that operates mainly in the evening and caters to adult students. Most colleges employ the coed model and do not give it a second thought. This model is an option that many single-sex colleges have used to expand their market because students no longer want to attend a single-sex college.

Traditional Student Model

The traditional model provides an undergraduate, residential experience for students who graduated from high school the previous spring. These are the colleges that everyone thinks of with the ivy-covered halls of academe. This model has the following characteristics:

- *Financial structure:* Tuition net of financial aid is the primary source of revenue. A substantial amount of income and cash flow is lost to financial aid. The evidence suggests that large chunks of new revenue are dedicated to ever-larger financial aid awards. Through the late 1990s, tuition discounts ravaged tuition revenue, cutting net tuition for the average college even though enrollment growth was strong. This began to change in 2000, suggesting that colleges were doing a better job of managing tuition discounting.[5,6]

  Many traditional institutions are borderline tuition-dependent, meaning that they receive most of their revenue from student sources (tuition, fees, residence hall, food service, and bookstore income). The rest of their revenue comes from annual funds and small draws from their endowment funds. Athletics may provide some income but is typically a net drain on the institution.

Classroom instruction remains the mainstay at most traditional undergraduate institutions, although some colleges are introducing online courses that could provide capital savings because they do not require additional rooms. Many traditional institutions have a small portion of their courses taught by adjunct faculty. Other costs, such as academic support, student services, and administration, are barely covered by the money remaining from tuition and fees net of financial aid and instructional expenses. Gifts or endowment income are needed to cover noninstructional services.

- *Enrollment and pricing strategies:* Enrollment is generated through a recruiting network usually tied to high school counselors and alumni. In the last decade, recruiting has become much more expensive because of tougher competition. Costs have increased as colleges buy expensive media advertisements, deploy large volumes of e-mail and direct mail messages, employ Web sites, and apply every trick in an advertising manager's handbook to build a pool of potential students.

Pricing necessarily works hand-in-glove with enrollment strategies as institutions try to set the right price for students in demand. Price involves determining the amount of financial aid to be awarded based on the characteristics of the students sought for the new class. The middle competitive set of colleges with good academic reputations and moderate-sized endowments sweeten financial aid packages as they fight for students not accepted at top universities. They face the predicament of devising financial aid packages that get the student but also generate enough cash to support the operation of the college. At most private institutions, many financial aid packages are unfunded, even at colleges with a sizable endowment fund.

Comments about the traditional model

The traditional tuition-driven model is common to many private undergraduate colleges and some institutions that offer nonresearch graduate programs. Most of these institutions look outside this model to find income because the cost of generating net income is very high. In fact, the net usually flows from gifts, which are restricted to the endowment fund. A huge amount of gift income is needed to generate $1 in endowment income. Endowment income is generally limited to 4 percent or 5 percent of a three-year average of endowment value, which means that $1 of endowment income must have $20 to $25 of principal supporting it. Therefore, a $1 million gift to the endowment fund will only produce $40,000 to $50,000 in annual income. That is not much money given the amount of time, effort, and cost put into getting a gift of that magnitude.

In summary, the tuition-driven business model depends on generating enough student growth to feed tuition and auxiliary services and to match operational and debt service growth. It works if financial aid, administrative expenses, student services, and capital costs are subsidized by gifts or student fees.

Two-Plus-Two Model

The two-plus-two model with most students entering the college for the third and fourth years of a bachelor's degree works best with adults who are employed and support themselves. These students are driven to finish the degree quickly with the least fuss because they are usually more mature and motivated than traditional-age students. Another attractive characteristic of working adults in two-plus-two programs is that attrition rates are much lower with these students, and they usually pay their bills on time. The two-plus-two model has these characteristics:

- *Financial Structure:* There is nothing unique about the source of revenue for this model; it is tuition revenue. This model can have periods of spectacular growth, and growth means everything with this model because endowments and gift revenue are miniscule sources of revenue. The model is noted for quick student turnover. Most students graduate within two to three years, so the college has to expend considerable effort to replace graduates and attrited students. If institutions using this model expect to succeed, they must grow to keep pace with inflation and to maintain sufficient cash reserves to cover normal operating expenses in addition to plant repair and replacement.

Even though institutions employing this model lose two years of revenue, they gain trade-offs by using adjuncts instead of full-time faculty for most courses and by providing minimal student services. Adjuncts are attractive for most transfer students because they find the field experience of their instructors relevant.

Many two-plus-two institutions carry relatively low levels of long-term debt. They are cash driven and highly dependent on the rapid collection of tuition. Because a large portion of these students work, they are not eligible for federal grants but are left with loans to fund their education. As recent history shows, credit crunches can raise the risk for two-plus-two colleges if their students cannot find loans for the next semester's courses.

• *Enrollment and pricing strategies:* Although there are many financial advantages with a two-plus-two model, the institution that takes this course needs a nimble administration and faculty that can quickly alter strategies and programs when markets disappear or appear. They have to keep in front of their competition because slower growth can severely weaken the financial condition of the college.

Many colleges that use this model tend to set tuition rates at what other institutions would consider the net tuition rate. In other words, a two-plus-two college does not offer tuition discounts; they offer only a low tuition rate. The reasoning is that these institutions find that a large segment of their first-year students enroll immediately before the start of classes and before the end of the drop-add date. These students do not consider tuition discounts; their enrollment decision is guided by the posted price. Net tuition only confuses them.

Comments about the two-plus-two model

This strategy works only when the administration and faculty recognize that they are serving students who demand convenience and immediate response to their needs. Colleges that survive the transition to the two-plus-two strategy have to learn that they cannot survive if they do not meet the needs of their students. These colleges are competitive with public institutions and with more hidebound private institutions because they provide responsive administrative services, flexible course scheduling, career-linked academic programs, and low tuition fees.

In summary, this business model works by having a strong student flow from community colleges or similar institutions that process students out in large numbers. Somehow, it must be embedded in the community college. Money is made through tuition revenue, financial aid is a small factor, administrative and student service expenses are minimized, and capital costs are limited by renting space until growth can sustain debt service.

Off-Site Model

Off-site models have been around a long time, but they have become cash cows for many colleges in the last 15 to 20 years. As noted, this model is relatively simple: a site is located in a geographic market that has a large number of students who would prefer to drive to classes and live at home. So that the site does not cannibalize enrollment at the main campus, it should be located more than 40 miles from the main campus. Delivery of the instructional programs is similar to the two-plus-two model where adjunct faculty members provide instruction. Administrative, academic, and student support is sparse so that it is relatively easy to generate a fairly substantial net from revenue.

The off-site model has these characteristics:

- *Financial structure:* The financial structure at most off-site programs is similar to the two-plus-two model with low tuition, adjunct faculty in place of full-time faculty, and minimal administrative and student services. The financial flow is simple at off-campus sites. Tuition revenue covers instructional expenses, administrative expenses, office expenses, and rental charges. Adjunct faculty is the primary instructional expense, and full-time faculty are there as faculty mentors or instructional evaluators. The economic advantages of adjuncts is simple: their compensation is about 50 percent and in some cases up to 70 percent less than full-timers.

- *Enrollment and pricing strategies:* The enrollment strategy is convenience for the student with flexible schedules so that the site can attract working adults or students who prefer to live at home rather than live on campus. Prices are usually set at the main campus rate net of tuition discounts* because most students who typically choose an off-site program select the institution based on posted price and not the discounted price. Because the college does not want to scare away potential students, it avoids using a high posted tuition rate.

Comments about the off-site model

Accreditation is a thorny issue with off-site programs because state agencies and accrediting agencies expect the full services of the college to be available if the program is given a campus designation. Even if the program is called a site, there are other accrediting issues, such as student services, library services, financial aid, veterans' benefits, faculty supervision and training, student contact with faculty, and course program continuity.

---

* Net price per course is deduced by dividing the net revenue after tuition by the total credit hours; the per course charge is figured at a three-credit standard course credit, which is typical of most off-campus courses.

Accreditation becomes problematic when a college steps outside its state or the geographic boundaries of its accrediting agency. State administrators charged with accreditation of external institutions are prickly about new colleges entering the state because state laws are usually written to protect the markets of in-state institutions. Opposition may be based on arguments that an external institution will duplicate programs offered by in-state institutions, not provide all instructional and support services to students, attempt to link with community colleges that are prohibited from offering four-year degrees, or fail to receive the support of in-state institutions for their programs. Similar problems may arise with accrediting commissions.

Under these circumstances the institution must strategize if it wants any chance of success in getting state and accrediting commission approvals. Merely filing voluminous reports by lawyers skilled in preparing accreditation reports will not overcome these problems. The institution must go beyond its lawyers and work the politics. The president will have to lead the political initiative; it cannot be left to a trusted underling. Political action means personal meetings, meetings, and more meetings with appointed and elected state officials and accrediting commissions. In addition, they need to find sponsors so that they can build a political alliance supporting the accreditation of the college. The president needs to find people who are influential and respected so that they can get a fair hearing. The college must avoid publicity about its plans. Do not meet with the press or make it apparent that the program is seeking a site and is ready to hire personnel for the site. These steps suggest that accreditation is in the bag. This presumption rubs government and accrediting commissions the wrong way. They are quite willing to show you are wrong!

Tuition discounts are usually minimal for off-site students because most colleges set tuition rates at the net tuition level for the main campus. Although tuition discounts are not a major problem, the institution should help students who apply for government and other noninstitutional aid. Making skilled financial aid officers available on site is very costly because they are highly paid and because there is not enough work at the site to justify the expense of a full-time assignment to the site. The alternative is some sort of a visiting or call-in center to provide financial aid assistance. In addition, the college should provide enough financial aid training for on-site administrators so that they can give basic information about financial aid and help the student fill out Financial Accounting Standards Board (FASF) forms.

Site relationship with the main campus increases in difficulty with distance. Close communications and regular visits help to keep site managers attuned to meeting their enrollment and budgetary goals. When the site is located too far for regular visits, technology must take over and provide reliable and continuous communications. The advantage is that technology has reached a state where continuous communications is available not only through text but visual means. The visual technology can make performance reviews at a distance more personal because the site administrator and main campus supervisor can have a long discussion on what needs to be accomplished. Phone conversations and e-mail messages do not provide this level of communication.

Goals are critical to the success of sites for two reasons. First, the site is some distance from any immediate supervisor. Second, precisely specified goals tell site administrators where they need to focus their attention, and where they should focus the efforts of their staff.

Colleges that use the off-campus model are now starting to move into online delivery of instructional programs. The president turns to site administrators to help launch online programs because they have the most experience in offering convenient and flexible student and instructional sources. Online programs are discussed in greater detail later.

In summary, the off-site model operates very much like the two-plus-two model. The big difference is that it works best when all expenses are kept to the bare minimum. Technology and visiting services should provide any extras.

Coed Model

There is nothing special about the model; as noted earlier, it is a strategic option to expand markets. There are few single-sex colleges left, and there are fewer every day. Most of the male colleges have disappeared; women's colleges have hung on the longest. In the last decade, many of them have made the transition to a coeducational institution. Catholic women colleges linger, but they have lost their market advantage, which rested on their religious orders sending nuns to teach and recruit at high schools. As members of the religious orders have aged, they have retreated to the convent, turning it into a nursing home. As a result, Catholic women's colleges have lost their main new student stream and have turned to the coed model to increase their enrollment. The financial model is the same as the traditional tuition-driven model. The only major difference is that the new coed college has to expend a tremendous amount of money on marketing, athletics, and capital construction for new student centers and residence halls.

PRICE–QUALITY MODEL

The price–quality model works within the concept that price is a signal of quality. The higher the price charged, supposedly the better the quality for the product or service. This concept also works in higher education. Students and families assume that higher tuition means higher quality, even if the evidence to support this proposition is difficult to find.

There are two categories of institutions that use the price–quality model. The first category includes top institutions such as Harvard or Yale, or second-level institutions such as Gettysburg and Wabash Colleges. The second category consists of institutions that play off the concept. These institutions push up tuition so that they can exploit the price–quality assumption, and the college boosts its revenue as a result. Because expenses indicative of quality (for instance, faculty credentials or campus appearance) are not increased, the pricing increment drops to the bottom line.

Price–quality strategies work best when the institution has a strong investment base so that it can buy the best students seeking a first-rate education with first-class living accommodations and services. Some colleges build Potemkin villages using high posted prices to imply a top-quality education with pleasant living conditions and decent student services. These strategies work best with students who have no other alternatives and parents who would like to see their children receive a quality education. The catch for students is that posted tuition is the only indicator of quality. The hook is set with a large financial aid package that looks like a bargain. For the naïve, it seems like a huge scholarship to be paraded before friends and family.

The price–quality model has these characteristics:

- *Financial Structure*: Income flows for the price–quality model are comparable to the traditional model except that they depend on income flows from large endowment funds and gifts with net tuition providing the balance. The chief use of the riches is to secure the best students with generous financial aid packages.

- *Enrollment and Pricing Strategies*: Enrollment strategies depend on convincing potential students and their families that the tuition rate is justified by the high quality of the programs. Of course, this is problematic if quality is not readily apparent. Colleges that exploit the price–quality relationship often raise tuition discounts so that their pricey tuition looks good enough to ignore the lack of an acknowledged reputation for quality. For the price–quality exploiters, tuition discounts can become a losing proposition as enrollments and gross tuition increase but net tuition and cash stagnate. Increasing the scale of tuition discounts at institutions such as the Ivies, Stanford, Duke, and other similar universities has no real effect on their financial condition because endowments essentially fund the academic program. The main concern of the best privates is not the scale of tuition discounts but how to balance attracting the top tier students while distributing admission to their institutions equitably across diverse segments of the population. The latter institutions see themselves as providing a luxury service at a discount while the former institutions see themselves as "using" price–quality to build enrollment to fund a run-of-the-mill academic program.

Comments about the price–quality model

Private institutions face an expensive dilemma resulting from the gap between sticker (posted price) and net prices (tuition net of financial aid). Sticker price gives "the perception of growing riches from ever-higher tuition rates, [or sticker price, which] translates into [a]… gap between perception and reality [that] can only serve to exacerbate the pressure to grow services on campus, negotiate the financial aid award, and decrease the rate of growth, if not the actual price, of attendance."[7] Some colleges have created a serious credibility problem using the high-price, high-quality strategy. The sticker price grows by leaps and bounds, seemingly taking parents' hard-earned money to fill college coffers, when they are merely covering the ever-widening breach between expenses and revenue.

Higher sticker price signals higher quality to purchasers, who demand higher quality by way of more expensive services. Whereas instructional quality is not easily shown to a purchaser, better dorms, new workout gyms, quaint brick walkways, massive student centers, classy shopping malls, high-toned food services, and fancier computers do offer tangible signs of quality. When colleges with meager resources try to match service value with richer competitors, they may be forced into a merry-go-round where enrollment increases fail to produce enough revenue to support the cost of buying the high-end residences and services to attract more students.

This model is vulnerable when prospective students hear rumors or find facts that the high price does not yield future incomes that are large enough to pay off debts and live in anything more than humble circumstances. Colleges that exploit the price–quality assumption by placing a high price on a low-quality product seem to enroll inadequately prepared and undermotivated students. The families of these students are not aware at the time that their child starts at one of these colleges that price is not necessarily a reliable indicator of academic quality. In fact, price was raised by these colleges beyond the level expected for it to attract large first-year classes. Sharp students will quickly discover that the college needs them as much as they need the college. When students make this connection at a high-priced but low-quality college, they can exploit the college by negotiating its academic standards and gaining large tuition discounts. Reisman saw this happening back in the early seventies when many colleges began to negotiate with their students on academic standards.[8] This business model may collapse if prospective students see that the price and quality linkage is not valid. When this happens, the college is left with a high-price, low-quality model and nowhere to go.

In summary, this model needs to be funded by endowments and gifts to make the price–quality equation work. Expenses will be similar to the traditional tuition-driven model; however, capital investments and instructional and student services expenses will be higher to convince students and parents of the quality of the college.

RESIDENCE HALL MODEL

This strategy is very close to the "field of dreams" belief that if you build new residence halls with lots of beds and comfy services for students, they will come. In the last decade, this seems to have been the case, but every so often this strategy fails. For example, Bradford College in Massachusetts built new dorms but was unable to fill them. Many institutions applying this model require that students live in the residence halls for at least two or three years of their attendance. The college does this to ensure a steady flow of income to cover debt and operational expenses. Additionally, in small towns this helps with town-gown relations. This model has the following characteristics:

- *Financial Structure*: The attractive part of this strategy is that residence halls are built with debt that is paid by "board" fees, and new residents produce more tuition revenue in addition to income from food services, bookstores, and other on-campus service revenue sites. Some smaller colleges are also trying to reach the optimal economic scale of students by using the residence hall strategy.

    This model typifies the expense structure and cash flows for most traditional undergraduate colleges. Full-time faculty in a classroom, intensive student and academic services, interest payments on debt, and a layered administrative structure define operational expenses. Cash covers principal payments through student fees when most rooms are filled.

Comments about the residence hall model

This strategy may impose both immediate and long-term risks on the institution, if enrollment does not materialize or if enrollment falls after several years. In both instances, the college will have capacity, but also debt with no way to support it. Lenders may call the debt if the institution is unable to make payments, or the president may have to "rob Peter to pay Paul" by taking money from operational accounts to cover debt payments. This tactic cannot last long; it will diminish the reputation of the college because it cannot sustain its academic programs or student services. Either enrollment will sink further or student quality will tail off. These conditions usually mean that the student body will lack the financial resources to sustain the high costs needed to sustain the institution's reputation for quality. When this happens, college leaders are forced into the circular trap of chasing their own tail.

In summary, the residence hall model works when there is a large enough pool of students who prefer not to live at home. Students who can afford it increasingly want to live on campus. However, with the changes taking place in demographics and higher debt and operational costs that will be passed on to students, the demand for living on campus could fall.

ATHLETICS REVENUE MODEL

The athletics revenue model is based on the proposition that athletic teams are simple devices to increase revenue at colleges that need a quick boost in enrollment. An athletic team can often recruit nearly double the number of team members required for putting a team on the field or in the field house because athletes must try out for their team each year. Coaches need new players to fill team slots of those who graduated and to challenge the team members who return so that the best players are selected for the team. If players fail to make the team, the chances are high that they will remain at college to finish their degree. If the college expects to attract good student athletes, it needs winning seasons, if not every year then at least once or twice, during a four-year period. Otherwise, student athletes will turn down enrollment and scholarship offers, which might threaten the validity of the athletic strategy. This model has the following characteristics:

- *Financial Structure:* Net tuition revenue is the main source of income with athletes being a key enrollment stream. This strategy works best when athletes produce enough net tuition to pay for the athletic programs and throw off extra income to help balance total expenses with revenue. Some institutions may receive a small amount of revenue from ticket and concession sales. In most cases, this is a minor source of revenue. Alumni gifts are what the big institutions want, and the alumni gifts are dependent on how well the team does. Most private colleges or universities find that big money flows freely only for big-time sports such as football and basketball. The downside of big-time sports and big-time gifts is that alumni sometimes will try to intrude into operations and game day planning. Interference by sports fanatics can be expensive, especially when they insist that the college fire coaches, build new facilities, or force movement to a higher National Collegiate Athletic Association (NCAA) level, resulting in larger financial aid awards and greater expenses for the teams. The worst transgression of colleges with an athletics revenue model is when they violate NCAA rules, which may result in sanctions, a loss of prestige to the institution, and even the removal of the president.

  A strategy based on athletic growth imposes a greater load on student services and academic support because many student athletes have problems balancing practice, games, and classroom work. Coaches, insurance, travel, conference fees, facility expenses, and general athletic expenses also add to the burden of the expense budget.

- *Enrollment and Pricing*: This enrollment strategy expects coaches to recruit enough athletes to increase enrollment. Recruitment strategies for many small and medium-sized independent colleges target students who lack the athletic and academic skills to enter larger schools. These potential students are committed to playing and are not ready to quit sports, so they will take any offer, no matter how meager, to play. The problem with this segment of the market is that they may not do well in their colleges and have to quit because they fail to meet academic standards to continue their enrollment.

  Pricing is highly controlled if the sport is played within the rules of the NCAA. The financial aid offers have to be carefully crafted so that they meet the conditions of the governing body. For example, DIII does not allow student athletes to receive athletic scholarships, but often government aid is insufficient because students just want to play.

Comments about the athletics revenue model

Although a sports team can appear to be a quick and easy fix to enrollment, it contains many potential problems. The first and largest problem is attrition. If the team member came to college only to play the sport, classroom work may take a low priority in his or her life. Also, some of these students are low income, so if they lose team eligibility because of poor academic performance, they will leave college. Attrition can be so high that some colleges find that they have to replace most of the team every year, which is very costly for recruiting and sports expenses.

ENDOWMENT- AND GIFT-DRIVEN MODEL

The endowment- and gift-driven model is the standard model for colleges that are not tuition-dependent. However, dependence on endowment draws and gifts can be risky for colleges with small endowment funds or colleges that have picked the wrong investments during a major stock market correction. When the market booms, as

FIGURE 6.1—COMPARISON OF NET TO REVENUE BY TUITION DEPENDENCY CATEGORIES, 1998–2002

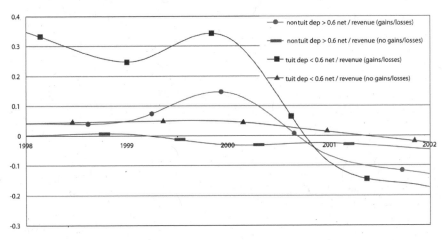

Legend:
- nontuit dep > 0.6 net / revenue (gains/losses)
- nontuit dep > 0.6 net / revenue (no gains/losses)
- tuit dep < 0.6 net / revenue (gains/losses)
- tuit dep < 0.6 net / revenue (no gains/losses)

Reprinted with permission from JMA Higher Ed Stats, Boulder, CO: John Minter and Associates, 2002.

it did in the 1990s, risks appear to be small, and endowments throw off huge amounts of new money. However, when the market turns bust, money dries up like a dry creek bed in a Texas summer. Figure 6.1 shows what happens to operational income when the market is strong or weak.

From 1998 until late in 2000, the market was very strong, but in 2000 the market turned down when the technology bubble burst. After September 11, 2001, the market fell even further. The impact on endowment draws lagged the downturn because they work on a moving three-year average, which meant that they did not pick up the effect of the 2000 market decline until 2001.

During the period from 1998 through 2000, net to revenue remained strong for tuition-dependent[*] and nontuition-dependent institutions,[†] when unrealized gains are included. After that period, net to revenue dove into negative territory as the impact of the

* Tuition equals more than 60 percent of revenue.
† Tuition equals less than 60 percent of revenue.

severe market decline of 2001 and 2002 was taken into account in endowment draws. When unrealized gains and losses are removed, net to revenue for tuition-dependent institutions shows that deficits are commonplace in good and bad markets. Then again, nontuition-dependent institutions remained above the deficit line, but barely so, until 2002.

This suggests that even though endowment draws are only a small portion of total revenue for tuition-dependent colleges, they keep these institutions above the deficit line during good markets. The market masks the weakness of net income from operations for these colleges. On the other hand, the market provides the impetus to wealth building in nontuition-dependent institutions because they can add massive amounts of wealth during strong markets. Although weak markets, as happened in 2000 and 2001, diminish the value of this wealth, the losses were less than the growth of endowment principal during the 1990s.

The endowment- and gift-driven model has these charactertics:

- *Fund Structure*: Endowment and gift income is the chief source of revenue. Endowment draws are controlled by the prudent stewardship rule discussed in an earlier chapter, which requires the principal to be protected for future generations. Draws from the endowment fund usually fall between 4 percent and 5 percent of the principal. Recent committee hearings at the national and state levels suggest that legislators expect that institutions with large endowments should provide more financial aid for students from endowment funds. The wealthiest colleges are already reacting to government pressure by offering financial aid packages that completely pay for a student's tuition bill. Private colleges with small endowments that compete with wealthy institutions (that grant full rides to those students) for the best high school graduates, may find that they are forced to match those liberal awards if they want to enroll the best students. Going up against the wealthiest colleges could be a losing game for the less affluent institutions because large unfunded grants could seriously impair their financial stability.

- *Enrollment and Pricing*: Enrollment and pricing work hand-in-hand for wealthy institutions because they want to find and enroll the best and the brightest students subject to various internal goals and social interests. Most top private institutions restrict enrollment because tuition revenue is not needed to balance expenses. In fact, larger enrollment classes for the top private universities are counterproductive financially because they prompt huge expense increases for more top-flight faculty, additional facilities, and expanded services.[9] However, Princeton is increasing its enrollment and Stanford is studying the impact of adding more students. Why would they do this if tuition revenue is unimportant and expense increases are so large as to render the exercise pointless? Are they just being nice by letting more students bypassed by their current enrollment restrictions attend? It is likely that this is not the case. An article in *The Chronicle of Higher Education* reports that one benefit of larger enrollments is that it gives the university the opportunity to offset the number of legacy[*] students because there is growing controversy in Congress and elsewhere about this preference.[10] Another reason, according to *The Chronicle*, is that Princeton could enroll more athletes with better athletic skills because Princeton stands at the low end of the sports ranks among the Ivies.[11]

Another, more plausible reason not mentioned in *The Chronicle* for increasing enrollments at a university such as Princeton rests on three propositions. The first is that the top private institutions depend on multi-billion-dollar endowments to support their academic programs and to burnish their reputation. The second is that endowments are fed not only by returns on investments but through epic gifts from alumni who have made Gilded Age fortunes. The third is that there are only a few alumni who have made the requisite fortune to make massive gifts to endowment

[*]Legacy students are the children of alumni and in many cases they are the children of large gift givers.

campaigns. Given these three propositions, it is in the institution's interest to expand the number of potential alumni, thereby improving the probability that the institution will continue to grow its endowment through its wealthiest alumni. Whether this is a valid argument is purely speculative but interesting.

Comments about the endowment- and gift-driven model

The wealthiest institutions use endowments and gifts to conduct research; instruction is a decidedly secondary interest. Research activities are usually supported by large grants from the federal government, foundations, or major corporations. Under these conditions, the revenue flow is endowment, gifts, and grants. The first two, endowment and gifts, are cultivated by managers devoted to growing endowment value and producing an ever more bountiful harvest of gifts. Endowment growth will depend on the acuity of the managers picking the right investments and avoiding big mistakes. Because most endowments are broadly diversified across many different investment sectors, mistakes and the impact of bad markets are minimized. The development manager must be like the undertaker—always there ready to convince well-heeled alumni or other friends of the college that the best testament of their life is a departing gift to their favorite college. Gift solicitation requires patience by the college's president, development office, and board members and the willingness of the president to spend significant time traveling and visiting with potential donors.

Research grants are another story because the skilled grant writer has to have an intelligence network that locates the latest source of funds and that understands what the agencies are willing to fund. Grant writing is an art because the writer must anticipate the donor's wishes and provide solid proof that the institution can deliver the sought-after service or products.

Many boards of trustees do not appreciate how hard it is to raise money from gifts, foundations, and businesses. The impression many board members have is that fund raising is a combination of a golden Rolodex, rich alumni, and a high-speed dialer. Golden Rolodexes buy little in today's world. Foundations tend to give to research or to a narrow interest that they have. Businesses give large grants only if they get a return on their investment, such as research that can be turned into a marketable product. When corporations cannot get research benefits from a college—in most cases liberal arts and business colleges lack the means to conduct research—they will offer a token gift of $20,000 or so to the college. This will happen if the business is geographically close to the college or a board member is a high officer in a business and can tell someone to send a check. For most private institutions, foundation and purely business gifts are small drops in a very large bucket.

Fund raising from alumni is no easier. Normally, alumni limit their gifts to $100 checks to the annual fund. Colleges may not see large gifts (*large* in this case means hundreds of thousands and not millions) from current graduates until long after the president has retired. Even when wealthy alumni, who made their money on their own, reach their late fifties, they are reluctant to part with their hard-earned cash. The *nouveau riche* think about bequeathing large gifts only on or near their deathbeds. Otherwise, they have too many irons in the fire to give away their money.

The hard and sometimes bitter task of raising money pits the board against their president. The board thinks that the president is a slacker if he or she cannot raise huge bundles of money quickly, and the president thinks that the board is hopelessly unrealistic. Firing presidents, development officers, and advancement officers because they have not brought in the dollars is counterproductive unless they are incompetent. Fund raising requires time, perseverance, and consistent relationships. Moreover, colleges enrolling first-generation students are going to have few fund raising resources.

In summary, this business model is really the quintessence of higher education and will fit the price–quality model. It works mainly on gift flows and the growth in endowment principal. Operational costs should be kept in check, but that is subject to the production of enough revenue to support a high-quality academic experience.

PARTNERSHIP MODEL

The right market and clever presidents can put together partner-ships that enlarge markets, expand program offerings, and/or cut expenses. Here are five common partnership options:

1. *Community college partnerships*: Four-year degree programs offered onsite at the community college at a reduced tuition rate.

2. *Complementary institutional partnerships:* For example:

    - Degree programs that use specialized faculty unavailable to one institution

    - Facilities and other assets, such as library services, classrooms, student services, academic support services, residence halls, food services, bookstores, athletic services, transportation vehicles, and whatever else that can be leveraged to advantage for several institutions

    - Online services and other technological services where several institutions can pool resources to reduce costs

3. *Outsourcing or partnerships where the cost of operations is reduced*: Examples include information technology, bookstores, food services, residence hall management, custodial services, and security operations.

4. *Research partnerships:* Partnerships with large corporations where the corporations provide funds, the university provides the intellectual capital, and they both reach an agreement on the splitting of benefits, if any.

5. *Business partnerships:* Partnerships arranged with faculty or busi-nesses that want to establish profit-making business schemes with an institution. Not-for-profit colleges need to scrutinize these plans carefully because the college may have to pay property taxes, business license fees, or income or corporate taxes.

This model has the following characteristics:

- *Financial Structure*: The revenue flow will depend on the nature of the partnership. Outsourcing and some service partnerships produce cost savings by reducing operating expenses and the cost of capital investments. Each partnership should be treated independently with its own financial arrangements and accounting system, which produces accurate and timely operational and financial reports. The institution entering into a partnership should also insist on financial and operational audits with access to the summary and management reports.

Comments about the partnership model

Any institution taking on partners has to live by the "due diligence rule." It must accept the costs of legal, financial, and other advice so that it understands the benefits, costs, and especially the risks of the operation.

In summary, partnerships are an opportunity to either control expenses in a particular area by diluting them among a larger set of colleges, or to increase revenues by developing new revenue channels with or through other colleges.

ONLINE MODEL

The original intent of online models was classes and instructional programs offered over the Internet. There is wide variation in how these programs are offered whether completely online, through a hybrid model with in-class work and online assignments, or with student meetings online and instruction in a traditional classroom.

The point of online models originally was to reach a broader market and to offer courses at a lower cost, but the cost of technology and the cost of designing the instructional package are expensive. If full-time faculty members teach the courses, then there may never be a payoff. Developing a course requires a densely written course design that includes lectures, presentations, visual displays, audio components, assignments, and tests. Faculty cannot cruise through an online course because instructional materials must be ready at the start of the course. In contrast, faculty teaching in a classroom often try to keep two classes ahead of the students, and they have the luxury of ad-libbing if they are well acquainted with the material. This is not possible with online courses, especially when the course is conducted asynchronously.* Teaching an online course may be more demanding than an in-class course because the instructor must respond to each student individually, and student discussion and assignments are arriving 24-7.

This model has the following characteristics:

- *Financial Structure*: Three factors shape the financial viability of an online program: course development costs, instructional costs, and growing enrollments. Course development, as noted, is both time consuming and expensive. Even though packaged courses are available, colleges usually hire an instructional designer or contract with the faculty to develop courses. Course development is expensive because, like a movie, the course must have a script that lays out every step in instruction including objectives, class material, assignments, class discussions, and tests.

  The college inevitably must sort out how to pay for faculty—adjunct or full-time. Customarily, full-time faculty are paid for an overload when they teach an online course. This is because adjuncts are hard to find for day-time instruction.

  Online courses' value to financial stability is greatest when enrollment comes from outside the institution. If courses are mainly filled with students from the institution and if online tuition is less than in-class tuition, the college could discover that online courses cannibalize campus programs. Moving students from classroom-based courses into the online program could undermine the financial stability of the institution. Colleges have to be wary about

---

* Asynchronous students do not meet online at a specific time for instruction. They do their work at times convenient for them.

this possibility. Enrollment growth for online courses should be drawn from outside the bounds of the campus because these new students will shore up the finances of online programs. Obviously, online courses will also need special expenditures for additional information technology resources and administrative support. For instance, course management software, high-speed communication, and 24/7 maintenance and student technical support are needed because students will link up at any time of the day or night.

Comments about the online model

Marketing is everything for an online program because it has to grow quickly to cover expenses and contribute to the financial viability of the institution. The big challenge is how to target the market and reach the prospective students in a cost-effective manner. Few administrators have any experience marketing online programs and only a handful of consultants know much about the subject. It is not easy to implement academically valid and financially successful online programs, and if online administrators and presidents are not careful, colleges can invite costly marketing mistakes. For instance, badly designed E-mail campaigns or Web mail ads could cost hundreds of thousands of dollars that get huge numbers of hits[*] and no interest. Only later does the college discover that the click may be a popup with little or no marketing value.

An online model will work only when the college has a sophisticated administrative, information, and instructional technology system to permit 24-hour connections, ongoing instruction, and rapid communication with students. Although online projects are technically challenging, they are technically feasible when they are well planned and tightly managed.

In addition to technical and marketing challenges, the registrar, bursar, and financial aid offices may oppose various forms of online enrollment because they may require major changes in how these

---

[*] A hit is when one person clicks into the site. Web ads charge by the hit. An ad campaign that generates a large number of hits with few enrollees may not cover the high cost of the Web ad.

offices operate. These offices are used to limited periods for students to enroll and tightly scheduled billing cycles. Online enrollment forces them to redesign administrative software, working hours, and policies and procedures. These changes increase the chance that mistakes will be made, students will be angry, and the president will be unhappy. Registrars, bursars, and financial aid officers see the problems as insurmountable and may propose paper-based solutions, which inherently go against the philosophy of online education. Opposition to online instruction may also come from librarians, who do not see how books or other media resources can be delivered online, and from the faculty, who think that change of this sort diminishes the interactivity needed for instruction.

Despite the fears of administrative officers, librarians, and faculty, legitimate online systems can be developed to manage enrollment, to deliver books, and to provide student-instructor interaction. Designing administrative systems that accommodate online students will also improve delivery of administrative services to on-campus students. Many librarians have found out that they can meet the needs of online students by turning traditional libraries into media centers that combine powerful media search engines with new methods to distribute books, articles, and other academic resources. Faculty who take the leap into online instruction soon discover that instructional software allows more and deeper interaction with students. These instructional programs give faculty the means to conduct thoughtful classes.

In summary, the online model depends on growth to survive and flourish. It needs flexible administrative and academic managers who work hard to ensure administrative integrity and academic validity. Online instructional systems offer two advantages to a college: they can stand alone in creating new revenue streams, or they can supplement traditional business models such as tuition-driven, two-plus-two, price–quality, off-site, athletic, and residence hall models. The trick is to build momentum in enrollment to generate sufficient income to cover expenses and produce a net greater than the average for the college (tuition net of financial aid and instruction).

MULTINATIONAL MODEL

During the last decade, as the Asian and Middle Eastern economies have taken off like skyrockets, more colleges are looking at moving overseas and tapping into these rich markets. Whether this is a realistic strategy depends on economic and political conditions plus a thorough due diligence analysis of the project.

The concept of a multinational university goes beyond the recruiting of students in another country, or offering study abroad programs, or even joint degree programs with an overseas institution. Multinational involves establishing a physical presence in another country where full academic programs are offered and are supported by the panoply of services and administration typical to a U.S. college or university.[12]

An institution considering a multinational university will confront problems that are beyond its normal experience. Each of the following areas is problematic for a new multinational in a new country: exchange rates, language, local governmental regulations, customs, information technology, communication systems, banks, and transportation. Exchange rates can have a significant impact as funds are brought back into the home country and as they are recorded on financial records. If the dollar increases in value, exchange rates could wipe out the financial rationale for the program. Language problems will occur between students, faculty, administrators, and even government regulators. The TOFL* examination can often turn into a breakpoint in recruiting a financially viable set of students. Of course, this assumes that the business and academic programs of the college are conducted in English. Because most Americans are deficient in foreign language skills, the problems of communicating with local officials can be difficult. Local governmental regulations may involve unexpected costs or regulatory quagmires. This can delay projects or force dangerous and unethical bargaining. Different customs can pose a challenge for project leaders. Information technology and support in technologically advanced countries may

---

*TOFL stands for *Test of English as a Foreign Language*. Usually a college will establish a minimum score to accept a student into an English language-based program.

not be a problem, but in some countries transmission speeds may be slow. Local banking customs can be a concern in some countries. It is not unusual to find that money is delivered in a bag on the back of a motorbike. Sometimes exhorbitant fees are charged to cover processing fees. Last but not least, transportation may prove unsafe and/or expensive in some parts of the world.

Even though a market is huge or looks like a promising opportunity, it does not mean that success necessarily follows from the establishment of in-country sites. Take the experience of one Australian university in Asia. They closed their sites after finding that even though the potential seemed vast, in reality less than half their expected enrollments materialized. Several quickly closed their doors.[13] These issues suggest that the success of an international strategy depends on strong planning and due diligence.

The multinational model has the following characteristics:

- *Financial Structure*: The financial model of multinational programs is fairly straightforward. It is driven by student tuition payments that should cover all associated expenses and allocations. The big issues are accurate forecasts of enrollment, correct estimates for expenses, currency exchange rates, pricing, debt, and regulations. Pricing decisions must balance price parity with the U.S. campus and the financial capacity of students in another country to pay the high price charged by U.S. institutions. If the price is at parity to keep foreign students at the U.S. campus from staying home and taking the education at a significantly lower price, tuition may price itself out of the overseas market.[14] Typically, foreign students come to the United States in hopes of finding high-paying positions. Price differences may not be relevant. This is not always a valid assumption in countries such as India where the income for technical professionals is growing fast enough to compete with U.S. pay scales.

   If a comparable scenario governs tuition pricing, then financial aid may play a significant role in pushing prices into an affordable range for local students. This scenario does not apply when a significant price differential may not cause problems with students enrolling at the U.S. campus. However, financial aid may be given as a matter of courtesy so that the national or state government can declare a benefit for allowing the U.S. institution to open its doors. Debt will probably have to be financed through the home funds of the home university, although local financial institutions with government support may provide some assistance subject to the granting of a service gratuity paid through financial aid for students. Governmental regulations in the form of customs laws and transfer of funds back home may have an impact on the speed of starting the program and the repatriation of cash. Because of the complexity of running a program overseas, Hal Irwin and Robert Thompson* in an excellent article on multinational programs suggest that institutions should expect that the parent institution must properly capitalize the venture and expect that several years will be needed to reach breakeven.[15] The institution needs to prepare itself to provide substantial financial support during this period and may decide that the program needs to be canceled if it is not at breakeven after a particular date.

Comments about the multinational model

Leaders need to think through exactly what the college expects to do, how it will be done, what obstacles will be encountered, what the benefits and costs are, and what information is needed to prepare a due diligence report effectively. Some private institutions conceive that establishing a foreign campus is similar to finding the lost city of gold sought by the Spanish conquistadors.

---

* If your college is planning to conduct programs overseas, the Irwin and Thomson article should be required reading because the authors provide insightful discussion of the challenges and considerations in developing an effective strategy. The citation for the article is Irwin, H., & Thompson, R. "Making it as a Multinational University," *Business Officer* (NACUBO July/August 2008).

MARKET NICHES

A niche market strategy concentrates on a narrow piece of the total market.[16] The niche may be defined by its geographic area, attributes, demographics, or uses.[17] The niche is viable only if the set of buyers is large enough to sustain the cost of production, if those buyers actually want the product or service, and if there are few competitors or if larger institutions do not believe that the market is worth their while.[18]

Several examples of market niches include Berkelee College of Music in Boston; Unity College in Maine, specializing in environmental studies; Wentworth Institute of Technology in Boston, known for its applied internship programs; Julliard College in New York, specializing in the performing arts; Cornish College of Arts in Seattle; St. John's College in Annapolis, where the academic program is based on the great books; Chatham University for Women in Pittsburgh, acknowledged for its wide-ranging leadership program for women; and Wilson College in Pennsylvania, recognized for its equestrian center of instruction. An exhaustive list would probably include a large proportion of private colleges or university degree programs because many purposely seek niches where they can thrive.

The market niche model has these characteristics:

- *Financial Structure*: Normally, there is nothing unique about the financial structure of a niche college except in those cases where the niche is capital intensive or depends on specialized faculty. Capital intensive programs require large investments in buildings, equipment, or grounds to support operations. For instance, an equestrian program requires grounds for exercising horses and facilities and equipment for housing and training the horses. The cost of hiring faculty with the skills to provide instruction depends on the size of the particular labor market. If there are few instructors with appropriate training, experience, and degrees, then faculty costs coupled with capital investments can render the project too costly to justify the investment.

Comments about the market niche model

The key to niche marketing is figuring out the niche and then nurturing it so that the prospective students immediately think of the college when they look for a program in that niche. Successful niche programs require continuous development of their reputations through investment in the programs, faculty, and plant, and by marketing their reputations. Regrettably, a niche strategy does not guarantee success because the niche may not be large enough to support the inherent cost pressures from administrative, academic, student, and plant operations. Therefore, tuition-dependent, and even marginally tuition-dependent, private institutions have to find new niches continually so that enrollment can grow to sustain their operational costs.

NEW MODELS

Three models that are now in the formative stage have not been widely accepted. They are not widely accepted because most have run counter to the traditions of not-for-profit institutions. These models are low price-high volume, minimized administrative and service support, and a combination of low price, low support, and partnerships. The review examines general features of each model and any obstacles to providing quality instructional programs and to producing enough income to make a particular model a worthwhile investment.

Low Price-High Volume

This model takes several different forms. The most common form at this time is the two-plus-two combination with the four-year institution embedded in a community college. The advantage to students is that they can leverage the low tuition rates of the community college into a low-cost bachelor's degree. According to Moody's Investors Service, some students may shift to lower price options because higher fuel prices and diminished home equity may reduce their capacity to fund a degree at institutions with high tuition rates.[19]

Another form of this model involving distance education has the possibility of coming to the fore but has not yet arrived. This form could be a true low price-high volume format. High volume means that large enrollments compensate for lower tuition rates by producing revenue that is much greater than the amount lost to lower tuition rates.

An institution could lower its tuition rates to produce a decent net income after it covers its online expenses and allocated administrative and capital costs. The reduction in tuition rates could be substantial if the college carefully manages its instructional expenses by mainly using adjunct faculty or full-time faculty under an overload agreement. However, the model will not work if the college loads the program with administrative expenses or offers academic programs with little or no academic quality.

There are two obstacles to the low price-high volume model: accreditation and faculty. Accreditation commissions have been concerned with the relationship of full-time faculty (a high-cost item) to distance education programs. The assumption is that adjunct faculties lack the academic experience and skills to deliver and evaluate their courses and the effectiveness of distance programs. The faculty may resist distance programs if they see the program as a way to sidestep their role in academic governance of the curriculum. In either case, accreditation or faculty resistance, the college must take both sectors into account or the program will fail, either because the college cannot elicit approval by the accreditation agency or the faculty senate. A low-price program will fail if expenses are increased to satisfy these two groups. This will preclude any price advantage because net income will disappear unless tuition rates are raised to cover higher costs.

Minimized Expenses

Expenses are the most intractable factor that drive inefficiency and higher tuition rates. If a college intends to reduce its tuition price or limit the pace of tuition increases, it must minimize expenses. As noted earlier, Moody's believes that significant changes in the ability to fund a degree at high-tuition institutions is forcing a shift to lower-cost options.[20]

Taking control of expenses is not beyond the realm of institutions, but it requires presidential grit. Presidents have to challenge vested interests in the administration, services, and even instruction. Before a process for producing a paradigm shift to cut expenses is suggested, it would be useful to see the options for reining in costs. Most of these options are recognizable; some are very difficult; some come from the for-profit sector; some are methods that have not been tried but could render real benefits if attempted. The basic notion behind several of these alternatives is that the institution acts as a buyer who can either purchase services from its employees or from the marketplace. The decision on where or how to make the purchase of administrative, student support, or instructional services would have to weigh the relative costs and benefits of each option. Obviously, because some of these options could lead to heated conflict in the college, taking action should not be done lightly. Table 6.1 on the next page is a brief list of cost-cutting opportunities.

Combination Strategy

The purpose of a combination strategy is to put together an organization that minimizes costs, maintains instructional quality, and keeps tuition rates from rocketing upward. Effective change means that the college has made a paradigm shift to take advantage of technology, to streamline and eliminate administrative levels, to provide low-cost student services, and to improve the delivery of services.[21] This shift rests on the assumption that the president can convince the major constituencies that it is in their interest and the interest of the students to step back and figure out what is important, what is not, and what can be replaced with technology. Enthusiastic support and firm direction by the trustees and president are a necessary condition for a successful paradigm shift. The value of a paradigm shift is that the leadership of the college has a real opportunity to make significant improvements in efficiency, to take control of costs, and to slow the seemingly unrestrained acceleration of tuition rates.

Before detailed work begins on the restructuring of the institution, all parties must understand and accept the premises for restructuring the college. Major restructuring projects are daunting tasks

TABLE 6.1—COST CONTROL OPTIONS

Personnel Savings
- Eliminate administrative positions that do not or no longer fit the college's mission.
- Thoroughly analyze all administrative work flows and remove redundant positions.
- Consolidate and dispense with middle-level administration by getting rid of unnecessary bureaucracy.
- Reduce secretarial services or use pooled secretarial services; very few formal letters or documents are generated below the top administrative levels.
- Require 40-hour work weeks from all administrators.

Curriculum and Academic Programs
- Close underenrolled instructional programs.
- End instructional programs that do not fit the mission and are underenrolled.
- End course duplications that are underenrolled.[a]
- Document demand for new courses; do not offer new courses if there is no demand.[a]
- Make sure that proposals to increase total credit hours needed to graduate should compensate for higher instructional costs with increased tuition revenue.
- Use responsibility-centered management analysis to identify programs that are not making financial contributions to the institution.
- If independent studies comprise most of the courses in an instructional program, find out whether the program should be revised or closed.
- Form consortia with other colleges to make programs or courses with low enrollments economically feasible.

Faculty
- Modify the full-time and adjunct faculty mix when the full-time proportion is higher in comparison to comparable or peer institutions.
- If faculty time devoted to instruction in their department is less than 15 percent of their total instructional responsibilities, review the demand for the department.[a]
- Get control of decisions to offer independent studies and internships.
- Assess the necessity for and quantity of release time from instruction.

Property
- Closely track space usage; know how much space per student is needed to produce income, and remember that depreciation, utilities, insurance, and other costs must be allocated to instruction.[b]
- Find ways to generate income from all property, buildings, and equipment. Money is too precious for most private institutions to allow these assets to sit idle.[b]
- Test whether renting, leasing, consortia, or other alternatives are better ways to add space or capital equipment before adding long-term debt burden to the institution.
- Refrain from construction for an instructional program if demand is weak or does not exist.

- Wait to provide nonrevenue space until the budget can support operational, repair, and debt service expenses.
- Sell the president's house[c] and pay the president a stipend for housing expenses because the cost of maintaining the house deflects resources from the mission.

Student Services
- Request bids on student services to see whether outside contractors can be as effective; include penalty clauses in the bid for failing to meet stated performance criteria.
- Only offer services that are mission specific.

Information Technology and Printing Services
- Cease the practice of providing free telephone, Internet, and cable hook-ups in student residences.
- Charge for downloading of music and video.
- Charge for electricity for refrigerators, large game installations, and televisions.
- Set-up consortia with other colleges to run computer services.
- Charge students for using copiers and printers.
- Solicit bids for printing services.
- Minimize printing of material by instructors; have them place it on the electronic course file.

Other Services and Auxiliaries
- Purposely redesign administrative services. Get rid of overlap, unnecessary procedures, conflicting policies, and systems that create superfluous workloads and methods that do not serve the students. Follow the old rule: keep it simple. Simplification is time consuming, conflict ridden, and hard work, but it can result in major savings for the college.[d]
- Solicit bids for marketing services.
- Outsource any auxiliary that does not produce positive net income.
- Outsource building and grounds, maintenance, security, custodial services, bookstores, food services, payroll, and any service that can be reliably provided by an inexpensive provider. Make sure to include background checks on their personnel and penalty clauses for nonperformance on stated criteria.

[a] *From Bugeja, M. (2008). How to fight the high cost of curricular glut.* Chronicle of Higher Education. *Retrieved September 19, 2008, February 1, 2008. http://chronicle.com/weekly/v54/i21/21a03301.htm.*
[b] *From Blumenstyk, G. (June 5, 2008). Lessons from for-profit institutions about cutting college costs.* Chronicle of Higher Education. *Retrieved August 21, 2008, from http://chronicle.com/daily/2008/06/3116n.htm.*
[c] *Providing a home for the president may result in a gross increase in income reported to the IRS. However, the higher taxable income is not often supported by increases in cash, so presidents may pay for this benefit from their own pocket.*
[d] *William Gauthier, Dan Lewis, and Michael Renfrow (February 2007). Solving the Process Puzzle;* Business Officer.

that depend on a strong president, who gives direction and keeps the project on track and on time. The president must keep everyone moving forward and prevent conflict from stymieing progress.

The first task of the president and key decision makers is to construct precise definitions of outcomes, costs, and constraints on the project, such as:

- Outcomes from instruction;
- Outcomes on student services and administrative support;
- Ranges for tuition rates;
- Ranges for unfunded financial aid;
- Average costs for:
  - Instruction by program;
  - Administrative services;
  - Student services; and
- Constraints on outcomes and costs.

Paradigm shifts are costly to presidents, who have limited supplies of time, energy, and tenure. Paradigm projects often bog down without accomplishing anything of value, or the project is completed but fails to deliver on its goals and promises. The costs are heavy for the institution and the president. The latter gains nothing and may have lost other opportunities to strengthen the institution's operating and financial condition. In the case of a costly failure, the president may bear the ultimate personal cost with loss of his or her job.

SUMMARY

The business model for higher education is not complicated. However, success requires diligence, discipline, and leadership. Leadership skills, more than understanding, shape the success or failure of a particular business model in higher education. The factors that determine success are bound in the personalities and interests of many different sectors in an institution, and understanding those personalities and interests is key to success. Leadership skills in higher education should be highly valued because they are not easily found; even business executives who take over an institution and try to manage the college using a simple business model can fail miserably.

ENDNOTES

1. Carlson, Scott (July 18, 2008). "Worsening Economy Could Cause Trouble for Smaller Colleges," *Chronicle of Higher Education*.
2. Ip, G. (2008). "The Declining Value of Your College Degree," *Wall Street Journal*. Retrieved September 15, 2008, from http://online.wsj.com/public/article_print/SB121623686919059307.html.
3. Nelson, John, personal interview, August 25, 2008.
4. McPherson, M. "The Demand for Higher Education." In *Public Policy and Private Higher Education,* edited by D. Breneman & C. Finn Jr. (Washington, DC: Brookings Institution, 1978), pp. 183–186.
5. JMA Higher Ed Stats. *Management Ratios: Private Institutions*, xls: *1997–2000*. (Boulder, CO: John Minter and Associates, 2002).
6. Ibid.
7. Lapovsky, L., & Hubbell. L. (February 24, 2001). "An Uncertain Future," *Business Officer*, http://www.nacubo.org/documents/bom/2001_02_future.pdf; 29.
8. Riesman, D. R. *On Higher Education.* (New Brunswick, NJ: Transaction Publishers, 1998).
9. Farrell, E. F. (2007). "Is Bigger Any Better?" *Chronicle of Higher Education*. Retrieved September 12, 2008, from http://chronicle.com/weekly/v54/i13/13a02301.htm.
10. Ibid.
11. Ibid.
12. Irwin, H., & Thompson, R. (July August, 2008). "Making It as a Multinational University," *Business Officer*, 20. http://www.nacubo.org/x10665.xml.
13. Cohen, D. (2007). "Australian Universities Cull Overseas Programs," *Chronicle of Higher Education*. Retrieved September 19, 2008, from http://chronicle.com/weekly/v53/i46/46a03201.htm.
14. Irwin, H., & Thompson, R. (July August, 2008). "Making It as a Multinational University," *Business Officer*, 20. http://www.nacubo.org/x10665.xml.

15. Ibid.
16. Thompson, A. A., Jr., Gamble, J. E., & Strickland, A. J., III. *Strategy Core Concepts, Analytical Tools, Readings* (Boston: McGraw-Hill Irwin, 2006), p. 129.
17. Thompson, A.A., Jr., Gamble, J. E., & Strickland, A. J., III. (2006). *Strategy core concepts, analytical tools, readings* (pp. 129–131). Boston: McGraw-Hill Irwin.
18. Ibid, pp. 130–131.
19. Carlson, Scott (July 18, 2008). "Worsening Economy Could Cause Trouble for Smaller Colleges," *Chronicle of Higher Education*.
20. Ibid.
21. Massey, W. F. "Remarks on Restructuring Higher Education." In *Straight talk about college costs and prices: Report of the National Commission on the Cost of Higher Education*. (Phoenix, AZ: Oryx Press, 1998).

CHAPTER 7

OPERATIONS: MANAGEMENT FOR SUCCESS

Operational management puts into practice the strategy as stated in the mission, goals, and policies of the institution. Strategy is a meaningless exercise unless it is put into operation and carefully monitored. Most presidents mind the store by carefully tracking enrollment and big-ticket capital expenditures. Otherwise, they use management by exception, that is, not paying attention to anything else until a problem pushes its nasty presence into the foreground. There are two problems with this approach to management. First, by the time the problem is apparent, it may be very difficult to whack it into shape. Second, if there is a single operational problem, it is usually sticky, dragging along other smaller and even larger issues that need attention.

Presidents must take a disciplined and comprehensive approach to operational management if they want early warning of problems or want to assure themselves that operations are under control. Of course, doing all the right things does not necessarily eliminate all problems, but it may make them more tractable to early action.

Operational management is not simply keeping the store in order for today or for this fiscal year. When operational management is done correctly, it carries out strategy and sets the stage for broader improvement in the state of the institution. Cost controls are a good example of long-term effects. The purpose of cost controls is not simply keeping the expenditures in line with the budget. They should be designed to minimize operational costs. This means that cost control has two parts: managing expenditures and improving operational processes to minimize costs. The latter is more demanding than the first because it requires good data and, most important, the cooperation of everyone affected by cost minimization projects.

Our main interest here is in management of operations that influence the financial condition of the institution. Financial condition is determined by more than the operations in the business office; it is shaped and driven by the operations in the rest of the institution. Enrollment management, academic departments, student support, institutional administrative services, plant and grounds maintenance, auxiliaries, and other offices will have direct and major influence on financial condition. If the business office is competently managed, it acts as a scorekeeper of how other segments of the institution are performing. Too many presidents and board members think that the business office has a magic wand or a secret stash of money (they usually do so that they can respond to small emergencies or the whims of someone else). In general, the business office depends on everyone else managing their expenses so that the college meets the budget or carries out cost minimization plans. Even though the business office cannot force others to change, it does have insight into financial weak spots throughout the institution that are undermining the financial condition of the institution.

Developing a solid operational management scheme becomes more important as students become choosier in selecting an institution based on price. The evidence suggests that the Hispanic population will be the impetus for the next major phase of enrollment growth. This population is large, but like African-Americans, it does not yet have the economic resources to buy expensive degree packages. Colleges that depend on enrollment to sustain themselves must significantly improve operational management to manage the effect that cost growth has on tuition.

OPERATIONAL STATEMENTS

Operational statements spell out performance standards, decision boundaries, authority relationships, policies, and procedures for each administrative office. These statements are ready reference manuals for managers and subordinates that ensure continuity and coordination within the office and across the institution.[1] Taken together, these statements catalog how operational activities work together to achieve institutional strategy.

Most operational statements in higher education are implied, not explicit. Everyone understands that the college must collect its receivables, keep net tuition from declining, produce positive net income, and build cash reserves. However, there are no explicit guidelines to define what these implicit measures are, so they are sometimes driven by internal pressures of the moment. When financial aid cuts into net tuition, the administration becomes single-minded in its desire to eliminate the decline. Yet, this single-mindedness may mean that other important principles are ignored, which could lead to stagnating cash, uncollectable receivables surpassing normal levels, or personnel costs rising beyond budget limits. When operational principles are not embedded in processes, decision parameters, and controls, the institution tends to lurch from one problem to the next. Operational principles should be incorporated into everyday work, and they should infuse all decisions made within the institution. Chief administrative officers need information flowing from all levels of the institution that indicates whether or not the institution is taking action within the parameters established by its operating principles.

Contradictions between strategy and operations create confusion, destabilize the institution, and weaken its financial condition as scarce resources are frittered away while factions pursue their own version of the correct strategy. Therefore, operational management should rest firmly on the principle that everyone in the institution must conform to strategic plans as approved by the board. The board and president must see that this principle is accepted and applied.

When this principle is not accepted by a segment of the institution, the president must take immediate action to bring the segment into conformity. Sometimes the action requires hard and painful decisions; failure to act expeditiously suggests that the strategic plans do not have to be taken seriously.

DESIGNING OPERATIONAL STATEMENTS

Designing operational statements is demanding because it requires attention to detail and a conception of how a particular function* fits into the whole. These statements should not be written in a perfunctory manner because they will be ignored as claptrap. Neither should they be exercises in filling file drawers with minutiae. Each statement should provide sufficient information to guide the administrator/manager in how the office is expected to work. Preparation of effective function statements requires input from managers and those on the firing line.

The only way that an administrator/manager† will follow these statements is if the statements become the foundation for supervising and evaluating the work of the office. This means that the president should establish a regular schedule of interim and annual reports on operational performances. Interim reports indicate whether the office is adhering to its standards, is progressing toward its goals, and is encountering problems. The annual report should cover the same issues as the interim report, and it should identify obstacles to meeting performance standards and plans to overcome those obstacles.

Effective statements should include these elements: operational description, strategic linkage, objectives, performance standards, policies, procedures, controls, and authority structure, as follows:

- *Operational description* defines the function of the office, its structure, and its contribution to the institution.

---

*A function is a group of common activities and responsibilities.

†The term "administrator/manager" is used here because individuals assigned to run the affairs of a particular office or function are more than administrators who see to the smooth flow of paperwork. They must see that the activities for which they are responsible accomplish the goals of the institution, which means that they should make changes and improvements. They also need to hire competent people and conduct training to ensure that their employees have the skills to do the work.

- *Strategic linkage* sets out the relationship between the work of the office and the strategic objectives of the institution.

- *Objectives* state a measurable target for performance for an administrator/manager.[2] These should be designed so that the targets are important, tied to the strategy of the institution, and are measurable. An example of an objective for the marketing department is that by May 1, 1,000 new students should be admitted and have paid their deposits.

- *Performance standards* refer to the expectations that the administrator/manager should achieve in the performance of regularly scheduled tasks. These standards will guide employees who perform a particular task, and they will also be the basis for supervising and evaluating employees. For example, a standard of performance is that checking accounts should be reconciled monthly or payrolls should be reconciled to monthly payroll reports.

- *Policies* are rules that govern decisions. Policy statements need to be in accord with the strategy and principles of the institution. Two common policies are a registration policy that defines the condition under which a student with late tuition payments can register for class and an employment policy that sets out the rules on when an employee is eligible for benefits.

- *Procedures* are the steps that someone must follow to complete a task. Procedures should be reviewed frequently to improve efficiency. Some procedures may be embedded in an administrative program; in this case, the procedures should be documented. Examples of procedures include the steps taken to enroll a student or to prepare a student bill.

- *Controls* are the methods used to determine whether an employee meets the criteria set for standards of performance or whether the manager is achieving the objectives assigned to the function or office.

- *Authority structure*[3] circumscribes the relationships of the administrator/manager to subordinates, the relationship among subordinates, and the relationship of the administrator/managers to parallel functions and to upper-level executives. The authority structure also encompasses the conditions under which an administrator/manager can make a decision deemed legitimate by the institution.

OPERATIONAL MANAGEMENT: ACHIEVING FINANCIAL STRENGTH

Private colleges and universities should develop operational plans in 11 operational functions that are critical to financial integrity: net tuition, income, production, costs, cost control, budgets, quality, cash, investments, development, and governmental regulations. Plans that clearly define management of these areas substantially improve the chance that the institution will strengthen its financial condition. These areas are not necessarily the province of any single office or manager. In most cases, they may cross several or all offices but are ultimately the responsibility of the president.

Effective operational plans are coherent, concise, cogent, and consistent, and they are mainly concerned with objectives and controls. The design of a particular operational plan will depend on the objective to be achieved and the information that the administrator/manager and president need to ascertain if the objectives are achieved. Even though the management of the 11 operational functions is unique to a particular institution, certain features should be considered during the design of the operational plans. The following commentary offers insight into the primary features that can improve the operational management of each function.

Net Tuition

There are four keys to managing net tuition: set a net tuition dollar value, establish a discount rate, devise a financial aid distribution matrix (see Appendix F: Financial Aid Grids for Net Tuition Rates and Net Tuition Revenue), and keep tight control on the admissions process. Net tuition reports should track financial aid awarded compared to financial aid goals, new student characteristics against goal, and net tuition actual dollars against its goal. The report should be produced daily during the recruitment season, monthly during the semester, and final reports composed for the semester and end of the year. These reports should go to the president and chief management team. This function drives the financial condition of most private institutions and must be carefully managed to ensure that it is achieving its goals.

Although attention to producing net tuition is important, it is crucial that every step of the admission process must be managed meticulously. It is here that the college generates the students who will produce the net tuition. The two primary concerns in admissions are producing enough students and getting the right types of students. Producing enough students means that you need to know more than whether they pay deposits, which is where most admission offices end their reports. It is as if the car sales staff performance was judged on how many people made a token payment of interest and not on how many cars were sold. You need to know how many remain in class after drop-add. Reports on the general state of admissions are not sufficient. You need to know who does the best job closing sales. Then, you need to evaluate admissions on the characteristics of the students. Excuses about the condition of the marketplace do not wash when you need enough students and good academic students to keep and build the reputation of the college. Therefore, admissions performance must be tracked constantly with formal evaluation conducted by the head of admissions and the reports submitted to the president for review.

Income Center Production

The president should establish as a basic operational principle that all income-producing centers should produce net income in excess of direct costs, depreciation, and allocated institutional administrative support and student service expenses. This principle should apply to instructional programs, auxiliaries, development, and athletics. To foster this principle, the budget should give the net income after allocation of depreciation, institutional administrative support, and student services. Budget reports should incorporate performance reports on income centers that are distributed to the president and chief management team. The report should be monthly with final reports for each semester and the year. These centers speak to the real issue of managing the income productive capacity of the institution. Administrator/managers of these centers must recognize that the net income produced by their centers is critical to the financial condition of the institution. These centers must be rigorously managed to their goals so that the institution can maintain and improve its financial resources.

Costs and Productivity

Costs comprise the cost of producing a product or service. Productivity is the measure of effective use of resources. Cost management assigns costs to the production of the outputs of the institution, such as graduates or credit hours. Assigning costs to graduates is difficult because the costs of producing a graduate must be spread across the years to get an average graduate cost. Collecting the data is often beyond the capabilities of small institutions, which do not have separate institutional research departments. The second measure involves collecting data on credit hours. This may be easier to handle than tracking student cohorts. However, the data should be aggregated by academic degree program. Productivity is measured by relating output to input; generally, the relationship for colleges is graduates to cost of producing the graduate or credit hours for a year with the cost of producing the credit hours (see Appendix C: Financial Measures for productivity measures). Each program should have its own productivity measure. Costs should be allocated in a fashion similar to that given for "income production centers." Management of costs and productivity depends on setting productivity measures in the budget, and then management reports will show whether productivity measures of actual performance are meeting their budgetary goals. These reports are distributed to the president and chief management team at the end of semesters and fiscal years.

Cost Controls

The purpose of cost controls is to manage, limit, and cut costs. Recent Congressional hearings suggest that the people who pay the bill for higher education—parents, students, and government—are very concerned about operational costs in higher education and its impact on tuition rates.[4,5] As a result of dissatisfaction with the price of higher education, real pressure could be placed on private colleges and universities to bring their costs under control. One proposal by Congress is to require institutions to appoint an efficiency committee charged with controlling and cutting costs. The work of this committee would be reported to the U.S. Department of Education.

Whether or not Congress passes legislation mandating cost controls, it is prudent for private institutions to undertake a continuing effort to bring costs under control. Private institutions in their own self-interest should seriously consider a cost control management plan because costs could propel tuition to a level that some income groups now sending their children to private schools could no longer afford.

Rather than suggest a laundry list of ideas for reducing costs, it makes more sense to establish an ongoing management process to monitor and develop long-term plans for cost controls. Private colleges and universities have to move beyond slash and burn tactics when costs are cut as a result of a financial crisis. Too often, the cuts lack any thought about their impact on the operational efficiency of the institution. What is even worse is when the cuts are either restored upon the arrival of happier days in the finance office or they mutate into new and larger costs.

Cost cutting makes sense only when it is done in the context of operational efficiency, which means that cost cutting uses information technology and operational designs to the fullest to reduce per unit costs. One example is to actively plan to reduce administrative personnel and restructure staff in the registrar, bursar, library, admissions, and financial aid offices so that managers act as internal office auditors and staff are direct service personnel that back up electronic service delivery. There are too many administrators and staff fulfilling Parkinson's Law that work fills the time available, or playing Sudoku and solitaire, or ordering gifts and new clothes from a catalog, or keeping in touch with friends. Too many administrators, poorly planned work flow, and too much idle time adds costs that have to be covered from revenue, which usually means turning to increased tuition rates to generate the necessary revenue.

If the president seriously intends to improve operational support, the following are the minimum requirements to get cost containment under way:

- *Data:* Data on the operational costs of instruction, administration, auxiliaries, and plant management are necessary.

- *Board support:* The board needs to send a clear message to the college community that the cost of operation must be cut.

- *Cost containment task force:* The board and president should appoint a task force from the key areas of the college— academics, administration, finance, auxiliaries, and plant. The charge to the task force would be to develop cost minimization plans for all areas of the institution. Plans should include changing work flows, eliminating redundant positions, cutting out levels of administrative support, and utilizing information technology to perform administrative and staff tasks. Set cost reduction goals in terms of costs per student (this clarifies the linkage with tuition) and set a deadline to introduce the changes. The task force should be reconstituted every several years so that improvements to the first round of changes and new changes can be introduced.

- *Reports:* The college needs to incorporate performance on cost reduction goals in its monthly, semester, and annual reporting system.

- *Incentives and sanctions:* Departments should be given incentives to meet or exceed targets; those that fail should be sanctioned.

- *Caution:* Cost reduction plans should not reduce the quality of the main product of the college, which is instruction.

Budgets

A budget should at least include revenue, expense, net income, enrollment, tuition rate list, personnel budgets, capital budget, and cash
flow projections. In addition, the president should ensure that objectives are stated for allocation of net income; estimates for enrollment
goals for at least five years; goals for average gift and number of gifts;
and goals for grants, returns on endowment, and cost productivity.
Budgets should also include as their appendix a master five-year
forecast with a performance report comparing performance against
forecast for the prior three years. The chief management officers
should look for answers to the following questions:

- Did performance match forecasts?

- Which income areas exceeded or fell below forecasts and
  what were the reasons?

- Which expense areas exceeded or fell below forecasts and
  what were the reasons?

- What plans were made or need to be made to get control
  of income or expenses that failed to achieve their forecast
  goals?

- Were plans introduced in the past to make improvements
  successful, and if not, why not?

- How do you provide incentives to go beyond ordinary steps
  to build revenue or minimize costs?

- What obstacles exist or are foreseeable that will prevent the
  budget goals from being achieved? What contingencies can
  be taken to reduce these risks on the budget?

Quality

There are two aspects of quality: academic quality, in which student outcomes are dependent on student characteristics, faculty,
instructional resources, and student support; and service quality, in
which quality is related to the reliability and value of administrative and student services. The reason for inclusion of quality as a
critical operational function is that low quality can have long-term

detrimental effects on the financial condition of the institution. Each aspect of quality requires objectives with measurable results that determine whether performance exceeds, matches, or falls below quality objectives. Performance reports should be available for the president and chief management team at the end of each semester and fiscal year.

Cash

Because cash is the *sine qua non* of financial survival, the budget should reflect its importance by including cash as a budgetary objective. The budget should include a dollar objective for cash after net income and cash to income ratio. The ratio should refer to benchmark institutions that are financially sound or refer to ratios reported by Moody's Investors Service. In addition, the institution should have a short-term cash policy that indicates where cash investments are made, a level of cash reserves, and when cash in excess of reserves is turned over to long-term investment managers.

Investments

Large, well-endowed institutions have detailed policies on investment practices; however, many small- or medium-sized institutions may not have developed an investment policy because the size of their investment pool is small. It is in the interest of institutions with enough money to make long-term investments to set investment goals and policies. Investments must do well because the draws are important generators of revenue; they also can buy quality, reputation, and financial stability.

The policy should set allocation ranges for various types of investments and investment agent expense ratios. It should also state the benchmarks for returns from different types of investments. Minimally, institutions should have a board investment committee that develops the policy with the president and oversees investment performance. As investment funds increase in size, boards should consider placing portions of the investment funds with different investment firms. If investments from a particular firm fall below market averages, the firm should be replaced. Investment policies and performances should be reviewed quarterly and annually by the board committee with the president and chief financial officer.

Development

There are two ways to grow investment principal: returns on existing investments and the addition of gifts or net income to investments. Gifts, small or large, as every president knows, do not voluntarily walk through the door. Sometimes board members who are unfamiliar with development practices and who are board members at a college that has not had a full-blown development office expect that all a president has to do is buzz up rich alumni or pull out the golden Rolodex and call foundations and business executives and that the money will flow like manna from heaven. The world of development does not work that way. It takes a long time and many contacts (intensive and personal) to turn someone into a willing donor. They have to be persuaded, cajoled, wined and dined, and turned into best friends of the president and the college. This is particularly true for the big-dollar donors. People with big money have a long queue at their door and too often at their deathbed looking for gifts. The winners are not the last ones to speak to a donor. Donors will only give their gifts to someone they know and trust. It is the job of the president and development officer to develop a trusting relationship.

Although the president may enjoy travel and dining perks of fund raising and the opportunity to meet exciting and successful people, the real story of fund raising is basically drudgery. Travel takes the president away for days and even weeks at a time. The hours are long and tiring. Sometimes the people are interesting, but it is not a given that a potential big-dollar donor will make the evening pass in pleasant conversation. Too often, meetings with donors turn into a demanding evening where the donor acts as a chief executive looking to hire another high-level executive. In many cases, successful business leaders think that they can do a much better job running the college than the president can. They are more than happy to prove that their skills and experiences are better and more useful. Real development is patience, diligence, and persistence.

The crudest way of stating the development problem is that it depends on a long-term relationship to make a sale. So, the issue is who are the best closers on the development staff? Given this issue, management takes a similar path as with admissions. The chief development officer must keep careful records on contacts and gifts to identify who are likely donors, the scale of their gifts, and who on the staff should be given credit for the gift. Because the success of capital drives is paramount to the success of a president in the eyes of the board and in respect to future positions as a president, development must be reviewed, evaluated, and taken seriously by the president. The president must figure out whether the development office is working at peak efficiency or whether it is floundering in its efforts. The issue, regrettably, must boil down to who stays, who goes, and who is hired. It also involves knowing how to keep board members who do not really like the president happy. This is a unique and necessary skill that must be developed by any president because presidents meet many people who do not like them or their policies, but they must learn how to keep their composure and not let contentious people destroy their focus on accomplishing important tasks.

Government Regulations

Congress continues to dally with the idea of setting strict standards so that: (1) endowment funds are used to reduce the price of education; (2) institutions are placed on a warning list if they have excessive tuition increases; and (3) institutions will have to appoint efficiency teams that are responsible for cutting costs. Colleges would report their activities to the government through new report procedures to capture what the college is doing with financial management. This would be done in conjunction with the usual plethora of government reports that are currently required—Integrated Postsecondary Education Data System (IPEDS) filed with the Department of Education, the 1990 tax report filed with the Internal Revenue Service, A-133 Audits of Federal Awards filed with the Federal Clearinghouse, Form 550 filed with the Internal Revenue Service, and Fiscal Operations and Application to Participate (FISAP Report) filed with the Department of Education. This is a brief list because it does not include other special reports that have to be filed on crime statistics, Occupational Safety and Health Administration (OSHA) rules, equal employment opportunity, grant reports, and reports to state and local agencies. If anyone wants to know why tuition prices are going up, just ponder all the hours and staff needed to prepare these reports. The burden on staff at small private colleges is especially excessive.

Regardless of our opinion about the reports, reports must be filed and filed in a timely and accurate manner. The best solution for a college, regardless of size, is to have a clearinghouse for reports that collects and reviews all reports prior to signature by the president and other chief management officers and prior to mailing them to the relevant agency. The review should include a simple one-page summary that gives the purpose of the report, a summary of the data, and any issues that may exist and that need to be resolved before the next report. The clearinghouse officer should keep a list of reports, data filed, mailing receipts, and items that need to be corrected. The correction items should become part of the president and chief management officer's regular status report.

OPERATIONS: CAPITAL PROJECT MANAGEMENT

Capital project management goes beyond financing a capital project; it is concerned with the period between the initiation and completion of the project. Management of most capital projects involves a level of technical expertise that is rarely possessed by the president or even by chief management officers. A capital project requires managers who are knowledgeable about construction of buildings, adding infrastructure, buying and installing equipment, or renovating buildings. Contractors will assure you that they will do the job, and the college does not need to spend the money on someone with technical expertise. Contractors act from their own self-interest. The institution needs someone to represent its interest and make sure that the work is done correctly. This person is responsible for constantly checking to see that work fits the specifications. They will also demand explanation when a change is requested. The internal manager or contracted construction manager should meet regularly with the president, chief financial officer, chief plant officer, and a board representative, if required. The purpose of the meetings is to report on progress, problems, costs, regulatory compliance, and any issues that may appear.

The second part of capital project management involves the contract for the project. Increasingly contractors present contracts that neither impose a bonding requirement[*] nor even require a penalty for delayed completion.[†] Arbitration clauses now are supposed to resolve complaints with contractors. A college needs to understand that arbitration does not fully protect its interest. If the company refuses to attend or pay fees, arbitration will stall. Also, arbitration is useless when a company goes bankrupt. This is why bonds were required in the past, but if the college requires a bond, check its validity. Is the bond agent reputable, and do they have the resources to make payment on the bond? Of course, part of the due diligence in hiring a contractor is to check their reputation. Be careful: just because the prior project was a success means nothing if the company was bought by someone else or if their Dunn and Bradstreet report shows that they are near insolvency.

OPERATIONAL CONTROLS

The heart of management is control, and control means getting the right information at the right time so that decisions can be made. Good operational management systems necessarily include good control reporting systems. Every major operation in the college needs to have a concise reporting system that shows what is being done, whether it is according to plans, and whether there are major problems that prevent carrying out the plans. Presidents must insist on control reports, and these reports should be presented in a forum such as a chief management officers meeting. Progress can be checked and problems resolved, in particular when a problem crosses multiple operational areas.

---

[*]Bonding requirement is when a contractor is expected to post a bond for the value of the contract or a major portion of the contract in case the firm goes bankrupt so that the college can complete the work with another company.

[†]Penalties for delayed completion are payments by contractors to the owner (institution) for failure to complete the project on time.

GOOD PEOPLE EQUAL GOOD OPERATIONS MANAGEMENT

There is a very simple rule in management: hire the best person to do the job. If you skimp on hiring quality, you will get full measure of a bad deal. Too often, private institutions think that they are saving money by promoting or hiring unskilled people into positions requiring complex technical skills. But unskilled employees have long learning curves and will make mistakes; hire the right person with the ready expertise.

SUMMARY

Operational management is the basis for translating strategy into practice. This works only when operations management is conducted in a rigorous, coherent, and concise manner. Managing by exception results in loss of perspective and discovering problems after they have become too large to hide. Effectively managing operations depends on presidential leadership. The president must know the outcomes of important decisions, the performance of the institution at all levels, the skills of the chief management team, the obstacles or challenges facing the institution, and the strategies and methods used to respond to obstacles and challenges. A president has to know what the chief operating officers are doing. Weak presidents leave a vacuum that either will be filled by one or more chief operating officers or by the faculty. The essence of leadership is knowledge, and not necessarily technical knowledge. The president must know what is happening on campus, why it is happening, who is a leader and who sits back waiting for someone else to deal with a problem, who is causing problems and why, and whether decisions and actions fit with strategic and operational plans. This is particularly important in small colleges and in any institution that is in financial distress. Otherwise, others will not take management seriously, and management will disconnect from strategy, leaving the institution to survive on fate and the sheer altruistic drive of subordinates. This is a very risky management principle.

ENDNOTES

1. Drucker, P. *Management: Tasks, Responsibilities, Practices* (New York: Harper & Row, 1974), pp. 101, 403–406, 414–418.
2. Ibid, pp. 99–100.
3. Weber, M. *The Theory of Social and Economic Organization* (New York: Oxford University Press, 1947), pp. 152–153.
4. Field, K. (2008). "Pending Bill Would Double Colleges' Reporting Burden, Critics Say," *Chronicle of Higher Education*. Retrieved September 5, 2008, from http://chronicle.com/temp/email2.php?ed=83n8MMcD5sdbfmjRz2cPzykpSV85xy4w.
5. Field, K. (2008). "Congress' Cost Cure May Have Side Effects," *Chronicle of Higher Education*. Retrieved September 5, 2008, from http://chronicle.com/weekly/v54/i22/22a00101.htm.

CHAPTER 8

STRATEGIC
PLANNING

Typical private college presidents tend to small crises by the hour and dedicate most of their professional life to enrollment budgets, new instructional programs, faculty hiring, and donor-wooing. They work with scant financial reserves and, thanks to a lack of accountability standards for administrators and faculty members, generally work alone. Out of necessity, this captain of a discombobulated crew is forced to rule from the helm, the watchtower, and the galley where he or she constantly puts out fires. Presidents have little if any time to map a strategic course, but they must nevertheless figure out where they want their institution to go. The inability of presidents to predict the future constrains long-range planning.[1,2]

George Keller, the author behind modern perspectives on academic strategy, asserts: "Presidents who do not look ahead, who do not plan, become prisoners of external forces and surprises most often unpleasant."[3]

Strategic planning is very difficult to do but easy to explain. Basically, strategic planning boils down to selling a service to a target market at a price so that a sufficient number of buyers buy the product to generate enough revenue to maintain the financial integrity of the institution. Anything less than this is an unworkable strategy! This chapter works from the premise that strategies must start with the marketplace. It discusses one of the main problems in strategic planning in higher education—incrementalism, when strategy is defaulted to doing what has been done, but just doing a little more of it. The last section deals with a trusted approach to the development of strategic plans in higher education. This approach is based on George Keller's proposition that good strategic planning requires the effort and support of everyone in the college.

MARKET-DRIVEN STRATEGIC PLANNING

> When faced with the kind of revenue shortfalls that now confront higher education, most college presidents and their institutions simply hunker down by making the preservation of current jobs and operations their top priority... The result, despite everyone's best intentions, is an institution even more dependent on its current markets and less able to invest in its own future.[4]

The preceding quotation succinctly states the dilemma faced by the strategic planning efforts at most colleges. If the only goal is to preserve the present, the strategy will fail because the market for higher education is too dynamic. College administrators must look to the legitimate demands of the marketplace as they formulate their strategic plans. This is the basis of sound strategic planning. Potential students *want* a quality education that is in tune with relevant labor markets or graduate schools' demand for students. Students depend on their colleges to know these markets and to offer relevant training. This is only possible if, as Robert Lenington suggests, the strategic plan is "market-oriented and... contains alternatives to a market position that goes awry."[5] According to George Dehne, college administrators must know their colleges and their competitors.[6] They can do this by pulling information from student interviews and surveys, state planning offices, the Internet, and the National Center for Education Statistics. Colleges must extricate the dynamics of student choice, that is, the differences in prices, programs, services, or other institutional characteristics that drive a student to a given college (or its competitor). Before crafting market and pricing strategies, the college must comprehensively collect and evaluate data on itself, on its competitors, and on the phantoms who never showed up after paying their deposit.

Student demographics and economic conditions change, and so too do colleges need to change their internal and external market research and market goals. As markets and economies shift, college missions should be updated; and, after the missions are rewritten, the market will undoubtedly shift yet again. The college that wants to survive 30 more years of change would do well to remain attentive and flexible to accommodate student demands and open to alternative market strategies.

STRATEGY VERSUS INCREMENTALISM

Strategic plans establish a single route of travel, checkpoints, and an estimated time of arrival. Simple as it sounds, strategic planning is laden with difficulties in higher education. Collegial governance runs contrary to timeliness and singleness of purpose, but the process of coordinating and monitoring the efficient movement of several divisions (e.g., academic, financial, and marketing) toward a single goal in the unknowable future is *not* impossible for a private institution. The president *can* resolve financial problems strategically and must begin the process despite dissension among participants and unforeseen roadblocks.

In the absence of a strategic plan, financially distressed colleges (a very large number of colleges, in fact) tend toward the path of least resistance, commonly known as "muddling through" but formally deemed "incrementalism." Incrementalism is a process whereby small decisions nudge an organization toward some undefined future point, which results in insignificant and uncoordinated growth. The scarce resources of many institutions, along with the energies of department heads, are depleted during vain attempts to synchronize and monitor divergent and contradictory incrementalist strategies.

Given the lack of oversight and restraint associated with incrementalism, presidents of independent colleges and universities find that they are vulnerable to countless pressure from self-interested parties. Multiple small-scale decisions, which are apparent during budget planning, grow from nubs into twisted tentacles that choke future action by the whole system.[7] As a mediator during budget negotiations, the president forges small deals among various departments to produce a balanced budget (or at least a budget that appears on its surface to be balanced). For example, the vice president of academic affairs pushes for a new faculty position to assuage a department chair that earlier cut a deal on instructional policy. At the same time, the vice president of administration wants to beef up campus security patrols to deter pilfering in parking lots. The president wants to support the faculty to keep the peace, and because of growing safety concerns among students and employees (as expressed in the campus newspaper), the president cannot ignore the administration's security patrol request. The president compromises, allowing for a half-time faculty position and a part-time security guard.

But this small compromise may haunt the president later, for nearly all half- and part-time positions outgrow themselves. Though the president agreed to the equivalent of one full-time position at the budget meeting, within a year the college will be paying two full-time salaries. Without an overarching strategy to direct the budget, bundles of small favors explode into potholes of money that can confuse the course of an already wayward institution. Like a traveler in a foreign land with only a street map, the imperiled college without a strategy has no concept of its ultimate destination, how it will get there, or how long it will take. Without a larger view, the traveler shuffles through numerous tolls trying to find the way, only to end up where he or she started—like the college, facing a long journey with a nearly empty pocket and a small-scale map.

Strategic planning demands a huge shift in perspective and requires significant resources. One irony in higher education is that those institutions with a highly refined strategic planning process are the least in need of it. Wealthy private institutions have the resources to invest in strategic planning because they have the means to build intricate economic models that guide budgetary decisions. Small college presidents struggle not only with inadequate financial resources but also with a real or perceived lack of time, skills, and support. In lieu of strategy and elaborate planning models, presidents of less wealthy colleges "live by their wits... improvising[,] groping in the darkness, [and] grappling in the confusion and blood of [everyday existence]."

Strategic plans move the institution from ad hoc decision making to a systematic approach linked to a strategy that sets out the direction, resources, and plans to reach some desired place in the future. Strategic planning is a methodical process in which key leaders follow a rigorous planning regimen to develop an institutional strategy. The regimen moves through these steps:

- *Team development*: Select who is involved in strategic planning and the ground rules.

- *Diagnostics*: Analyze the current and future condition of the college.

- *Strategic goals*: Set the goals based on the diagnostics analysis.

- *Strategic objectives*: Establish what is to be accomplished and when it is to be accomplished to achieve a particular goal.

- *Strategic plans*: Prepare a statement of goals* and action plans.

- *Monitoring schedule*: Establish a regular reporting schedule.

When the institution takes on this or any strategic planning regimen, the president must guide, oversee, move everyone forward, and maintain control of the plan.[9] Otherwise, the institution will remain a muddle where strategy is shaped by pressures brought to bear on the board, president, faculty, staff, alumni, or students. In too many cases, strategy deteriorates into a set of digressions be-

---

*Goals are statements that this book treats as something that a significant functional area in the strategic plan expects to accomplish. Objectives state the specific things to be accomplished in a particular time frame. Goals and objectives may also be used interchangeably by others.

cause the mission is ignored, or there is no overarching guide in the development of the strategy. Incremental strategies are attractive precisely because no one is responsible for them. The incremental-ist dynamic does not depend on the hard work of figuring out the best approach, given the mission, goals, markets, and price of the institution. Incrementalism defaults to the past and it can be blamed for today's or tomorrow's failures.

STRATEGIC PLANNING 101

Once intent for the plan has been conveyed, debated, and cham-pioned, the real process of strategic planning begins. This chapter introduces joint planning committees or task forces; strategic diagnostics or goals; and implementation schedules, performance benchmarks, and monitoring schedules. In the spirit of successful strategizing, whether on a grand scale or limited to financial strategy, we then consider how strategy should respond to Robert Lenington's suggestions on applying a market-oriented perspective to strategic planning.*[10]

A major difficulty with selecting goals is that presidents and their key decision leaders cannot reliably predict future economic or student market conditions. As a case in point, 10-year strategic plans that list specific yearly program additions could prove illusory because leaders cannot possibly predict future markets with complete accuracy, especially 10 years out. Instead, specific steps could be taken *toward* a strategically desirable state within a reasonable time frame, which suggests that strategy must implement changes that will allow institutions to retain flexibility in tactical operations as they enter the constraints of a new long-term framework.†

Another consideration in strategic planning comes from Gary Wirt, vice president at a small financially viable (but once struggling) college.[11] In his work on accreditation teams, he found that most 5- to 10-year strategies fail, not for lack of leadership but because of

---

*Lenington's book, *Colleges Are a Business*, provides specific insights on college planning that come from his career as a college administrator and business executive.

†Tactical operations are any plan or decision that influences only the current year of operations.

the lack of precise goals. Until conditions change that require major modifications in strategy, the board and president need well-drafted goals and objectives that can be matched to actual performance. They need these management statements so that they can determine whether they are on or off track with their strategy.

Strategic change must consider the impact on interrelated systems and functions within the college. For example, a close look at the specific project's fit with the college's mission and geographic location can help to ensure sensible and flexible building designs, adequate parking, and compliance with zoning regulations.

PLANNING UNDER FINANCIAL DURESS

Colleges that are in deep fiscal trouble may have to wait until more propitious circumstances prevail to introduce the joint planning group. This group works best when a college has the luxury of time and resources.

If the college is on the brink of failure, strategic planning will fall on the shoulders of the president, who will have to pull together key decision makers to produce a rational strategy. They must work together, and if certain members are contentious, divisive, and push unworkable solutions, then they must be removed from the team. Administrators who cannot abide by the simple rule of working toward the solution should leave the college. If they remain, they can tear the college apart and turn strategic planning into a debacle.

The president must be accepted as the champion of the institution with the full backing of the board of trustees. If the board believes that the president lacks the skills to carry off the strategic reconstruction of a dying college, then they must find someone who does have those skills. If the board is not willing to commit the funds to hire the best, they can hope for the best talent and hire who they can afford. In some cases, talented presidents can be found from the dross that applies to a financially damaged college. Those cases are rare and far between.

Strategic planning under financial duress must still follow the main rule that strategy follows from the fit among mission, services, markets, and price. A president needs the wit and wisdom to know how to make the mission relevant to the market, how to define the target market, how to design services to fit the market, and how to price and sell those services so that the target market chooses to enroll in the college.

PLANNING UNDER CONDITIONS OF FINANCIAL STRENGTH

Joint Planning Group

When a college has the resources in time and money to approach planning without the stress of its impending failure, a president can turn to a joint planning group to develop the strategic plans for the college. Under these circumstances, the establishment of goals and options, as well as the choice of people and deadlines associated with the strategic plan's implementation, take place within the forum of the joint planning group. [12] Membership of the joint planning group should represent the major constituencies within the institution, such as the board, key administrative offices, the faculty, and other positions deemed important for the successful development of a strategic plan.

As head of the joint planning group, the college president must maintain familiarity with, as well as ultimate control over, the strategic plan's progress. The president must trust and expect each hand-picked member of the joint planning committee to reasonably participate in and debate the college's strategic direction. John Stevens points out that nothing is more dispiriting than to have a workable strategy deemed worthless by a few major players who missed out on their fair share in its development. [13]

Presidents must exercise authority and political savvy to keep the process on track when power factions threaten to bring it to a grinding halt. Beyond serving as an aid to participatory governance, the joint planning group will eventually spur the formation of task forces, members of which will construct the specific targets, plans, and monitoring systems necessary to the larger strategic plan.

Task Forces

Task forces review strategic options within the members' area of responsibility and contribute to the larger strategy. Members meet regularly to devise, debate, and revise their piece of the plan. Each task force must have a leader, assigned by and accountable to the president.* The greater the president's involvement at as many task force meetings as possible, the greater the esteem and enthusiasm of task force members as they influence necessary program cuts and identify areas of opportunity. Specifically, task force members develop action plans, implementation schedules, benchmarks, and performance monitoring schedules for the president and key leaders to review and approve before the documents are blended into a formal task force report.

Strategic Diagnostics

Any useful strategy must rest on a reliable assessment of the institution's market and financial positions because the former has a direct influence on the latter. During this phase, data are collected from budget reports, financial statements, cash flow reports, cost analyses, financial and market trends, admission reports, and known facts on competitors.

The first step in strategic planning takes place when the president reviews diagnostic data with the joint planning group. Before this can take place, key administrative officers must prepare reports on finances, admissions, instructional programs, grounds, maintenance, capital campaigns, and the recent history of the institution's main competitors. Gathering operational, strategic, and competitive data at small colleges may prove difficult because the colleges might not have an institutional researcher or an effective system for collecting and analyzing data. The president may recruit the help of auditors or contract with an institutional research agency to assist the college with several phases of strategic diagnostics.

---

*Accountability must not be diluted through joint or group decisions because the task force that disintegrates into a leaderless debate society will ultimately contribute nothing to the strategic planning process.

Strategic diagnostics phase 1: The first phase of strategic diagnostics establishes the type of data to be collected and who is to collect the data. In this phase the institution needs to determine the financial and time resources needed to produce a solid report on the strategic condition of the institution. Then, the president and the board must allocate funds.

Strategic diagnostics phase 2: Phase 2 involves collection of data on the financial, marketing, academic, and operational conditions of the college. Each sector responsible for data collection must make an exhaustive study of the conditions in its area that have a direct and immediate impact on the institution. A sampling of the data typically required to evaluate the strategic condition of the college includes the following:

- Academic programs data include accreditation reports; performance reports on achieving the requirements set by the accrediting agency; enrollment by program; attrition rates by program; graduation rates by program; outcomes assessment by program; and faculty, staff, and administrative compensation benchmarking data.

- Marketing office data include admission reports (inquiry through the end of the add-drop period for new students), market strategies, market costs to enroll a new student, and enrollment and admission comparisons with competitors.

- Finance (operations) data include audit and management reports; trend[*] reports for cash flow; standard report format[†] for financials; management ratios[‡] on net income, liquidity, debt, and return on net assets showing marginal[§] changes for one- and three-year periods for revenue, expenses, cash, and

---

[*]Trends cover a period in time, such as the prior five years or a forecast for five years.

[†]Ratios are based on revenue and assets for each line in the respective statements of activities and position.

[‡]For computation of net income, liquidity, debt, return on net assets, and other ratios that could be included, see Appendix C, Financial Measures.

[§]For computations of annual and multiyear margins, see Appendix C, Financial Measures.

debt; and the Composite Financial Index.*[14] In addition, the financial office should design a financial model† to forecast financial statements for a period between three and five years. The forecast will need information on how the college produces and spends its funds compared to benchmarks and its competitors.

- Plant operations and conditions reports are needed on the condition of campus buildings, systems, and plans for repairs and replacement for the period covered by the financial forecast.

- Information technology reports should be on the condition of the information and communications technology (hardware and software); identification of major problems and weaknesses; and plans for upgrades, repairs, and replacement for the period covered by the financial forecast.

- Auxiliaries data are needed on the condition of residence halls, food services, the bookstore, and other income-producing services; financial reports on the productive capacity of each auxiliary; and a plan for repair, replacement, or additions for the period of the financial forecast.

- Institutional research should assist in the preparation of all data reports that will be needed for the financial, marketing, and academic plans.

- Administrative and student services reports cover the senior offices in the institution and all buildings that are set aside for administrative and student services. The reports should include compensation analysis, major strategic issues, and other recommendations.

---

*Composite Financial Index computes weights and strengths for four standard ratios. See Appendix G: Composite Financial Index Computation Table plus the CFI Excel worksheet on CD.
†See the Forecast Model on CD, for one example of a basic forecast model.

The diagnostic report should be published as a single document with summary tables so that the board and president do not have to plow through minutiae. The institutional research office (if the institution does not have this position, the chief financial and academic officers usually make a good team to produce the report) should coordinate the production of the report. Without the knowledge afforded by the general diagnostic process, the president will be ill equipped to perform the more detailed financial diagnostics to come.

The diagnostic analysis for the preceding areas should be presented as a report to the president and the members of the joint planning group. The meeting should be run by either the president or a neutral facilitator so that a clear, coherent, and cogent list of major diagnostic strategic issues can be identified. The diagnostic analysis should cover the following areas:

1.   *Environmental and SWOT analysis:* Strategic diagnostics should include an environmental analysis and SWOT (internal strengths and weaknesses, external opportunities and threats) analysis. They are essential elements for determining the strategic condition of the institution before setting strategic goals. Both types of analysis should be conducted in a group setting after the group has had an opportunity to review and discuss the preceding diagnostic reports. The president or a neutral party should lead the session to facilitate discussion and to identify critical environmental and SWOT factors needed to understand the position of the college and generate an actionable report for selection of goals.

     • *Environmental analysis:* Identify economic, political, demographic, and social changes that may have a positive or adverse affect on the institution; and

     • *Strength, weakness, opportunities, and threats (SWOT) analysis:* Identify the internal strengths and weaknesses of the institution and the external opportunities and threats facing the institution (refers to the environmental analysis).

2. *Goals:* Goals embody the college's expected destination based on its given strategy and its desired new academic, operational, marketing, student services, and financial condition. Goals are the domain of the board and the president with the advice of key sectors of the college or university community. They should flow naturally from the mission of the institution and reflect the college's big targets, for example, a learned student body, community service, or the highest standards of research. Goals are general statements of where the institution expects to be at some time in the future. There should be a goal for each major component of the strategic plan. A typical goal statement could state, *"in five years the college expects to have improved the reputation of its graduates in the job market."*

3. *Objectives:* Objectives are precise statements about how an institution expects to achieve its goals. The statement should reflect performance-based measures of what and when the objective is to be accomplished. There should be a small number of objectives for each goal so that the institution is not bogged down with measuring every activity in the organization and reporting it to the president or the board. The president, nevertheless, must insist that each sector should be responsible for its respective institutional goal and its related objectives, which should also be linked to the institutional strategy.

4. *Financial goals and objectives:* A strategic plan regardless of the size or mission of the institution should guide a college toward financial stability; without financial stability, the rest of the strategy is rendered meaningless. Therefore, the strategic plan needs specific financial goals and objectives. In fact, every sector of the institution should have a financial objective that expresses its responsibility for the financial stability of the institution.

    Financial goals and objectives for a particular sector of the institution will depend upon the institutional strategy. Examples of financial goals and objectives include balancing long-term revenue and expense growth rates through new pricing strategies, markets, net income requirements for academic programs, donor campaigns, research grants, or investment strategies.

5. *Strategic options:* Exactly how a college meets its strategic objectives depends on its financial condition and the relevant options the college selects. In light of established goals and objectives, colleges may opt to enter new markets, upgrade instructional programs, simplify the administration, revamp student services, cut operational costs, or find new ways of distributing the college's services. Strategic options should change the present course of the institution while working toward long-term financial stability.

Strategic options have to be developed soon after agreement is reached on strategic goals. At least three options should be developed for the major functions of the institution: academics, markets, finance, auxiliaries, and the plant. Each option should be diligently tested before inclusion in the strategic plan. The purpose of the tests is to evaluate the contribution that each option makes to the function and to the institution. Here are several questions that can help guide the evaluation of the options:

Academic option

- Will it significantly improve the skills of graduates seeking employment or acceptance to graduate school?

- Will the option generate new funds? If so, its risks, financial plans forecasts, and operational assumptions should be tested. Also, financial estimates should be tested using net present value analysis.

- Will the option increase or decrease expenses? If so, how does the college expect to fund the expenses, and what is the impact that higher expenses will have on institutional productivity (credit hours/costs)?

Marketing option

- Will target markets buy the new programs or services?

- Can the marketing division reach the target market effectively and at a reasonable cost?

- Will the price be discounted and is the discount large enough to convince prospective students to enroll?

Finance information technology option

- If the option calls for a new administrative and financial system, do the costs include infrastructure, training, and sufficient personnel to support the system?

- How will a new system improve the operational productivity of the institution?

- Will new financial systems produce accurate and expeditious reports that pull data from all major functions of the institution?

Capital option

- What are the capital and operational costs of the project?

- What are the risks (legal, regulatory, funding, safety, or other risks)?

- Will the project payback generate revenue to cover debt service and operational costs? If it does, the estimates should be evaluated using net present value analysis.

- Will the project generate only extra expenses and no revenue? If so, does the college have the resources to implement it, and what impact does it have on institutional productivity (credit hours/costs)?

Administrative and student support option

- What is the purpose of the project, and is it critical to the mission of the institution?

- What impact will it have on institutional productivity?

6. *Selection of strategic options:* After the options are tested and rigorously deliberated, the next step is to select the most promising options for inclusion in the strategic plan. This is where problems arise if the choice of an option is made just to satisfy constituencies. These are necessarily nonoptimal decisions because they supplant the interests of the institution with the interest of the few. The single criterion that is essential to optimizing strategic plans is presidential leadership. It is the duty of the president to represent the interest of the institution and its clientele. Otherwise, strategic plans are informed not by rational decisions but by self-serving interests. Here are several other suggestions that can help optimize the choice of strategic options:

    • Select options that produce net revenue by choosing options that maximize their net present value.

    • Select options that do not produce net revenue by choosing options that minimize the impact on productivity.

    • Select options that must meet accreditation, governmental regulations, or safety requirements in terms of the requirement while minimizing the impact on productivity.

7. *Action plans:* Action plans lay out precisely who will do what and when for each component of the plan. An action plan may be the most important part of the strategic plan and, as such, should be carefully drafted and critically reviewed. A slapdash plan of action, void of precision and purpose, will render the college just as lost as it was prior to its strategic awakening.

8. *Performance benchmarks:* The purpose of performance benchmarks is to determine the current condition of the college in reference to the national standards or some set of institutions and to understand the future state of the institution as it puts its strategy into operation. The benchmarks must be relevant to the strategic goals and measured against other (preferably competing) colleges. Benchmarks are targets that the college tries either to match or exceed, depending on its current condition.

Benchmarks often reference these factors: admissions yields, enrollment growth, class sizes, student-faculty ratios, assets per student, net income, receivables, financial reserves, and debt targets. Strategic monitoring reports compare actual performance to established benchmarks and identify any variances. If performance falls substantially below a benchmark, the college must identify the cause and adjust operations.

9.   *Monitoring schedule:* The monitoring schedule should establish a regular schedule to review the progress of the institution so that it can ascertain whether it is meeting its strategic goals and objectives. Minimally, the schedule should call for meetings every quarter and before every board meeting. According to George Crouch of Georgetown College, colleges must revisit strategic goals annually, revising them in accordance with current market conditions.[15] All reviews should be conducted in formal meetings where reports are presented for each sector of the institution. Written reports will likely be set aside and ignored.

10.   *Implementation schedule:* After the compilation of goals, objectives, action plans, performance benchmarking, and the monitoring schedules, the strategic plan document goes to the board for review. The president should reserve discretionary authority to revise each piece, in keeping with the time frame, scope of the goals and objectives, and the resources available to the strategy. Any changes that the president intends to make to the strategic plan should also be submitted for board review and approval. Following the approval of the final plan by the board, the president should then introduce major goals and objectives to offices and departments. The initiation of the strategic plan must involve a review of the responsibilities and accountability of each staff and faculty player who is assigned a role in the implementation of the strategic plan. The president may need to meet individually with key players to help them prepare their own objectives, plans, and monitoring systems.

TABLE 8.1—SEVEN CRITICAL IMPLEMENTATION EVENTS

1. Meetings with departments and offices responsible for carrying out the strategic plan
2. Implementation of major changes in the organization
3. Meetings with departments and offices affected by such changes
4. Production of policies and documents supporting the strategic plan
5. Establishment of data systems to support changes in the organization and produce performance reports
6. Purchase of supplies or equipment
7. Training schedules for employees whose duties have changed

---

This schedule lays out a timeline for implementation of the strategic plan that covers what is to be done, who is responsible, when it is to be initiated and completed, and when reports are due. The president must ensure that everyone adheres to this schedule. If a critical part of the schedule is lagging, the president must find out the reason and take appropriate action. Table 8.1 is a summary of critical implementation events to guide the president and the college.

11. *Strategic planning summary:* Strategic plans for private institutions should reflect a market-oriented perspective. This means that the academic programs, student services, auxiliaries, administrative support, and information technology should respond to the demands of the student market and improvement in delivering services and managing costs by competitors. Markets drive the success of private institutions; private institutions typically do not have direct access to government funds. So, their survival depends on the leadership ability of the president and key decision makers to appreciate how markets are changing, what markets want from the college, and how the college can deliver the sought-after services. If the college employs something less than a market perspective, it will hobble the success of the strategic plan.

Strategic plans should be considered living documents. Each year, the goals and objectives should be reviewed and updated. The purpose of the review and updating is to take into account changes in the marketplace, problems encountered in putting the action plan into operation, and new information that requires correction of assumptions or plans. The president will want to meet with the persons responsible for goals or objectives that are not being completed according to the action plan so that the problem is understood and solutions are identified. In addition, the president should report to the board and the campus community when goals and objectives are completed so that they are aware that progress is being made. The strategic process should accomplish the following tasks:

- Prepare diagnostics like the current state of the institution, forecasts, environmental and SWOT analyses;

- Select and rank order the major strategic issues;

- Develop, test, and rank order strategic options; and

- Prepare a strategic plan, action plans, monitoring plan, and implementation schedule.

BASIC BUSINESS PRACTICES

For-profit businesses ensure that strategic and operational decisions are based on the impact of the market on the business. Responding to the market means that an organization must offer products and services, minimize costs, and target prices to attract customers. Ignoring the broadest impact of the market on strategic operational plans dilutes their effectiveness. Private institutions have the same need to respond to the market. Too often colleges only pay attention to markets when they are developing student recruitment plans. Then, they are interested in what motivates students and how price affects a prospective student's decision to enroll. This single-minded interest in students and enrollment can lead to fancy recruitment strategies and complex tuition discounting plans. However, when the college turns to cost, the assumption is that costs are a problem of revenue and not a problem of minimizing costs so that the college can sharpen its pricing. Because pricing is treated independently of costs, tuition discounting turns into a dog-chasing-its-tail story where discounts run higher to capture more students. At some point in this circle of price and discounting, the college generates lots of tuition revenue and very little cash. Of course, if the budget ignores tuition discounts, it may be creating a fantasy budget in which revenue and expenses are equal but cash is insufficient to pay the bills. When tuition discounts are included in the budget, revenue is netted for financial aid, and the expense problem of not having enough revenue persists. The deficit issue, when costs' impact on price is ignored, results in haphazard budget cuts that too often rest on the political skills of administrators to maintain empires.

Another failure is when private colleges neglect to scrupulously evaluate large campus investments. When contemplating new construction, planners tend to overlook alternative locations, zoning requirements, architectural layouts, parking considerations, operational costs, and financing methods. Only when the county cites the college with a zoning violation or parking shortages turn into traffic nightmares or students trip over each other down short and narrow hallways do planners discover their design flaws. Given scarce resources, leaders must commit to customary business practices, some of which are considered in the following sections, to ensure the highest return on their decisions and investments.

Seek and Evaluate Alternatives

There is rarely a one-size-fits-all strategic goal, objective, or plan. The president must seek optimal solutions by encouraging options and testing those approaches to find the best course of action.

Look at the Big Picture

Leaders must consider a proposed major investment's impact on other systems and functions within the college. A close look at the project's fit with the college's mission and location helps to ensure

TABLE 8.2—FORECAST GUIDE

- Calculate the net present value for each alternative.
- Determine the probability that expected outcomes associated with each investment alternative will occur.
- Multiply the probability factors by the relevant net present values to determine the expected financial value of each alternative.
- Rank alternatives in order of the financial value of their outcomes. Revenue projects are rank ordered in terms of net income, and expense projects are rank ordered in terms of minimal impact on institutional expenses.
- Debate the top two alternatives.

sensible and flexible building designs, adequate parking, and compliance with zoning regulations. Do the following when considering the overall impact:

- *Treat major financial decisions as investment decisions.* After establishing goals for the proposed project, planners and financial leaders must evaluate operational revenue and expenses. The first step in evaluating financial decisions requires a forecast model to test the plan's financial impact on all sectors of the college. The second step is that each financial option needs to have its own budget to be tested by the forecast model. Table 8.2 is a guide for conducting a forecast.

- *Justify the decision.* Presidents should assume nothing but the burden of proof. Leaders must persuade their boards of the need for change through concise, coherent written statements and analyses. A board should not approve a decision or project unless it understands how the decision or project will best serve the institution. They can do this only by seeing summaries of the evaluation of decisions or projects.

    Caution: The strategic plan is not…

- *A knee-jerk reaction to current events:* Planning without discipline and risking without care has pushed more than one college over the brink. A residence hall built on a hunch can lead the college to its demise when students fail to enroll in the numbers needed to cover debt service. From the brash to the timid, examples of thoughtless yet destructive actions abound. Risk-averse administrators, the norm within higher education, implement minor changes to instructional programs, student services, or admissions and ultimately contribute nothing to service improvement or to revenue. Strategy and reason must supplant impulsivity and fear.

- *A perfunctory exercise:* Key leaders cannot approach strategic planning as a way to placate the board or as an excuse to meet annually for coffee and donuts. The successful strategic plan has substance and will be implemented by strong leaders who will insist that updates and meetings are taken seriously.

- *A wish list:* Strategic planning must not be confused with personal needs. The strategic planning committee should reject staff and faculty wish lists for computers, desks, chairs, lights, buildings, new faculty, new staff, benefits, and the kitchen sink before such ridiculous examples of self-interest reach the chief financial officer. Scarce resources, time, and money should under no circumstances be devoted willy-nilly to spending that has no relation to institutional goals.

- *Just another appointment on the president's calendar:* The president must delegate the mundane as well as some of the critical daily processes she or he traditionally handles. Administrative assistants must not deliver messages to the president that trash was left in the halls, that security did not lock a door, or that a student is unhappy with an instructor. If appointed managers cannot handle this fog of daily battles, management training should be introduced as a component of the strategic plan. The president who resists delegating authority out of ignorance or mistrust is spread too thin to maintain strategic planning as a priority.

- *An isolated financial strategy:* Financial strategy must be integrated with the larger strategic plan. As such, the chief financial officer must participate fully in all planning aspects. The confidentiality of budgets, heretofore restricted to the president and chief financial officer, may need to be compromised to facilitate the melding of financial strategy with other strategic components. Key leaders must understand the link between financial resources and strategy. This linkage must go beyond the assumption that only administrators understand strategy and finance, but it is an indispensable thread in the strategic safety net that all segments of the institution comprehend the relevance of finance and strategy. Simply put, everyone needs to understand the concept of scarce resources. Planning in higher education sometimes is impeded by the simplistic expectation that everything could be done if more money was available. Obviously, that is true, but the problem is that private colleges and universities cannot print their own money, so they must learn to work and plan within the constraints of their resources.

- *A straitjacket:* Strategy provides a context for presidents to balance opportunities with risks and college goals with student needs. Strategy need not constrict to direct. Instead, strategy should allow the small college to mobilize quickly and opportunistically, anchored only by expressed goals and guidelines.

- *Avoiding mistakes:* Everyone connected with strategic planning wants to avoid the big mistake that drives the institution into a box canyon where the only escape is back through the mess that was created. The preceding discussion on strategic planning and business practices should help to reduce the possibility of major mistakes. Table 8.3 on the next page presents 10 points to keep in mind during the development of a strategic plan that can improve its prospects for success.

TABLE 8.3—TEN WAYS TO AVOID STRATEGIC PLANNING MISTAKES

1. **Do the data.** Regardless of the demand involved, good data collection is a prerequisite for good strategy.

2. **Involve critical segments of the college.** Instruction, student services, and finance departments must interact.

3. **Be realistic about goals.** A poor or invisible college cannot become a Cinderella overnight. (It just might need a rich prince to transform it.)

4. **Find alternatives, and test them.** Explore ways beyond the obvious, resisting the urge to implement the first plan that comes to mind.

5. **Make managers accountable for carrying out the plan.** Passing the buck will impoverish the strategy.

6. **Measure performance.** Objectives must be measurable and benchmarked to good practices.

7. **Monitor progress.** Assume nothing. Establish formal monitoring systems.

8. **Review and revise regularly.** Annual strategic review meetings should be supplemented as necessary throughout the year.

9. **Support the plan with policies and procedures.** A toothless plan is a worthless plan.

10. **Include options in the plan.** Allow for the unexpected by keeping viable alternatives handy. There's more than one way to skin a strategy.

KEYS TO FINANCIAL STRATEGY

Small colleges are crumbling beneath the weight of daily pressures, and many private colleges and universities are cowering at the prospect of yet another beating from the market. For leaders at these colleges, strategy has been reduced to a frenzied search for the next new dollar, without reasonable regard for management practices, market position, or long-term operational efficiency. More often than not, time, energy, and revenue are wasted on stop-gap financial measures. Even those colleges that have prospered under an intuitive leadership are not safe from closure, for success based on the hunches of particular leaders often ends with their tenure; many an institution has faltered, if not fallen, during changes in management.

Strategy acts as insurance against vagaries in management. It complements a leader's intuition and keeps chaos at bay. The president as keeper of the strategy will be a model of integrity, gaining the college safe passage to a world of financial stability. Most of the strategy and leadership tips in this chapter are simple and familiar to the greenest of leaders, but the work will certainly be slow and difficult at times. Problems and challenges will call, but a course of action and peace of mind will emerge for the progressive manager who trades in an incrementalist mindset for long-term security.

The financial component of the institutional strategy provides the resources necessary to accomplish a college's mission and to ensure its financial viability for future generations. Inadequate financial resources can prevent a college from delivering education, research, or other services to students, parents, and the community. The keys to a successful financial strategy are not esoteric. They follow from economic theories such as those of Clotfelter, Hopkins and Massey, and ratio analysis such as CFI and Moody's Investors Service.[16,17,18,19]

To implement a successful financial strategy, a small college must take into account 20 keys to financial strategy, as laid out in Table 8.4 on the next page.

SUMMARY

The president and senior officers must seriously commit themselves to development of a financial strategy. They must disseminate it throughout the institution, not just print it and send it through the mail, but convey it personally to all who will bear responsibility for its implementation. If the leadership takes the strategic plan seriously, so too will the larger college community. The president, to be believable, must follow established protocol, hold everyone accountable for errors, grant rewards for good decisions, and scrutinize changes to the strategy. In conclusion, the president and chief financial officer must anticipate economic shifts and design effective strategy to withstand them.

TABLE 8.4—TWENTY KEYS TO FINANCIAL STRATEGY

1. Eliminate deficits by balancing revenue with expense growth rates.

2. Build a coherent net pricing strategy.

3. Raise funds to reduce unfunded financial aid.

4. Focus strategy on main income flows into the college.

5. Diversify the main income flows to reduce risk.

6. Trade gifts for debt to raise the debt ratio above 2:1.

7. Formulate budgets by:
   a. Making forecasts, goals, and plans of major business operations;
   b. Adding employees discriminately;
   c. Containing expense growth;
   e. Estimating revenue conservatively and before expenses;
   f. Increasing revenue conservatively and scrupulously; and
   g. Designing incentives to improve college efficiency.

8. Build a reinvestment fund for renovations and replacement.

9. Provide a contingency fund.

10. Monitor financial performance with internal and external measures.

11. Install budget controls with policies for:
    a. Handling overexpended budgets;
    b. Tracking variances between actual and forecast revenue and expenses;
    c. Deciding what to do with budget variances (positive or negative); and
    d. Limiting the addition of new employees during the fiscal year.

12. Conduct regular financial review meetings.

13. Bill students monthly and enforce collection procedures.

14. Set a bad-debt goal with a not-to-exceed goal, for example, 2.5 percent of receivables.

15. Set cash and short-term investment goals equal to 16 percent of expenses.

16. Require auxiliaries to achieve their net income.

17. Outsource auxiliaries, administrative services, or other operations that fail to meet financial goals.

18. Ensure that income from alumni relations equals or exceeds its expenses.

19. Set recruiting and retention goals for athletics.

20. Use strategic options to promote flexibility.

ENDNOTES

1. Lindbloom, C. *The Policy Making Process*. (Cambridge, MA: Harvard University Press, 1968).

2. Wildavsky, A. *Budgeting, 2nd Rev. ed*.(New Brunswick, NJ: Transaction Books, 1986), p. 107.

3. Keller, G. *Academic Strategy* (Baltimore: Johns Hopkins University Press, 1983), p. 67.

4. Zemsky, R., Wenger, G. R., & Massey, W. F. *Remaking the American University* (Piscataway, NJ: Rutgers University Press, 2006), p. 7.

5. Lenington, R. *Colleges are a Business!* (Phoenix, AZ: Oryx Press, 1996).

6. Dehne, G C. *Student Recruitment: A Marketing Primer for Presidents*. (Old Saybrook, CT: GDA Integrated Services, 2001).

7. Keller, G. *Academic Strategy* (Baltimore: Johns Hopkins University Press, 1983), p. 112.

8. Townsley, M. K. (1991). "Brinkmanship, Planning, Smoke, and Mirrors," *Planning for Higher Education, 19, 19*.

9. Keller, G. *Academic Strategy* (Baltimore: Johns Hopkins University Press, 1983), p. 61.

10. Lenington, R. *Colleges are a Business!* (Phoenix, AZ: Oryx Press, 1996).

11. Wirth, G. (Vice President and Director of Admissions, Goldey-Beacom College, Wilmington, Delaware), personal interview, October 11, 2001.

12. Keller, G. *Academic Strategy* (Baltimore: Johns Hopkins University Press, 1983), p. 61.

13. Stevens, J. (President and Chief Operating Officer, Stevens Consulting, Vermont), personal interview, September 11, 2001, and September 18, 2001.

14. Salluzzo, R. E., Tahey, P., Prager, F. J., & Cowen, C. J. *Ratio Analysis in Higher Education* (4th ed.). (Washington, DC: KPMG, & Prager, McCarthy & Sealy, 1999).

15. Crouch, W. (President, Georgetown College, Georgetown, Kentucky), personal interview, September 13, 2001.

16. Clotfelter, C. T. (1999). "The Familiar But Curious Economics of Higher Education: Introduction to a Symposium" *Journal of Economic Perspectives*, 13-1, 3–12.

17. Hopkins, D. S. P., & Massy, W. F. *Planning Models for Colleges and Universities*. (Stanford, CA: Stanford University Press, 1981).

18. Salluzzo, R. E., Tahey, P., Prager, F. J., & Cowen, C. J. *Ratio Analysis in Higher Education* (4th ed.). (Washington, DC: KPMG, & Prager, McCarthy & Sealy, 1999).

19. Moody's Investors Service. *Private Colleges and Universities Outlook 2001/02 and Medians*. (New York: Moody's Investors Service, 2001).

CHAPTER 9

LEADERSHIP, POWER, AND AUTHORITY

WHEN LEADERSHIP GOES MISSING!

Though we know the benefits and general requirements of a strategic versus an incremental approach to financial stabilization, we have yet to characterize the leadership that will manage the strategic plan.

Presidents often find that their management prerogatives are severely circumscribed because higher education blurs the lines of authority with its most important segments—instruction and research. Management as a process of leadership is further compromised because in most cases presidents are drawn from the academic side of the house where decision making is dependent on consensus before action is possible. Under these circumstances many presidents do not have the opportunity when they are young to learn many of the basic management techniques—delegation, supervision, evaluation, or monitoring performance. In stark contrast to a management approach, wherein self-interests are subordinate to the larger organization, a Machiavellian approach presides, and self-willed decisions trump institutional goals.[1]

The good news is that old ways are changing among academics as they take hold of program evaluation, which requires them to write performance goals, track performance, evaluate outcomes, and determine how resources should be allocated. Even as these changes take place, presidents must remain adept at working within a dual authority structure that often requires finely tuned political skills that may at times have to override the classic methods of management.

The president is charged with strategic oversight and with demanding accountability by breaking through collegial stalemates, and in the words of George Keller, the president has to get the "right things… done," keep "spirits from flagging," and "wave… the flag for all to see."[2]

WHAT MAKES A LEADER?

Peter Drucker, who was instrumental in describing modern management theory, can find no substitute for leadership at the institution that plans to embrace change.[3] The president's leadership underpins everything; the president must be everywhere and prepare everyone for the strategic revolution to come and must convince the board, students, faculty members, and administrators that despite miserable conditions and despite the growing pains ahead, the college's future is certain. Resistance to new approaches will undoubtedly surface, with some influential members of the institution working at cross purposes with the leadership. But the president, invested with the confidence of the board, key members of the administration, and the college community, must authoritatively push the strategic plan ahead—noting, rather than entertaining, dissension.

According to James L. Fisher, a 30-year leadership veteran and a noted author on the American college presidency, the president must keep the true state of the institution free from presumptions, clichés, and controversy.[4] The president must ignore the siren calls of a smug or passive status quo, remain impervious to the jostlings of powerful interest groups, be a mediator, and be seen as the epitome of impartiality. Forsaking the comfort of routine and ordinary progress, the successful president will "hold out visions of potentialities and worthy objectives that motivate others to perform beyond the ordinary."[5] The college that embraces strategy, but whose leader indulges mediocrity or conflict, will find that its plans will be for naught.

Great colleges, on the other hand, are run by great presidents.[6] Superior leaders know their college, its weaknesses, its strengths, its possibilities, its workings, who within its walls impedes change, and who inspires changes. They maintain communication with subordinates, drawing on them for information and assistance. They deduce as well as intuit what needs improvement and win swift approval for strategic patchwork and overhauls alike. As they influence necessary changes, they delegate and demand accountability, yet they get their own hands dirty in the demanding work of setting policies, reviewing programs, controlling budgets, and monitoring performance.[7]

The president must enjoy ultimate authority; however, the work of strategy cannot succeed without a supportive partnership between the president and board of trustees. After all, the board appoints the president, and they concoct either a recipe for failure in their choice of a passive president who is content with mere survival or an incompetent president who drives the college over a cliff, or they choose a powerful president, who insists on leading the college forward in an atmosphere of excellence.[8] Board members must "give [the] president adequate authority and staff, and their own support in the difficult task of encouraging constructive change—realizing that periods of change are also periods of unusual tension."[9] The private colleges and universities with progressive boards and a dispassionate president will likely fulfill Fisher's proposition that leadership can propel a college to its highest potential.

If the competent president also has the savvy to make sense of the financial condition of the college, then you have a private institution that just might be around through this century. According to John Nelson, senior vice president at Moody's Investors Service, "Colleges have the best chance of surviving [when] the president understands finances, works well with the chief financial officer, and [when] the board takes a critical role in [financial] decisions."[10] Ruth Cowan, in her writings on presidential leadership, believes that overcoming financial paralysis at a college calls for hard work, long hours, and continuous effort to keep the college on the right financial track; in contrast, a college that waits for economic turmoil to stabilize will not build strength.[11] Rather, when the president, board, key financial leaders, and the college community come to believe they can change their college's destiny from the inside out and when they begin to act accordingly, financial stability returns.[12]

SHARED GOVERNANCE: A COMMON THEME IN HIGHER EDUCATION

Michael Cohen and James March have arguably claimed that the ambiguities of shared or collegial governance equate to organized anarchy.[13] This state of affairs takes place when professionals, faculty, or administrators make decisions by pushing aside the interests of the college, by ignoring the consequences of their decisions, by mismanaging the actions that flow, and by avoiding central control and accountability standards.[14] In this case, the most a president of a college can do, then, is ride the issue carousel and hope to glimpse the brass rings of presidential power and strategic financial success. Baldridge compared shared governance to a political system, wherein a cycle of chaos, inactivity, conflict, and negotiation follows every decision posed to a disjointed interest group.[15] A president operating within a political ring can only hope that every wrestling match ends in a truce. In any case, shared governance equates to fragmented governance, wherein the formal authority of the small college president is indistinguishable from the professional authority of in-house faculty members and administrators.

No wonder presidents find themselves hemmed in on all sides.[16] Having little influence over tenured faculty, departmental budgets, or such basic college policies as the student-faculty ratio, a president may turn to manipulation and bargaining to juice up the collective decision-making apparatus. Once self-interested parties have supplanted leadership, no brand of exploitation will prevent mediocrity. In effect, shared governance substitutes meandering decisions that send the college off in directions that are not pertinent to its well-being. At its worst, shared governance simply becomes the sum and average of multiple self-interests and it has the unfortunate capacity to devastate a leaderless institution.[17] As Keller notes, "Every society and every major organization with[in] a society must have a single authority, someone... authorized to initiate, plan, decide, manage, monitor, and punish its membership."[18] Leadership is imperative if the president and institutional leaders want to achieve the values laid forth in the mission statement.

MANAGEMENT-STYLE GOVERNANCE

According to Robert Lenington, organizational structures within higher education, from the autocratic to the diffuse, suffer from "lack of professional management and good business practice[s]."[19] Too often, chief executive officers equivocate when it comes to delegating work. In the absence of clear directives, the person assigned a task may not know what is expected, when it is due, or who is in charge. Vague leadership style may successfully keep people off balance, but it accomplishes little in the long run. It conveys a lack of both knowledge and responsibility on the part of the president.

Herbert Simon, a noted author on organizations and leadership, contends that colleges are led largely by amateurs.[20] Most presidents and key leaders have not worked previously within a management framework, and they are not trained in management practices once they walk through the doors of higher education. One could say that management is scorned within higher education, for it interferes with the anarchic and political tactics, ranging from the passive to the cut-throat, that typically abounds there. An administrator lacking in management skills but well versed in avoidance might adopt the role of the kid in the back of the classroom. Back-benchers avert their eyes when called upon, hoping to avoid revealing too much of themselves to the teacher or their peers. Amiability and invisibility are key to a system where job survival depends less on achievements (one person's progress is another person's setback) than on avoiding retribution.

The challenges of the coming decade ought to give leaders pause, for neither ambiguous nor Machiavellian tactics will succeed. Presidents must familiarize themselves with management practices because they describe how an office is expected to carry out its responsibilities, how it is held accountable, and how authority is distributed to the office and in relationship with other offices. Authority need not incite rage or fear; rather it can and should be even-handedly delegated within the boundaries of governance to achieve compliance and productivity. The scope of assignments, their deadlines, their objectives, their participants, and accountability standards can and should be determined and then conveyed unequivocally to academics and administrators alike.

MANAGEMENT PRACTICES

Five basic management practices can minimize conflict and contribute to smoother operations if college leaders apply them. These practices are coordination and control, delegation of authority, unity of command, simplicity, and esprit de corps.

Coordination and Control

Nothing destabilizes a small college more than fragmentation of loyalties and bickering among offices over designated workloads. Leaders must clearly define and reasonably assign responsibilities. All participants in a given task should understand why a task has been assigned (i.e., its objectives), to what extent they are accountable for the task's success or failure, how performance will be measured and coordinated, who is in charge, and to whom (and by whom) findings will be reported. The president can communicate command of important processes and activities through regular staff meetings and performance evaluations. Ripe for coordination and control are (1) the flow of work and students through admissions, registration, and payment processes, and (2) the scheduling of classes, which requires that various offices work together to coordinate the availability of classrooms, parking, supplies, staff, and instructors.

Delegation of Authority

The president who fails to delegate will drown in detail. Whether out of ego, pity, or fear that the subordinate will not do the right thing, doing subordinates' work dooms a leader to a skewed perspective.

The president becomes the end all and be all who is responsible for everything and nothing at the same time. Everyone else is simply a servant waiting to be told what to do. They lose the chance to learn and to acquire skills needed to run a complex institution like a college. The last thing a president facing strategic change needs is a desk cluttered with memos from subordinates who don't have the knowledge, confidence, or desire to handle even the most trivial of dilemmas. This all-too-familiar practice of delegation avoidance keeps the cycle of poorly prepared college administrators in place. Table 9.1 presents several simple rules for delegation of authority.

Unity of Command

Confusion and conflict erupt when work is assigned willy-nilly. Tasks are duplicated when various departments have implied authority over

---

TABLE 9.1—DELEGATION RULES FOR PRESIDENTS

1. **Assign tasks appropriately**. Don't assign similar duties to different offices. Do assign tasks to offices with relevant responsibility. If you want a new marketing plan, don't ask the marketing department and the academic division to develop it. Assign the task to the marketing division, and have that division solicit the assistance of the academic division.

2. **Put the assignment in writing**. Summarize the nature and objectives of the work to be done; list the names and characterize the authority of leaders and participants; record the amounts (and designation) of any financial resources dedicated to the project; and outline relevant performance measures, reporting schedules, and deadlines. An appropriately informative written statement should also be distributed to staff and offices who will be affected by or support in any way the completion of the assignment.

3. **Insist on timely progress reports**. Your assistant should ensure reports are submitted on time. If reports are late, call personally and clarify your expectations.

4. **Measure performance**. Establish criteria for measuring performance in all departments. Back up criteria with a timetable for reports.

5. **Enforce accountability**. Presidents who delegate to task forces and committees must take special care to follow the preceding rules and to assign to one person explicitly accountability for work performed and decisions made.

---

them. Work is left unfinished when glitches arise that no single person has the expressed authority to handle. Responsibility can diffuse to the point where no one knows or cares what the task's original objectives were. The president must definitively empower one office, one committee, or one person to see every task to its end.

Simplicity

From the course catalog to accounting office protocols to the layout of the library, college campuses are in need of simplification. Managers can and should translate goals, policies, procedures, and orders into forms digestible by staff and students. All will celebrate the reduction of superfluous costs and lengthy waits associated with unnecessarily tedious processes.

Esprit de Corps

Presidents would do well to herald any significant changes (e.g., strategic financial rejuvenation) with a few symbolic adjustments. Whether in the form of painted classrooms, tidied grounds, small awards, or prompt payment of employees, small efforts signify a leader's intent to see progress through. Ruth Cowan offers several pertinent suggestions to small college presidents:

- Conduct frequent face-to-face meetings.
- Acknowledge individual accomplishments no matter how trivial.
- Reestablish rituals and organize celebrations.
- Invite prominent people to the campus so that they can witness the changes taking place.
- Take visible risks, such as raising salaries, even if only slightly.[21]

Scott Miller, a successful president at several different colleges, advises new presidents and presidents facing new challenges to "make a splash," that is, to employ charisma, originality, and goodwill as they strive to better manage their institutions.[22] Leaders with confidence and vitality will elicit the same from their staff and students.

Power and Authority

The duality of power and authority is what defines the boundaries of leadership, in particular leadership in higher education, where the ambiguities are so great that power is constantly shifting and authority has no real substance. It is within the vacuum between the clarity of authority* and the ambiguity of power† that a president's leadership must produce some sort of effective action.[23] Presidents have a legitimate assignment of authority over the institution. Yet, they must contend with the bifurcation of authority over the curriculum in which the faculty has legitimate rights. These competing rights fuel ambiguities and lead to the capacity of the faculty and others to go beyond the legitimate boundaries of authority to employ power to effect or to block action by the president. This nether land too often leads to chaotic floundering where nothing changes and frustration and pointless arguments characterize decision making.

Because of the ambiguities, presidents in higher education need a higher level of management, political, and intuitive skills than chief executive officers in business. If they can bring the savviness of a horse trader, the foresight of Warren Buffet, the management skills articulated by Peter Drucker, and the perseverance of Sisyphus, then the president may have a good chance of effecting real leadership. Unfortunately, success today does not mean that the road is now clear for future decisions. Each opportunity for action is a unique drama with no clear plot, in which the players change depending on the setting.

So, how are these ambiguities of power and authority resolved given the prior discussion on management skills and leadership? They are resolved only through the personality, energy, skills, and determination of the president. The president cannot acquiesce to chaos even under the circumstance of great wealth because no university

---

*A legally established right within an organization to expect others in a defined position to obey the decisions or actions of another holder of a position based on a set of rules and responsibilities, and the ambiguity of power.
†Where one person can expect compliance by another through some means not necessarily rooted in a legally defined position.

has an infinite supply of inertia given the uncertainties evident in the market or created by the government. The purpose of management skills is to bring discipline over decisions so that action can proceed forward. Because of the ambiguities of power and authority, the president must learn how Machiavelli's commentary on leadership can be applied to isolate and limit resistance to action.[24]

Leadership success requires political skills that complement management skills. Practical political skills require timing, persistence, coalition building, negotiating outcomes, humility, gaming outcomes, controlling emotions, keeping your own counsel, and "serving the needs of others."[25] Timing requires sensitivity on when to pursue or back off on taking action or getting others to take action. Persistence is critical to successful action. If the president is easily thwarted and abandons a plan of action with the first sign of opposition, nothing will be accomplished. The president has to persist but calmly, quietly, and humbly in the pursuit of a goal.

Presidential coalition building requires the people skills to find supporters and to get them to act in agreement. This is where humility comes into play. Sometimes in pursuing a goal it makes more sense to have others move it, while the president remains in the background. Gaming outcomes call for the skill to understand the set of moves and the parties who have to be involved to reach a desired outcome. Gaming skills also require the president to be able to assign probabilities of success to each move and to understand when a particular set of moves will work or fail.

Presidents should control emotions. This simply means not getting angry in public, not belittling opposition, and being pleasant with those in support or opposition. Franklin Roosevelt was a great president because he kept his own counsel. He knew what he wanted to accomplish, he understood who would support the action and who would oppose it, but he did not reveal his intentions or gloat when he succeeded. Presidents cannot succeed unless they "serve the needs of others."[26] The president must understand the underlying needs in which some will support a decision and others will oppose it. When presidents understand those needs, they then have the key to building support and allaying opposition.

Some are born with a natural inclination to political and management skills, while most others need to learn and practice these skills throughout a career. After every action, whether successful or a failure, a leader should reflect on what was done, figure out what needed to be done to succeed, and ask others what could have been done better. Success often comes after the bitter fruits of defeat, and the bitter fruits of defeat can quickly follow success. There has been more than one American president who has experienced defeat, and then success, and success, and then defeat. When either success or defeat happens, move on, learn from it, and do not assume that what happened in the past will always happen in the future.

THE CONUNDRUM OF SHARED GOVERNANCE

Shared governance is incorrectly interpreted by many to imply that the faculty has a right to be involved in every decision made by the president or the board of trustees. Shared governance is an advisory role where the faculty advises the president on academic matters of the institution. This is not meant to imply that they have a right to veto a president's decision regarding an academic issue. Neither does it mean that their advisory statement must be incorporated into the decision. If the decision involves funding for an academic project, the faculty needs to have information on funding constraints, which could limit the scope of the project.

The president should work with the faculty and solicit their advice. A wise president should be aware of what the faculty would accept or oppose before presenting the proposed course of action to them. Opposition will not be a surprise, but it can provide valuable information to the president as the issue is refined prior to a decision.

SUMMARY

Private colleges are crumbling beneath the weight of daily pressures and concerned about the prospect of yet another beating from the market. For leaders at these colleges, strategy has been reduced to a frenzied search for the next new dollar, without reasonable regard

for management practices, market position, or long-term operational efficiency. More often than not, time, energy, and revenue are
wasted on stop-gap financial measures. Even those colleges that have
prospered under an intuitive leadership are not safe from closure, for
success based on the hunches of particular leaders often ends with
their tenure. Many an institution has faltered, if not fallen, during
changes in management.

Strategy acts as insurance against vagaries in decision making.
It complements a leader's intuition and keeps chaos at bay. The
president, as keeper of the strategy, must be a model of integrity,
gaining the college safe passage to a world of financial stability. Most
of the strategy and leadership tips in this chapter are simple and
even familiar to new leaders, but putting them into practice will
certainly be slow and difficult at times. Problems and challenges
will call, but a course of action and peace of mind will emerge for
the progressive manager who trades in an incrementalist mind-set
for long-term security.

The greatest challenge for presidents is the balance between
leadership and collegial relationships. Too often the latter gets in the
way of the former, and leadership simply turns itself into higgledy-
piggledy activity with no purpose or direction. Leadership requires
forethought, tenacity, tireless activity, decisive action, and bold
decisions. This means that the president cannot wait for events to
force action. In today's economy, presidents must purposefully and
decisively move the institution forward. This should not be taken as a
call to dictatorship. Rather, it demands of presidents the perspicacity
to take strategic action and to have the personal skills to bring others
into the fold who are critical to carrying out the strategy.

ENDNOTES

1.   Cohen, M. D., & March, J. G. *Leadership and Ambiguity: The American
     College President*. (New York: McGraw-Hill, 1974).

2.   Keller, G. *Academic Strategy* (Baltimore: Johns Hopkins University
     Press, 1983), pp. 123–125.

3.   Drucker, P. F. *The Practice of Management* (New York: Harper & Row,
     1954), pp. 159–160.

4. Fisher, James L., personal interview, Baltimore, Maryland, September 5, 2001.
5. Keller, G. *Academic Strategy* (Baltimore: Johns Hopkins University Press, 1983), p. 125.
6. Keller, G. *Academic Strategy* (Baltimore: Johns Hopkins University Press, 1983), p. 35.
7. Balderston, F. E. *Managing Today's University*. (San Francisco: Jossey-Bass, 1975).
8. Carnegie Commission on Higher Education.*Governance of Higher Education* (New York: McGraw-Hill, 1973), p. 37.
9. Ibid.
10. Nelson, John (Senior Vice President Moody's Investors Service), personal interview, New York, August 7, 2001.
11. Cowan, R. B. (1993). "Prescription for Small-College Turnaround," *Change, 1*, 37.
12. Ibid.
13. Cohen, M. D., & March, J. G. *Leadership and Ambiguity: The American College President*. (New York: McGraw-Hill, 1974).
14. Ibid, pp. 33–34.
15. Baldridge, V. J., Curtis, D. V., Ecker, G., & Riley, G. L. *Policy Making and Effective Leadership*. (San Francisco: Jossey-Bass, 1983).
16. Riesman, D. R. *On Higher Education* (New Brunswick, NJ: Transaction Publishers, 1998), p. 297.
17. Keller, G. *Academic Strategy* (Baltimore: Johns Hopkins University Press, 1983), p. 35.
18. Ibid.
19. Lenington, R. *Colleges Are a Business!* (Phoenix, AZ: Oryx Press, 1996), p. 7.
20. Simon, Herbert. (Winter, 1967; volume 48). "The Job of a College President," *Educational Record*, 69.
21. Cowan, R. B. (1993). "Prescription for Small-College Turnaround," *Change, 1*, 37.
22. Miller, Scott I. (President, Wesley College), personal interview, Dover, Delaware, August 10, 2001.
23. Weber, M. *The Theory of Social and Economic Organization* (New York: Oxford University Press, 1947), p. 152.
24. Machiavelli, N. *The Prince*. (New York: Simon and Schuster, 2004)
25. Dwyer, C. *Managing People* (2nd ed.). (Dubuque, IA: Kendall/Hunt, 1996).
26. Ibid.

CHAPTER 10

FINANCIAL DISTRESS

There are two kinds of financial distress: episodic and chronic. Episodic financial distress is a temporary lapse into deficit spending and usually happens when unexpected changes take place in the market or in government regulations or budgetary allocations. Chronic financial distress, on the other hand, is not a temporary lapse into the red, but a continuous and pervasive condition.

Episodic distress occurred following the bursting of the technology bubble in 2000, 9/11, and the credit crunch of 2008. The problem is how to survive these events without destroying the integrity of the college. The effects of each event are unique, but the result is the same. For example, the credit crunch could result in the loss of students who want to go to college but are unable to pay for their education, do not have the academic or athletic ability to qualify for large scholarships, and have a credit rating too low for a loan. Credit crunch is an externally created financial crisis that could turn into chronic financial distress if the problem is not resolved.

Considerable evidence suggests that many colleges do indeed exist in chronic financial distress. During a five-year period in the 1990s, which was one of the strongest growth periods in U.S. history, 33 percent of private

FIGURE 10.1—PROPORTION OF PRIVATE INSTITUTIONS REPORTING DEFICITS UNDER TWO REVENUE CONDITIONS BETWEEN 1998 AND 2000

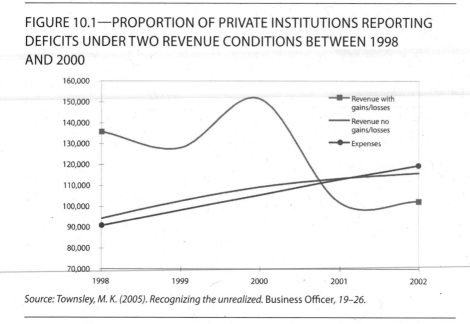

Source: Townsley, M. K. (2005). Recognizing the unrealized. Business Officer, 19–26.

colleges reported deficits for three of the five years.[1] The trend on deficits was exacerbated when the double whammy of the tech bubble burst and 9/11 hit the financial markets.

The period covered in Figure 10.1 starts during the supposed "good times" for technology investments leading up to the famous "Y2K" event. It clearly shows that even when the damaging effects of unrealized losses during the 1998 to 2002 period are removed, a large segment of private colleges (nearly 40 percent) operate with deficits. This does not necessarily mean that the same set of colleges and universities had deficits every year. However, 40 percent is a relatively high rate of probability that a college will have a deficit in fat and lean years. So, boards, presidents, and chief financial officers need to understand the dynamics that can thrust colleges into a period of recurring deficits.

For those colleges struggling daily with financial distress, wit, pluck, and luck are absolute necessities.[2] Their boards and administrators spend most of their time trying to find enough cash to keep their doors open. Planning revolves around simply finding the money to pay faculty and vendors rather than focusing on strategically improving instructional programs or responding to the marketplace. Colleges in chronic financial distress survive from registration to registration on the dribs and drabs of donor gifts, from one bridge loan to the next. For them, long range does not even exist.

No matter how redeeming a college and its mission may be, events and a severely weakened financial structure can push it to close. Several events qualify as college killers: revocation of the right to grant federal aid to students, withdrawal of accreditation, banks refusing to provide short-term loans, loss of a reliable funding source, and catastrophic enrollment declines. Regardless of the specific event or combination of events, the college is finished. There are numerous examples of colleges that have hit the wall. Antioch[3] and Upsala College[4] closed when their markets collapsed and the old reliables stopped making gifts. Bradford College[5] shut down when the "field of dreams" residence hall plan failed to generate enrollment, plunging the college into a hopeless debt crisis. Sierra-Nevada[6] could not attract a market, gifts, or bridge loans; and Sheldon Jackson[7] in Alaska could not keep up with rising costs or find money and was too isolated to build its enrollment.

The rare colleges that close their doors follow similar paths. The college secures short-term bridge loans, complete with conditions and restrictions and guaranteed by the president or board chair (an ominous, desperate sign of trouble). The college is probably forced to apply all excess operating income to short- and long-term debt reduction. In any case, credit analysis eventually indicates the hopelessness of the college's financial condition, and its bank cuts its losses. Donors shun the college, too, unwilling to throw good money after bad. Accrediting agencies review the financial condition of the college and withdraw accreditation. This is followed quickly by the U.S. Department of Education's order to cease issuance of federal financial aid grants. These losses leave the college no choice. In the absence of a miracle, it closes its doors.

WARNING SIGNS OF FINANCIAL DISTRESS

Chronic financial distress is not a set pattern in which the road is clearly lit and flags are being waved that action has to be taken now or the college financial condition is terminal. Initially, a college may have a single problem that continues to grow until its many problems signal that financial health is deteriorating and reaching a critical state. In the end, most financial problems boil down to a continuing cash crisis, where the college barely survives each payroll. When it comes to chronic and critical financial distress, John Minter has found that warning signs of trouble are usually apparent well before the college finds itself in dire circumstance, but someone must be awake at the switch or the opportunity to intervene might be lost.[8]

The problem for board members and presidents is that they are not versed in the complexities of financial reports and can be too easily swayed, thinking that the sweet siren of the next change will finally turn the problem around. What they need is some way to recognize classic warning signals of trouble ahead. Table 10.1 contains a list of warning signals. The idea of the list is not for the board member or the president to sit down and do the computations necessary to tease out the warning signals. The chief financial officer should provide an annual report that speaks to these warning signals. Also, a prudent step that every board should take is to meet in closed session with the auditors and ask them to report on the financial condition of the college. The board should also require the auditors to review the management report, to explain what problems exist in the financial operations of the college, and to suggest what should be done to correct those problems.

THE BOTTOM LINE OF FINANCIAL DISTRESS

Obviously, cash is everything in surviving and flourishing. However, this tells us nothing about how colleges lose the capacity to generate enough cash to pay their bills and make payroll. The fundamental reason for financial distress lies in a college's disconnect among mission, services, markets, and price. For example, the college has an

TABLE 10.1—WARNING SIGNS OF CHRONIC FINANCIAL DISTRESS

Business Operations
- Audit management reports indicate that the business office makes numerous and large errors that underreport the financial condition of the institution.
- Uncollected accounts receivables are growing faster than tuition.
- The checking account statement has a large number of large overdrafts.
- Payables for a large proportion of vendors are more than 120 days late.
- The IRS regularly places a penalty charge on tax deposits.
- Employee benefit coverages lapse for several months.

Revenue and Expenses
- Enrollment is declining in academic programs providing the major share of revenue.
- Independent studies are reaching the point where they represent a substantial portion of all sections offered during a semester.
- Revenue is growing slower than expenses are.

Finance
- Credit lines are growing at a fast pace and becoming a large portion of current liabilities.
- The cash account as reported in the audited statement of financial position is less than 8 percent of expenses and shrinks every accounting period.
- Endowment principal is used to provide cash flow.
- Fixed assets are being converted to cash.

Composite Financial Index
- The index score for the Composite Financial Index (CFI) is less than 1.
- The CFI has been declining for the past several years. (Go to Appendix G, Composite Financial Index, for a full explanation of the model.)

obsolete mission. Antioch College is a good example; the mission no longer matched its market. In the case of Sierra Nevada College and Bradford College, services were no longer valued by their markets. Out-of-line pricing was Upsala College's fate. Financial distress is omnipresent when the college, its board, president, and alumni lose touch with the economic realities of its existence. No matter how virtuous a college's mission is, if leaders lose sight of the necessary connection of mission, services, markets, and price, the college will slip into financial distress with a high probability of failure.

HOW TO AVOID CHRONIC FINANCIAL DISTRESS

Vigilance is the watchword: vigilance during the fiscal year, vigilance with plans for the future, vigilance against bad ideas becoming reality, and vigilance by getting the best information possible. The board, the president, the chief financial officer, and the chief academic officer need to keep their eye on performance and make sure that it matches strategic goals and that strategy is not being replaced with planning and action by whim. The rules of vigilance listed in Table 10.2 should become a part of the institution's regular review and planning process.

Private institutions that avoid financial distress will find that discretionary assets such as cash and short-term assets grow and provide the board and president with the ability to handle short-term calamities and to strengthen the academic quality and reputation of the institution. Colleges that are in constant financial distress gain no maneuverability so that whether the stress is small or large it is a potential catastrophe. Boards and presidents of these colleges have no room to maneuver or improve their institutions. Everything that is done is reactive; there is no time to plan; errors multiply; and the cost of errors further slices into whatever paltry financial reserves there are.

TABLE 10.2—RULES OF VIGILANCE

- Find out causes of large and continuing budget variances and hold department chiefs accountable.
- Carefully test every risky project; steer clear of projects that seem too good to be true.
- Prevent financial disequilibrium by constantly searching for new revenue sources and ways to cut or keep spending under control.
- If current student markets do not provide sufficient revenue, find new markets.
- Set aside a portion of new cash for a safety net and for new projects.
- Know what your competitors are doing; figure out what you have to do to keep ahead of them.
- Keep the connection running from mission, services, markets, and price.

Long-term financial distress forces the following question to the forefront: is the college doing anything worthwhile, or is it fooling itself and doing a disservice to its students? Under those circumstances, it makes sense for the board to examine the costs and benefits of merging with another college. Of course, merger is only appealing if the college has anything to offer. If it does not have a market niche, and if its pool of students is stagnant or shrinking, then the college may have little value to another institution.

What does the college do then, especially if it wants to do the right thing for its students? The board needs to find a partner. If it is not possible to find another partner, the board needs to seriously examine how to bow out of the market gracefully and keep from unduly damaging enrolled students. This means that the board needs to find another college that will take the full credit history of current students and merge them into relevant majors.

SUMMARY

If there is one statement that defines the challenge to the president of an independent college it is this—"constant vigilance is necessary if the college is to be kept from harm's way." Vigilance means more than stacks of reports lying on the desk of the president waiting to be read. Too often a president is inundated by administrative meetings, fund raising, board meetings, alumni relations, or work with regional and national groups. The result is that the reports are either ignored or not read until months after action needs to be taken.

For vigilance to be effective, reports must be timely and concise. Reams of budget reports that are decipherable only by the business office are not very useful. The business office needs to provide reports that show the current and expected condition of the college, and a list describing the current state of the institution. A list is preferred over paragraphs because it is easier to quickly see the point being made. Vigilance is not solely the responsibility of the president. For vigilance to be effective, everyone has to recognize the importance of their contribution to monitoring the condition of the institution.

ENDNOTES

1. National Science Foundation. (2001). Sheet 08180820: Unrestricted and restricted fund types 1987–1996. *WebCASPAR Database System*. Retrieved August 5, 2001, from http://caspar/nsf.gov/.

2. Townsley, M. K. (1991), "Brinkmanship, Planning, Smoke, and Mirrors," *Planning for Higher Education, 19*, 19.

3. Fain, P. (2007). "Antioch's Closing Signals End of an Era," *Chronicle of Higher Education*. Retrieved September 19, 2008, from http://chronicle.com/weekly/v53/i42/42a00101.htm.

4. Mercer, J. (1995). "Death Throes at Upsala," *Chronicle of Higher Education*. Retrieved September 12, 2008, from http://chronicle.com/che-data/articles.dir/articles-41.dir/issue-32.dir/32a04101.htm.

5. van der Werf, M. (2002). "The Death of a Small College," *Chronicle of Higher Education*. Retrieved September 17, 2008, from http://chronicle.com/weekly/v48/i36/36a03502.htm.

6. van der Werf, M. (2006, September 29). "The End for a Private College—With Big Assets," *Chronicle of Higher Education*, Retrieved February 24, 2009, from http://chronicle.com/weekly/v53/i06/06a03301.htm.

7. Fischer, K. (2007). "Small Alaska College Suspends Operations," *Chronicle of Higher Education*. Retrieved September 12, 2008, from http://chronicle.com/weekly/v53/i45/45a02403.htm.

8. Minter, J., E-mail interview, John Minter and Associates, January 15, 2001.

CHAPTER 11

WHEN PRIVATE COLLEGES FAIL

Failure may come in many shapes, but typically it is the very small colleges that struggle to stay open. Seventy-one percent of the colleges that closed between 1988 and 1997 enrolled fewer than 1,100 students. Some of these colleges may have been larger at one time, but they shrunk dramatically as they passed through the crucible of failure. With an average enrollment of 566 students, they were in a size category all their own. The following accounts of six colleges that closed over the past several years were compiled from recent articles and other documents. Read these accounts as cautionary tales rather than as complete case histories. These six examples focus on themes common to most failed colleges: *too much debt*, *too little cash*, *lost markets*, *crumbling campuses*, and *not enough leadership by boards and presidents*.

ANTIOCH COLLEGE

Antioch was not a fly-by-night college. It had a 155-year history of innovation, social liberalism, and influential alumni. Far from the madding crowds, free discourse took place on its pleasant tree-lined campus situated in the peaceful village of Yellow Springs, Ohio. Its fame was grounded in lively debate during the social revolution of the late 1960s and early 1970s, but Antioch's time had long since passed. By 2007, Antioch was a hulk of "spalled bricks, outdated classrooms, and grungy dormitories [that] scared away prospective students."[1] The condition of the campus was indicative of the financial death spiral in the college's last years—only 125 new students the last year, enrolling only 309 total students, seven years of deficits averaging $5 million for its last two years, and a bloated budget of $78 million.[2]

Antioch had viable off-campus sites, which were frustrated by ever-increasing demands to support the Yellow Springs campus without any apparent benefit to them. The animosity turned into outright conflict, as the off-campus sites sought independence from the main campus. This only added impetus to the eventual closing.

Before the demise of Antioch, the board and a group of alumni tried to reach an agreement to keep the college going or at least intact, but they were never able to reach agreement, and by the spring of 2008, time ran out. There have been several whistling-in-the-dark announcements of reopening in 2012, presumably when all the fiscal problems are resolved and the campus is returned to a pristine state.[3] Closing doors is not conducive to encouraging enrollment, gifts, faculty, vendors, or administrators to take the risk of being there when the doors reopen.

Was there recourse for Antioch? The evidence suggests that the problems went beyond finances and maintenance to the very core of the institution. The Yellow Springs campus was respected for its roots in social justice going back to the abolitionist and early women's movement in the 19th century.[4] Although the demand for social justice continued to flourish in Yellow Springs, its urban sites in Los Angeles and Seattle did not see this as a winning strategy. The students at the urban sites wanted curricula that readied them for a career.

Student expectations for career relevance drilled down to Yellow Springs where its social justice framework turned into an irrelevancy and a joke. Too many stories came out of Antioch about proposals such as "verbal consent" for intimate relationships.[5] Pushing the lifestyle envelope had an adverse impact on parents and students seeking a stable environment for a college degree.

Structural conflict, loss of market to its mission of social justice, and the desire of today's students for career-centered curricula were the trebuchet that knocked down Antioch's reputation and then shattered its financial viability. As Terrence MacTaggart points out in his article in *The Chronicle of Higher Education*, money woes obviously bespeak weaknesses, but boards and presidents should pay attention to deterioration of leadership, reputation, relevancy of programs, and the strength of the relationships within the college community.[6]

UPSALA COLLEGE

Upsala College was formed to serve New Jersey's Swedish Lutherans. Indeed, up to the college's last days, students from Sweden traveled to Upsala to pursue college degrees. In the late 1960s, however, a denominational change removed the firm underpinning of the Lutheran church from Upsala, leaving it to its own devices to fill a void left by the dwindling enrollment of middle-class Swedish Lutheran suburbanites. Upsala was left with an inner-city campus in East Orange (adjacent to Newark, New Jersey) and no good ideas about how to generate revenue from a market of students with relatively little money and weak academic skills. As the college scrambled to boost enrollments, it saw a rise in the number of African-American enrollees (from 18 percent of total enrollment in 1976 to 47 percent in 1994), but few of them could afford an upscale education.[7] When government aid did not cover the full cost of tuition, these students were not making up the difference. Increased enrollment may have indicated higher revenue, but it did not guarantee the college *cash*.

Enrollment peaked in 1984 at 1,822 students but shrunk thereafter for several reasons.[8] The college instituted new admissions standards, reducing the size of the freshman class and requiring that returning students pay tuition and fees prior to reenrollment. In addition, a full one-third more students were finding themselves on academic probation.[9] As enrollment declined, Upsala's operating deficit ballooned.

To reverse the situation, Upsala hired a consulting firm to recruit students, which it did with a vengeance! From a low point of 1,138 students in 1990, enrollments climbed quickly to 1,556 students.[10] Once again, many of the new enrollees did not have the financial wherewithal to pay for their classes or the academic ability to do the work. Federal financial aid made up some of the difference between what students owed and what tuition cost, but the rest was spread out over payment plans. By the early 1990s, nearly 50 percent of the accumulated operating deficit was a result of uncollectible tuition accounts—a situation exacerbated by Upsala's irregular billing practices.[11]

Without cash, Upsala could not pay its bills. Some bills were outstanding for more than two years.[12] The endowment fund was depleted to meet operational expenses and accounting legerdemain obscured the fund's erosion. In the days of fund accounting, the appearance of a stable endowment fund could be projected by treating the transfer of endowment funds as either a receivable or as a loan to fund current operations. The endowment fund would continue to show an acceptable balance, but there would be no reality behind the number.

In midcrisis, Upsala's president decided that any external sign of his college's financial quandary would engulf the college in rumors, pushing it deeper into financial distress. The chimera of enrollment growth was allowed to perpetuate the delusion that just a few more students would resolve the financial strain. Even though the college was unable to pay bills, each new student hid the reality that larger numbers did not increase tuition revenues. In reality, larger enrollments only pushed the college closer to the brink of extinction because more students did not produce enough cash to cover the additional instructional costs.

The college was becoming a Potemkin village. Four new vice presidents had joined Upsala's administration during the early 1990s to help ease the financial crisis. At that time, the vice president of finance warned that the college would have to close unless drastic measures were taken. He was promptly fired. The new chief financial officer indicated that the college would need a substantial cash infusion to survive. The board agreed but established no targets.

The college did sell some property; two sister colleges loaned funds; and the city of East Orange, a city that could ill afford being bilked for its generosity, guaranteed a $4 million bond issue.[13] However, Upsala applied the money to capital projects, not to its ever present and mounting cash deficit. The drumbeat of impending doom continued into the mid-1990s when the U.S. Department of Education determined that the college was no longer able to meet its financial obligations. Upsala would have to provide a letter of credit for $1.5 million to continue to receive federal financial aid support, but bankers would not provide the letter. So, in 1994, the Commission on Higher Education of the Middle States Association of Colleges and Schools ruled that accreditation would be discontinued December 31 of that year.[14]

Upsala was stunned. Many people had been "lulled… [into believing that growing enrollment and the new loans meant] that the college was turning the corner."[15] A fleeting ray of hope appeared in the form of a South Korean industrialist, who pledged $12 million to the college; it never materialized because the South Korean government required that such a large gift be devoted to a charitable organization within Korea.[16]

Ultimately, Upsala failed because it had not figured out how to accommodate itself to the loss of its original student market. The disappearance of a financially reliable market was also severely complicated by a delusional enrollment strategy, failure in the leadership of Uppsala's president and board, and an ineptly run financial office.

The board, and the students in particular, might have been better served if it had taken a hard-nosed approach to the financial and market conditions facing the college. Although financial measures (ratio, trend analysis, and CFI scoring) discussed earlier might not have prevented the downfall of the college, at least they would have provided a realistic base on which to judge the future. Many boards make the mistake of granting *a charity assumption* to the administration; that is, assuming that because the operation is a charity it does not have to be held to rigorous financial standards common in business. Board members, who see their role as only honorary and a community service, abdicate oversight of the college to the administration. They willingly adhere to the belief that only its practitioners understand the inherent complexity of higher education.

When a board takes its fiduciary responsibilities lightly, it is interested in only a cursory review of the financials and expects only perfunctory reports from the chief management officers. Some boards avoid the effort to understand a complex financial statement, and sometimes even ignore audit management letters.* These same boards allow chief administrators to orchestrate the relationship with auditors by keeping auditors far away from audit committee meetings.

Boards of trustees at nonprofits are expected to be the eyes and voice of the public; when they ignore common sense rules of fiduciary responsibility, they damage the viability and credibility of the college. As Upsala shows, unwise plans were submitted by administration and the board accepted them without a keen analysis of assumptions, prospects, actions, or consequences.

When the board finally voted to close Upsala, it brought in a retired accountant to oversee the closure. To his horror, the accountant found that financial records were out of date, had been kept inaccurately, or had not been kept at all.[17] How a board could allow this situation to occur given annual audits can only be surmised. Upsala may have been an egregious case of board members with business experience granting dispensation of business rules to college administrators they never would have trusted to handle the same functions in their own businesses.

BRADFORD COLLEGE

Originally, Bradford College was a small finishing school for fashionable young women in the Boston area. Its mission was abandoned as fewer and fewer women sought to become handmaidens to their husbands' careers. Going coeducational was the first step in its makeover. When going coed was not enough, Bradford sought a niche in the

---

*The audit management letter is a report by the auditors about weaknesses in financial operations or violations of government regulations.

1980s by instituting an "applied liberal arts" curriculum that would integrate training for a specific career with the classic disciplines.[18] Yet, this niche soon became crowded as more colleges in Bradford's market turned to similar degrees as their own device to remain marketable. Competition led to drops in enrollments, and Bradford compensated by adding new majors, eventually offering nearly 40 majors despite having only 35 full-time faculty members.[19] It was not long before Bradford's marketing strategy followed the simple but indiscriminate rule of all struggling colleges to enroll any and every student it could find. They snagged students by offering them huge tuition discounts that further destabilized the institution. By the late 1990s, the harder that Bradford tried to keep afloat, the worse things got. This is a story of wealth smothered by circumstance overwhelmed by bad decisions.

In 1989, Bradford brought in as president a money-raising whirlwind who had been an executive director of Oxfam America. His charge was to rebuild the financial health of the college. His fund-raising reputation was well deserved because he increased Bradford's endowment fund from $7 million in 1989 to more than $23 million in 1998.[20] Despite his fund-raising prowess, deficits became commonplace, running around $1 million during his tenure, which ended in 1998.[21] The deficits forced him to spend a good portion of his valuable time raising money that quickly disappeared down the annual deficit rabbit hole.

As part of the president's strategy, $7 million of the newly raised money went to major improvements in the appearance of the campus and to upgrades in its infrastructure. Enrollment did improve 41 percent during his presidency but, as noted earlier, more students and more tuition could not end the string of deficits. The board, fearing that the college's chronic financial weakness would become irreversible, contracted with a noted small college marketing specialist, who recommended that Bradford "define its specialties, concentrate on them, and get rid of everything else."[22] In other words, rationalize the curriculum, reduce costs, and put more money in a straightforward marketing campaign that would emphasize the college's strengths.

The president, in early 1998, thought that he had a better plan. As his last big move to push Bradford over the top to financial nirvana, he proposed with two bold strokes to build new dorms and make major investments in art facilities.[23] The college would pay for this with a bond issue with repayment based on these conditions:

- Increase enrollment from 512 students in 1998 to 725 students in 2000; and

- Decrease discounts from 30 percent in 1997 to 28 percent of tuition in 1998.

Failure to achieve these enrollment and discount targets would adversely affect reaching financial equilibrium.[24]

Enrollment after the bond sale went nowhere, with only 175 new students enrolled, even though 225 students had been promised in the bond proposals. Continuing student enrollment deteriorated with the loss of 36 Asian students after their local currencies collapsed. Even worse, the new students were given greater-than-predicted tuition discounts of 48 percent.[25] By the end of the 1998 fiscal year, the deficit was $6 million out of a $14 million budget.[26] In 1999, prospects simply fell apart when only 497 students enrolled and the discount rate rocketed to 60 percent. The college expected to receive $9 million in tuition income, but the discounts consumed $5.5 million of it.

By the end, the president was gone and a new one was hired who discovered that the place was in its death spiral.[27] For bondholders, Bradford was a disaster; performance was miles away from the forecast given to them. The board panicked and decided to announce the college's closure in the newly renovated auditorium. The last class graduated in June 2000, with the doors banging shut after they left. The parting comments by a member of the faculty and the board say all that needs to be said:

- One faculty member teaching history, said, "We were complicit in our silence."[28]

- The chair of the board said, "The trustees probably did not question administrators enough. At a small college, a board has to break out of the traditional mode of trustees. It has to be far more challenging and inquisitive. I think that we did that on and off. I don't know how I can say, in closing a college, that we [had done] enough."[29]

Why did Bradford fail? It was too small, and it had no financial reserves to counterbalance its size. Competition ate away mercilessly at its student market, forcing the college to offer financially unsound tuition inducements to convince students to enroll. The coup de grace was the failed dorm strategy that drove the college into the ground when it became evident that Bradford did not have the cash to pay the obligations on the debt service or to fulfill the covenants imposed by the debt instrument. In summary, by the time Bradford's leadership recognized and accepted the college's woeful condition, it was too late to take further reasonable action except for a last-minute Hail Mary pass. For Bradford, it was the wrong road taken with insufficient resources.

SPRING GARDEN COLLEGE

Spring Garden College had a long and hallowed history as one of the first technology schools in the nation. Originally located in central Philadelphia, it moved in 1905 to Chestnut Hill, an affluent suburb bordering the city. There the small college prospered and slowly grew for nearly 80 years. In 1971, its enrollment experienced a growth spurt, bringing the number of students to 1,051.[30] The following year, enrollment plummeted by more than 30 percent.[31] Not until 1978 did enrollment edge back above its 1971 level. That period of low enrollment had a devastating effect on the college's financial condition as fund balances dramatically shrunk and Spring Garden's deficit grew to $1.1 million.[32]

In 1983, hoping to turn the corner and get away from its frail image, the college moved to the recently closed Pennsylvania School for the Deaf, a 33-acre Victorian campus. But the administration had failed to anticipate the costs of plant maintenance, and it did not analyze the impact of a larger debt load. The decision to move put Spring

Garden on the road to financial calamity. Initially, enrollment did improve, reaching a peak enrollment of 1,667 in 1985. Enrollment generated more tuition, which had a salutary effect on the college's fund deficit, which was at its lowest level in seven years.[33] The peak soon turned into a downhill run as enrollment fell back to 1,084 students in 1989. This also sent deficits skyrocketing to $3.8 million.[34] At the end of the next academic year, the college was in such an abject state of poverty that it had to defer its summer payroll until September. Like our other financially desperate examples, Spring Garden frantically sought ways to salvage its financial structure. More than 30 members of its staff were released, and a fund-raising campaign was started to offset the deficit.[35]

It was too little and much too late to save Spring Garden. In 1992, enrollment collapsed to 681 students. A last-ditch effort to sell the campus to another college and then lease it back failed. Spring Garden, laden with weak finances and mired under higher expenses following a bad geographical move, closed its doors in 1992 after 141 years of service. The end of Spring Garden meant another tombstone for colleges that lost the battle to weak management, falling enrollments, big deficits, and unanticipated costs.

MARYCREST INTERNATIONAL UNIVERSITY

Marycrest is a classic case of what happens when financial disequilibrium eats away financial resources and ravages the faculty-administrative comity needed to turn around a college in decline. Marycrest closed in 2002, even though enrollment had grown in two years from 265 students to 650 full- and part-time students.[36]

The college tried several of the old tricks, going coed in 1969 and selling its property to Teikyo University. Marycrest still could not control its costs. According to the college's president, "We are tuition-driven. If your revenue from enrollment can't cover operational costs, you don't have much of a future."[37] Finding enough revenue was not the sole problem at Marycrest. A few months before the closing announcement, North Central Association of Colleges and Schools placed the college on probation because "the College's trustees, administrators, and faculty and staff members had a significant disparate vision for the future and the College was not channeling enough money into faculty development, or repairs and upgrades of buildings."[38] Probation by North Central led to a severe decline in new student enrollment.[39]

Marycrest's position in 2002 could not have happened overnight. Problems had to be apparent when the college moved from a male institution to a coed college in 1969. Moves like that are usually motivated by the desire to increase the pool of potential students and thereby augment enrollment. Single-sex colleges that go coed are signaling that enrollment is declining, which suggests revenue is not keeping pace with expenses.

This college had failure neatly lined up with enrollment declines, an inability to cover costs, and probation. Their one-trick pony, going coed, failed to deliver in the long term and the leadership had no bright ideas, so they closed. Whether this was because of a failure of leadership, markets, or accreditation is not evident, but the combination was deadly to its survival.

MOUNT SENARIO COLLEGE

Mount Senario College's problems were self-inflicted from its birth in 1962. It was located in a rural county with high unemployment and low per capita income, and a long way from major cities in Wisconsin and from cities in surrounding states.[40] Recruiters had a tough sell and had to fudge the truth to get students to enroll. In addition, the students who did enroll had lower than average ACT test scores. Students rarely finished their degrees. For instance, only 19 percent of students graduated in six years and less than 10 percent of athletes made it to graduation.[41] The lousy retention rate was disabling to Senario's strategy of using athletics to spur enrollment. High attrition rates meant that enrollment went nowhere.

Enrollment problems were coupled with pointless fund-raising efforts in which each board member only gave $650. Thus, the noose was tightened further. The college's location did not help because it was located in a region bereft of graduates or friends with the income needed for large gifts.[42] For example, a fund-raising campaign directed at 20,000 alumni cost $500 in returned postage yet raised a paltry $757.[43]

The path to the end was greased by an accrediting team report that the college had a negative net asset position; in other words, it was bankrupt.[44] Obviously, with no net assets, it could not pay a $500,000 past due bill on payroll taxes, and vendors were paid only when they came to the college and begged for their money.[45] The U.S. Department of Education put another nail in Senario's coffin when it ordered the college to refund $100,000 to students and the federal government because the college did not have adequate controls on disbursement of financial aid.[46] This package of problems lay on top of bad expenditure decisions to build new softball fields, to end low-cost contract services, and to buy trailers for dorms that did not fill.[47] The last step to Senario's doom was probation by its accrediting association, which despite desperate efforts to get grants and to sell parts of the campus, was the end of the line. Mount Senario College closed in 2002 due to declining enrollment, financial problems, and probation.[48] (Note: there is an excellent case study about the closing of this college by Martin Van Der Werf in *The Chronicle of Higher Education*, June 14, 2002, titled "Mount Senario's Final Act.")[49]

OTHER SAD STORIES

There are many more sad stories of colleges that through one or more unfortunate circumstances were forced to close their doors. These reasons follow a similar depressing pattern: something happens—enrollment declines, tuition no longer covers costs—and the doors close. Here is a brief list of colleges that closed their doors when declining enrollments and other financial misfortunes pushed them past the brink:

- Nazareth College closed in 1991.[50]
- Notre Dame College of New Hampshire closed in 2001.[51]
- William Tyndale College closed in 2004.[52]
- Sheldon Jackson College closed in 2007.[53]

WHAT ARE THE LESSONS FROM THESE FAILURES?

There appears to be a bit more to failure than declining revenue and financial problems. Many of the colleges were small like Antioch, Spring Garden, Upsala, and Marycrest. They did not have adequate financial reserves or enrollment to compensate for their relatively minor positions in the education marketplace. Another problem apparent in many of these cases is a dreadful lack of leadership by their trustees and presidents. Where there was leadership, a president sent the college down a blind alley (refer to Bradford and Upsala), or the president tried to give away the college hoping to build enrollment (a tactic tried unsuccessfully by Bradford and Upsala). Then, there is the classic mistake such as announcing the temporary closing of the college (Antioch made this mistake, which resulted in a real closing of the college because no rational student or their parents would willingly invest in a failure).

A quick look inside the workings of Bradford and Senario offers additional insight on how to avoid failure. Leaders at these two colleges made egregious errors. Bad judgment under stress is not uncommon, but colleges that hope to survive difficult circumstances must find leaders who do not fold in crisis and can tell the difference between winning ideas and ridiculous ideas.

For instance, Bradford College's management tried to bolster enrollment levels by discounting tuition excessively. The year that Bradford closed net tuition fell to 40 percent of tuition. Apparently, their leaders had predicted that short-term spikes in enrollment and revenue would translate into cash gains. Not so! Unfunded financial aid translates into a *loss* of cash; the difference between sticker price and net price (i.e., the amount of the tuition discount) is lost to the college. Unfortunately, for colleges in times of crisis, cash is king. Colleges fail when they don't have money to pay bills. At that point, competition, tuition discounts, and net income take a back seat to the issue of how the college will make the next payroll or pay its vendors and the bank. Employees and vendors can be put off for a while, but when a college can't pay the bankers, the game is over.

Bradford also borrowed huge sums to finance a residence hall and fuel a pipe dream. Without enrollments and reserves to fall back on, Bradford collapsed under its own weight. When Bradford closed, its cumulative operating deficit for the previous nine years was $3.8 million, deficits were reported for six of those years, and net assets/total assets had declined 30 percent. Bradford seemed to violate nearly every rule of prudent financial management. Excessively high debts loads and continuing deficits are ready signs of financial problems.

Leaders of the colleges cited here failed or were unable to address the loss of equilibrium between revenue and expenses early enough. These colleges were in financial distress long before they closed their doors, typically having accumulated deficits that amounted to a sizable portion of their annual incomes. Rare is the college that by sheer pluck crafts a successful turnaround in its final hour. Once the colleges entered financial crisis, they had lost a most precious commodity—time! In a state of crisis, there is no time to judiciously prune programs, conduct another fund-raising program, build a strategic competitive plan, or formulate an effective marketing program.

Major problems with marketing and responding to an aggressive competitor can put the college on the road to disaster. Recall that Upsala lost its original student market and was never able to figure out how to deliver services effectively to another market of low-income students. Bradford tried to offer too many programs within its market, thereby diluting its image and mission. To project a competitive reputation, small colleges must focus on what they do best. They must keep in touch with their students and remain vigilantly aware of what the big college down the street and the small competitor across town are doing to secure enrollments. When students shop for an education, they look to colleges with broad reputations, quality services, and up-to-date facilities. Swift evaluation of trends and a competitive strategy are crucial weapons that a small college can use against larger colleges prepared to trump it, as is shown in Chapter 8 on strategy.

When the end comes it is usually swift. Most of these colleges were able to drag themselves from year to year with a modicum of new money through gifts or loans. Although tuition dependency supposedly signals financial risk, the emergency transfusions of gifts at most of these colleges temporarily raised their tuition dependency rate to levels well above 80 percent. However, the gifts never produced surplus income that could be translated into endowments. Despite the generosity of donors, these colleges could never gain traction; deficit financing* became the norm and absorbed every new dollar. Donors grew tired of throwing good money after bad or could not afford to keep giving money to these colleges. Banks would no longer loan them money. When gifts stopped or loans were due and not paid, these colleges closed their doors.

So, who should have seen that Antioch, Upsala, Bradford, Spring Garden, Marycrest, and Mount Senario were on the fast track to doom? Who should have made or at least overseen the quality of marketing decisions? Just who *was* calling the shots when "mistakes were made" regarding bad tuition discounting decisions or adding debt based on hope because the college did not have a realistic plan for paying for the debt? The presidents of these colleges served them poorly, either misunderstanding financial dynamics in general or ignoring the potential financial implications of their individual actions, in the hope that their colleges would somehow squeak by. Board members deferred to presidential pipe dreams, perhaps not demanding enough evidence or information to justify critical financial decisions. And faculty members, left to fend for themselves as forgotten players in the game of rebuild versus collapse, tried to carry on instruction while the college was collapsing around them.

Were there obvious signals of impending doom? These colleges reported rising debt loads, continuing deficits, shrinking net assets, falling enrollment, switching investments into fixed assets, and dwindling amounts of cash leading up to their demise. These conditions are major factors in either the CFI scoring system or in other basic

*Deficit financing occurs when a college is forced to dip into its net assets to pay for operational costs because deficits do not provide cash.

financial measures. Deteriorating CFI scores and declining trends in other financial ratios would have signaled serious problems to the president and the board. If they had tracked their financial trends using these ratios, it would have been apparent that their financial and marketing strategies were failing miserably. Their financial and marketing strategies, instead of improving their financial condition, were making it markedly worse. Knowing these strategies were abysmal failures would not necessarily lead to the conclusion that a successful strategy could have been formulated. However, they could have improved their chances of success by targeting the ratio factors to improve their financial condition. Moreover, attention to financial performance could have given them more time to look at reasonable alternatives to a precipitous closing. Alternatives evaporate as a college's fortunes decline because potential suitors will prefer the carrion over the cost of buying a half-dead corpse.

As John Nelson, senior vice president at Moody's Investors Service, suggests, "Small colleges have the best chance of surviving [when] the president understands finances, works well with the chief financial officer, and [when] the board takes a critical role in decisions."[54] Small colleges need decisive, creative, inspirational leaders. The shrewd president of a small college will design a financially viable course and demonstrate it to the board, the faculty, the students, and the larger marketplace. Find a president with perspective and foresight, make sure that he or she refuses to humor the administration, and true leadership is created.

Antioch, Upsala, Spring Garden, Bradford, and the others reached the end because they lost their markets, made bad decisions, were no longer economically viable, and in the end tried to make an obsolete mission work. Closing of colleges like the ones discussed here, though sad and demoralizing to those involved, should not become a reason for preserving the inept or the inefficient. The discipline of the market can do a better job of allocating resources within higher education. In some ways, it is amazing that more small colleges do not drift off into oblivion because some of them seem to stumble from one catastrophe to another. They barely have the resources to stay open let alone deliver an education that prepares their students for the labor market.

SUMMARY

The six cases are studies in mission failure. Mission failure happens when boards, presidents, chief administrators, faculty, and alumni lose sight of the fact that a viable college requires a mission that produces services that the market wants and will pay for. If the mission is obsolete, as was the case at Antioch, new presidents, new programs, new advertising campaigns, and new tuition rates will not convince students to enroll. A mission is obsolete when it no longer serves the market. The market will dictate what a college should offer and how it will do it. Trying to do something else is both shortsighted and ultimately unfair to donors and to the few students who enroll. Colleges that are on track to failure take students' money, push students through courses, and saddle them with debt and a degree from a failed institution. Graduates may unfortunately find that their earning potential from such a college is diminished. Colleges should not devise plans merely to take money from students so that the college can continue to bump along with low-quality programs flowing from a worn-out mission. If the college's mission cannot produce instructional programs that draw enough students to provide the revenue to cover expenses, then the college must either redesign the mission or plan its closing in an orderly fashion.

Coincident with mission failure is the loss of financial reserves that are needed to buffer independent institutions against emergencies and major changes in the economy. Private institutions could soon face economic conditions not seen since the Great Depression. Although the depth and length of this recession remains an unknown at this time, financial signs suggest that this recession could last for two years before a sluggish turnaround begins. Hunkering down during an economic crash waiting for the economy to turn around is no longer a safe option!

It is already apparent that endowment valuations and donations have hit nontuition dependent colleges hardest. Moreover, several major institutions placed a significant portion of their endowment principal in private equity investments, which may have lost most of their value. Shrinking income from endowments and donations could lead to a short-term liquidity crisis as these institutions seek cash to cover daily operations. It is ironic that endowments and institutions that were supposed to have adequate financial buffers to protect them from the vagaries of the marketplace may be as vulnerable to this financial crisis as a struggling college solely dependent on tuition income.

Since most private institutions are tuition dependent, they must take into account the impact that the recession has on the decision to enroll or to continue in college. Most institutions will depend on loans to fund their students' education. Fortunately, the federal government has increased subsidies for loans and taken over the loan market so that students are not caught by the inopportune effects of a credit freeze by private loan makers.

What should private colleges do that barely have the reserves to tread water in good times let alone survive the current crisis? First, they need to make their cost structure more productive, because revenues will not be available to grow or to maintain expenses at current levels. Second, they should form synergistic partnerships to expand markets and improve economies of scale. Third, colleges should not forsake the idea of a merger with a stronger college. Colleges on the verge of financial collapse will have difficulty finding prospective merger partners. A prudent board and president will search for partners before the financial crisis is full-blown so that they can protect their students from the shock of an unexpected closing.

ENDNOTES

1.   Carlson, S. (2008). "As Campuses Crumble, Budgets are Crunched," *Chronicle of Higher Education*. Retrieved September 19, 2008, from http://chronicle.com/weekly/v54/i37/37a00101.htm.

2. Fain, P. (2007). "Antioch's Closing Signals End of an Era," *Chronicle of Higher Education*. Retrieved September 19, 2008, from http://chronicle.com/weekly/v53/i42/42a00101.htm.

3. Fain, P. (2008). "Antioch Announces It Will Close Its Doors," *Chronicle of Higher Education*. Retrieved September 12, 2008, from http://chronicle.com/weekly/v54/i27/27a01502.htm.

4. Fain, P. (2007). "Antioch's Closing Signals End of an Era," *Chronicle of Higher Education*. Retrieved September 19, 2008, from http://chronicle.com/weekly/v53/i42/42a00101.htm.

5. Ibid.

6. MacTaggart, T. (2007). "The Realities of Rescuing Colleges in Distress," *Chronicle of Higher Education*. Retrieved July 17, 2008, from http://chronicle.com/weekly/v54/i07/07b01101.htm.

7. National Science Foundation. (2001). Sheet 10463025.wk1: Enrollment level: 1988–1997. *WebCASPAR Database System*. Retrieved August 5, 2001, from http://caspar/nsf.gov/.

8. Ibid.

9. Kimberly, A. M. *The Response of Small Private Colleges to Financial Distress in the Nineties*. (Ann Arbor: University of Michigan, 1999).

10. Mercer, J. (1995). "Death Throes at Upsala," *Chronicle of Higher Education*. Retrieved September 12, 2008, from http://chronicle.com/che-data/articles.dir/articles-41.dir/issue-32.dir/32a04101.htm.

11. Ibid.

12. U.S. Department of Education. *In the Matter of Upsala College*. Student financial assistance proceeding. (Washington, DC: Compliance and Enforcement Division of the Office of Postsecondary Education, 1994).

13. Mercer, J. (1995). "Death Throes at Upsala," *Chronicle of Higher Education*. Retrieved September 12, 2008, from http://chronicle.com/che-data/articles.dir/articles-41.dir/issue-32.dir/32a04101.htm.

14. Ibid.

15. Ibid.

16 Ibid.

17. Ibid.

18. van der Werf, M. (2002). "The Death of a Small College," *Chronicle of Higher Education*. Retrieved September 17, 2008, from http://chronicle.com/weekly/v48/i36/36a03502.htm.

19. Ibid.
20. Ibid.
21. Ibid.
22. Ibid.
23. Ibid.
24. Ibid.
25. Ibid.
26. Ibid.
27. Ibid.
28. Ibid.
30. National Science Foundation. (2001). Sheet 15565881.wk1:
     Opening fall enrollment: 1967–1997. *WebCASPAR Database System*.
     Retrieved August 5, 2001, from http://caspar/nsf.gov/.
31. Ibid.
32. National Science Foundation. (2001). Sheet 08180820: Unre-
     stricted and restricted fund types 1987–1996. *WebCASPAR Database
     System*. Retrieved August 5, 2001, from http://caspar/nsf.gov/.
33. National Science Foundation. (2001). Sheet 15565881.wk1:
     Opening fall enrollment: 1967–1997. *WebCASPAR Database System*.
     Retrieved August 5, 2001, from http://caspar/nsf.gov/.
34. National Science Foundation. (2001). Sheet 08180820: Unre-
     stricted and restricted fund types 1987–1996. *WebCASPAR Database
     System*. Retrieved August 5, 2001, from http://caspar/nsf.gov/.
35. Chronicle of Higher Education. (1992). "Spring Garden College
     Fails to Meet Payroll," *Chronicle of Higher Education*. Retrieved Sep-
     tember 19, 2008, from http://chronicle.com/che-data/articles.
     dir/articles-36.dir/issue-38.dir/38a00203.htm.
36. van der Werf, M. (2002). "Marycrest International University
     Will Shut Down at the End of Spring Semester," *Chronicle of Higher
     Education*. Retrieved September 16, 2008, from http://chronicle.
     com/weekly/v48/i18/18a03601.htm.
37. Ibid.
38. Ibid.
39. Ibid.
40. van der Werf, M. (2002). "Mount Senario's final act," *Chronicle of
     Higher Education*. Retrieved September 16, 2008, from http://
     chronicle.com/weekly/v48/i40/40a02401.htm.
41. Ibid.
42. Ibid.
43. Ibid.

44. Ibid.

45. Ibid.

46. Ibid.

47. Ibid.

48. van der Werf, M. (2002). "Mount Senario College Will Close," *Chronicle of Higher Education*. Retrieved September 16, 2008, from http://chronicle.com/weekly/v48/i36/36a03502.htm.

49. van der Werf, M. (2002). "Mount Senario's Final Act," *Chronicle of Higher Education*. Retrieved September 16, 2008, from http://chronicle.com/weekly/v48/i40/40a02401.htm.

50. Chronicle of Higher Education. (1991). "Board Votes to Shut Down Nazareth College," *Chronicle of Higher Education*. Retrieved November 14, 2008, from http://chronicle.com/che-data/articles-37.dir/issue-29.dir/29a00302.htm.

51. Williams, A. V. (2001). "Notre Dame College of New Hampshire Will Shut Down" *Chronicle of Higher Education*. Retrieved September 17, 2008, from http://chronicle.com/weekly/v48/i16/16a02801.htm.

52. Gravois, J. (2004). "William Tyndale College to Close Its Doors," *Chronicle of Higher Education*. Retrieved September 12, 2008, from http://chronicle.com/weekly/v51/i15/15a02702.htm.

53. Fischer, K. (2007). "Small Alaska College Suspends Operations," *Chronicle of Higher Education*. Retrieved September 12, 2008, from http://chronicle.com/weekly/v53/i45/45a02403.htm.

54. Nelson, John (Senior Vice President, Moody's Investors Service), personal interview, New York, August 7, 2001.

55. National Center of Education Statistics. (2007). Table 187: Total fall enrollment in degree-granting institutions, by attendance status, sex of student, and type and control of institution: Selected years, 1970 through 2005. In *Digest of education statistics*. Retrieved February 25, 2009, from http://nces.ed.gov/programs/digest/d07/tables_3.asp.

CHAPTER 12

HOW PRIVATE COLLEGES TURN AROUND AND FLOURISH

"A specter is haunting higher education: the specter of decline and bankruptcy." In 1980, George Keller opened his book, *Academic Strategy*, with that line.[1] The specter looked real then, owing to the end of the Baby Boom. Now, ominous changes in demographics, the delivery of courses, and financial markets are cause for predictions that financially fragile, tuition-dependent colleges or universities may not survive for long. Yet, there are private institutions that reached the brink but then carried out a successful turnaround. This chapter looks at several colleges that stared down the "the specter of decline and bankruptcy" and lived to tell about it. If the previous chapter left you wondering whether there is any hope for small or financially fragile, tuition-dependent colleges, let the struggles and successes of this chapter reassure you. These colleges prove that with hard work, decline and financial distress do not have to mean bankruptcy or closure.

Inherent in each story are themes of vigilance, leadership, and wise financial planning. Colleges exist in a precarious education market. Without caution, agility, and steady guidance, many would fall to competitors or to a volatile economic climate. Think of financial distress as a vast pool of quicksand with the path around it poorly marked. The unwary traveler missteps and disappears. The foolish traveler tries to take a shortcut and disappears. Even the experienced traveler, having avoided the quicksand before, traipses along not carefully enough and disappears. Recall that credible sources thought Bradford College in Massachusetts or Upsala in New Jersey had made successful turnarounds; but within a short time, thanks in large part to foolhardy guidance, these colleges sunk.[2]

Now, we look at several colleges that did conduct successful financial turnarounds and have continued to flourish long after the turnaround. It is not impossible to do this; but what it takes, as will become evident, is the vision, leadership, and tenacity of the president. Everything else pales in comparison. Others may help, but it is the president who makes the turnaround happen, and it is the president who pushes the college to flourish and not slip back into financial instability.

There are six case studies that offer insight and lessons on what it takes to do a turnaround that flourishes. These institutions are Wesley College in Dover, Delaware; Georgetown College in Lexington, Kentucky; Marylhurst College in Portland, Oregon; Nichols College* in Dudley, Massachusetts; Wilmington University in New Castle, Delaware; and Gwynedd-Mercy College in Gwynedd Valley, Pennsylvania. It is interesting that two of these institutions are located in Delaware; but each one took a different path toward the turnaround, and each has flourished in its own way.

WESLEY COLLEGE

Wesley College is the oldest private college in Delaware, the proud first state of our nation.[†] Located in Dover, one of the premier pre-Revolutionary cities on the East Coast, Wesley is within walking distance of many pre-Revolutionary war homes, such as the Gov-

---

*The author needs to disclose that he is the husband of the president of Nichols College. This college was included in the set because it made a turnaround from a very low point and was near the brink of survival when the president came on board. This was more than 10 years ago, and the college has grown, strengthened its finances, and is recognized in Massachusetts for the quality of its academic programs and the leadership of the president.

†In addition to interviews with Dr. Miller on August 10, 2001, E-mails were exchanged with Dr. Miller on July 31 and August 3, 2008. Other information about Wesley College came from *Wesley Today* (Winter 2007), pages 18–23.

ernor's Residence, Woodburn Mansion. Caesar Rodney, the first signer of the Constitution, came from Dover. Another signer of the Constitution, John Dickinson, lived on one of many old plantations within driving distance of the college. Delaware is the only state east of the Mason-Dixon line; and like other southern cities, it has retained a southern flair.

The president of Wesley College at the time of the turnaround was Scott Miller. He does not fit the stereotype of the "slower Delawarean," however. A fast-paced leader, he assumed control of the moribund college in 1997. His rare energy was a powerful asset to a college that was at one time sinking rather quickly into financial oblivion.*

By 1997, Wesley had barely survived enrollment shrinkage of more than 20 percent.[3] In response to questionable terminations, former faculty members had filed lawsuits against the college and its former president, an overbearing preacher notorious for meeting dissension with fire and brimstone. A new college nearby sought to usurp the continuing education market, which had been keeping Wesley afloat. Until 1997, the college had survived rough patches through the beneficence of the United Methodist Church (John Wesley himself had founded Barratt's Chapel just down the road). But willing friends were becoming wary of backing Wesley. The blows from low enrollments, bad leadership, lawsuits, and competitors were apparent on campus, where even buildings were beginning to look downtrodden. Rumors were spreading and bets were accumulating about how long it would be before the college had to merge to survive.

Enter Dr. Miller. He found the money to settle the lawsuits and to begin building renovations. He gained the favor of the powerful Gannett paper, *The News Journal*, which championed his efforts to change Wesley's image. The newspaper was instrumental in establishing Wesley as a leader in Dover. Wealthy benefactors began to open their doors in response to the good press. (What good press it was— one of Wesley's generous donors happens to be the chairman of the

---

*Sitting across a desk from Dr. Miller during my first interview, listening to his untempered enthusiasm, I almost expected him to leap over the desk, and me, on his way to construct a new building.

board of Wesley's most formidable competitor!) But completing the small college's transformation from penury to prestige would take more than facelifts and testimonials. Dr. Miller meant business.

After making his splash, Dr. Miller moved ahead with his long-term strategy. Enrollment grew by more than doubling (617 to 1,500) in the traditional programs, building a powerful revenue base. Wesley no longer needed to troll for applicants. Dr. Miller narrowed Wesley's market by gearing advertising toward students with strong academic backgrounds and adequate financial resources. The numbers bear out that those students tend to complete their coursework. Wesley's retention rate rose to 88 percent.

Another factor in boosting Wesley's revenue has been Dr. Miller's initiation of a feeder system. In partnership with the Boys & Girls Club of Delaware, Wesley invites 400 high school students to use the campus for their various activities. In addition to the revenue that offsets the cost of using campus buildings, Wesley benefits from having potential students actively engaged on its campus. The second feeder channel is the charter school developed on campus in 1998, enrolling 300 students in grades 1 through 8 and another 400 students enrolling in a high school component that opened in 2001.

A third facet of Dr. Miller's strategy was the establishment of an ancillary campus for students in upper Delaware. The site is within a mile of the very college that sought to lure continuing education students away from Wesley's main campus. At its peak, more than 600 adult students enrolled at its off-campus center, generating nearly $3 million in operating revenue. (The competing college, by the way, has begun construction of a large campus on the main thoroughfare in Dover. Sometimes tit-for-tat can get out of hand.)

Dr. Miller also found creative ways to fund the college's debt. He employed off-balance-sheet financing to cover the cost of new construction. Of course, the cost of financing does not disappear; rather, it is replaced by finance charges, the goal being to generate enough revenue from the construction to compensate for such. But even if enrollments decline, Dr. Miller had a backup plan for the new buildings. One such building, a "wellness hall" with suite-style student housing, underground parking, a modern fitness center, laundry facilities, and the like, doubles as a conference center when classes are not in session. Another facility was designed for alternative use as offices or housing, in which case rents will offset the construction costs.

Another facet of Dr. Miller's leadership involved synergistic partnerships that added two facilities: the historic Schwartz Center for the Performing Arts in downtown Dover (jointly owned by Wesley, Friends of the Old Capital Theatre, and Delaware State University) and Barratt's Chapel and Museum (the "cradle of Methodism" in the United States), which is a learning laboratory for students.

Wesley College's turnaround can be attributed largely to Dr. Miller's energy and informed creativity. His aggressive problem-solving approaches have transformed Wesley from a directionless campus mired in controversy into a well-respected regional institution, and his sound judgment regarding markets and financing have rebuilt its distressed financial structure. Despite the risk of Dr. Miller's turnaround strategy, Wesley's liabilities as a proportion of assets jumped from 33 percent to nearly 43 percent over three years; but he used debt judiciously to build revenue, not to finance pipe dreams.

During his tenure at Wesley, Dr. Miller is credited with tripling the college's overall enrollment, doubling its endowment, increasing alumni participation from 5 percent to 29 percent, and raising $67 million (including more than $40 million for new construction) toward a strategic 10-year master plan. Significant growth was accompanied by major improvements in quality as the college earned top-tier regional rankings from *U.S. News and World Report* during his last four years.

After 10 years as president of Wesley, Dr. Miller took on new challenges in December 2007 as president of Bethany College (in West Virginia). At Bethany, a selective liberal arts college, he is expected to bring the same work ethic, creativity, and reputation as an "idea man" that he exhibited at Wesley and previously as president and executive vice president of Lincoln Memorial University in Tennessee.

GEORGETOWN COLLEGE

Like many colleges on American frontiers, Georgetown has religious roots.* The Kentucky Baptist Education Society opened the college in the winter of 1830 and chartered it in 1859. In keeping with the period, Georgetown offered a liberal arts education based on the classics, but it distinguished itself by offering academic and cultural blends of northeastern and southern influences. During the Civil War, the college closed as Kentucky became one of the early battleground states. Until the middle of the 20th century, Georgetown remained a liberal arts college. After offering its first professional degree in the 1950s, enrollment grew and so did the campus.

But enrollment began to decline in the 1990s, and it declined quickly. From 1990 to 1993, enrollments dropped 15 percent, from 1,595 to 1,370.[4] As enrollment plunged, deficits grew, a combination that inspired Georgetown's board to seek new leadership. In 1994, when Dr. Bill Crouch arrived, he set four goals for the institution and set about immediately to convince the board, the faculty, the students, and alumni that Georgetown could be the best college in its competitive niche.

First, he would modernize plant and equipment. Second, he would fatten the endowment fund that would support efforts to entice the best students. Third, he would instill the fiscal discipline the college would need to maintain financial stability. Fourth, he would improve faculty pay in recognition of the faculty's contribution to the college and in anticipation of hiring other high-caliber instructors. Bill Crouch, rising to one of George Keller's leadership standards, is a "quality monger."[5]

Dr. Crouch is well aware that small liberal arts colleges with limited endowments are struggling to find new sources of revenue. Some liberal arts college leaders have changed their mission from a liberal arts residential college to one with an emphasis on adult education and off-campus sites. They have taken this route so that they could improve their competitive position vis-à-vis proprietary

---

* The information on Georgetown was gleaned from correspondence with the president, college publications, and national databases.

schools. The leadership of Georgetown College took a different direction. They remain committed to their core mission while creating an exciting environment, which enables them to recruit a student population with the means to pay higher tuition rates with smaller tuition discounts.

Now, as Dr. Crouch moves into the second decade of his presidency, he has refined his strategy by fostering exciting new programs, building a diverse student population, and finding new overseas markets. This strategy is expected to carry the college into the next decade by sustaining enrollment, nurturing quality, and keeping the college financially strong.

His first step in the revised strategy led to the launching of the Programs of Distinction that include these three professional development programs for undergraduate students: Equine Scholars, Global Scholars, and First Tee Scholars (a partnership with the Professional Golfers' Association). The positive impact of these programs for the college is illustrated by the Equine Scholars. It enrolls 54 students from 12 states; 50 percent of these students have ACT scores higher than the average student. In addition, the institutional aid awards for these students are smaller because their financial need is less than the average. Another major initiative was the expansion of the graduate education program, which has grown to more than 500 students.

As a solid turnaround strategist, the president took steps to respond quickly to impending changes in demographics. In 2006, the college introduced a new recruitment strategy that significantly increased minority enrollment. Key to this strategy was a partnership with alumni at Bishop College, a historically black college in Dallas, Texas, that went bankrupt in 1988. Georgetown established a Bishop College Scholars program for alumni legacies so that they could enroll at Georgetown College. This strengthened enrollment and put the college in a position to improve its student diversity.

Letting no stone go unturned, the college partnered with the United States Equestrian Federation and the Kentucky Horse Park to create the United Nations of the Horse. They expect 2,000 young people from around the world to live on campus, participate in English as a second language classes, ride horses in the afternoon, and then take part in a Global Community program at night. The president sees this program as building international recognition while it provides a new enrollment feeder stream. It even has the potential of attracting new donors.

These are topsy-turvy days for small enrollment and endowed colleges. Georgetown's lesson is that college presidents have to be creative. What works today may fail tomorrow, or someone else could copy the idea with new twists and take your market. Presidents must keep their nose to the wind to figure out how the market is changing. Complacency is a disastrous frame of mind for struggling private colleges that think they have successfully made a turnaround. They must continue to be smart and creative risk takers. Georgetown College believes that this has put it on the right track.

MARYLHURST COLLEGE

In 1859, the Sisters of the Holy Names of Jesus and Mary followed Richard Henry Dana's route to the West through the treacherous currents of Cape Horn.* Their mission was to offer God's services to the pioneering women who had made the long wagon trip to Oregon. As entrepreneurs of the Catholic Church in Oregon, the Sisters established orphanages, a school for girls, and St. Mary's Academy in Portland. In 1893, St. Mary's began to offer bachelor's degrees, which was a leap forward for women's education in Oregon. The nuns, having succeeded in providing affordable education to women, eventually moved their academy in 1930 to Marylhurst, a suburb overlooking the city of Portland.

The Sisters offered their services to schools and colleges like Marylhurst at no cost. They required only shelter, food, and the opportunity to serve and educate young people (in this case young Marylhurst women) according to the teachings of the Church. Orders like the Sisters of the Holy Names of Jesus and Mary were

*Marylhurst College information came from college publications, an interview with president Nancy Wilgenbusch on August 28, 2001, an extensive article about the president and the college in *University Business* (April 2000, 3(3), 34–39), and from "Wilgenbusch will retire at Marylhurst" in the *Lake Oswego Review* (http://www.lakeoswegoreview.com/news/story.php?story_id=118177215379459500).

the bedrock of Catholic education until the changes wrought in the 1960s. The Vatican II, a growing feminist movement, and the general social upheaval of the times drained religious orders. Young sisters embarked on journeys of self-discovery, leaving convents to the care of older nuns.

As nuns retired from educational service and retreated to their convents, student pools in the feeder schools dwindled as female students moved to larger coeducational colleges and universities to complete their educations. Marylhurst, having lost most of its students *and* its inexpensive yet most experienced labor source, the nuns, eventually closed as a women's school. Later, under the direction of a lay board, the college reopened as a coeducational college with no tenured faculty.

Marylhurst's coed reincarnation did not significantly increase its fortunes, however. Enrollment continued to stagnate with most students attending part-time. As deficits mounted, the threat of default on federal loans forced the college to look outside the order for a new leader. They selected Nancy Wilgenbusch, dean of continuing education and vice president of marketing at St. Mary's in Omaha, Nebraska.*

Dr. Wilgenbusch found Marylhurst in disarray; its buildings and grounds seedy from years of neglect; its curriculum a veritable hodgepodge. Students had customized degrees on whims, stretching personal service to its limit; and the students, along with Marylhurst's reputation, were suffering for the abuse. It would take a miracle to reverse damage to finances, to the campus, and to the educational system, and Marylhurst turned to Dr. Wilgenbusch for a sign of just that.

Fortunately for the college, it found a president with the same spirit, loyalty, and straightforwardness that Marylhurst's founding nuns had projected. Wilgenbusch set about changing Marylhurst's image, a task that initially involved convincing many Portlanders, who thought the college closed sometime during the 1970s, that it was indeed open. Dr. Wilgenbusch spoke to any civic or service group that

---

*Dr. Wilgenbusch retired in the spring of 2008 after serving 23 years as president. Her story is included because she provided wonderful insight into the management of a difficult turnaround when she was interviewed in 2001.

TABLE 12-1—WILGENBUSCH'S RULES

1. Mission determines finances.
2. Knowledge is power.
3. Inflation caps tuition.
4. Tuition discounting must be kept in check.
5. Gifts are dangerous.
6. Budgets are promises.

Source: Feemster, R. (2000). Faith in financials. *University Business, 3(3), 39.*

would have her, eventually generating gifts enough to begin sprucing up the campus. Beyond inspiring donations, Dr. Wilgenbusch's public engagements led to business alliances that would later bring new revenue streams to the college.

Dr. Wilgenbusch's overall strategy went way beyond face-lifting Marylhurst. She hired the very best faculty members and administrators (her vice president of finances and facilities came from Stanford University). She streamlined Marylhurst's curriculum, accompanying any changes to it with new brochures and view books that emphasized the link between courses, degrees, and the student market. Dr. Wilgenbusch used the six principles listed in Table 12.1 as her guide during the turnaround.

The most interesting rule is that "gifts are dangerous." According to her, excess reliance on gifts can place a college at risk when gifts dry up.[6] Small or moderate-sized colleges that depend on substantial gifts from a single benefactor can be at considerable risk. Also, many small gifts from middle-income families can evaporate during periods of economic disruption.

She made every part of the college financially accountable. Departments that proposed new instructional programs had to file a business plan that showed expected return on investment. Also, the finance office tracked fiscal performance of each department in terms of its contribution to the college's margin. When an instructional department reported a decline in enrollment or margin, it had to file a report explaining the problem and proposing a solution. The department was held accountable for the implementation of its turnaround plan.

Dr. Wilgenbusch expected every asset to perform to its maximum. Rooms or buildings that were empty part of the week were leased to outside organizations, maintaining a revenue stream in the absence of direct educational service. She further bolstered revenue by identifying holes in the marketplace and developing relevant new programs to fill them. Despite fears of enrollment or margin declines caused by competition between new and existing programs and despite the risk of profit sharing (inherent whenever a college contributes significant resources to a new program), enrollment rose substantially under Dr. Wilgenbusch's guidance.

Wilgenbusch delivered on her miraculous intentions to bring Marylhurst out of the red and into the black; however, she faced criticism for her efficiency. Some faculty members thought that she ran the college too much like a business, a complaint commonly directed at presidents after they overhaul a troubled academic institution. The faculty prefer the *benefits* of the structured approach, yet they would prefer the lack of accountability inherent in the good old days of lax financial procedures and self-serving administrative standards. They forget the penury wrought by those years.

Decision making in a vacuum of faculty and student interests exemplifies Michael Cohen and James March's famed "garbage can model,"[7] which likens collegial decision making to a manipulative game that rarely serves academic interests. Large, rich, private universities may be able to afford the waste of resources associated with a full-blown collegial decision system wherein precious time and energy are invested alternatively listening and arguing, and obstructing and conceding, but small colleges cannot. Their resources are too dear and their financial condition is too fragile to wait for faculty egos to reach consensus.

Dr. Wilgenbusch, although she ascribed to the philosophy that leaders ought to be accessible to their front-liners, steadfastly demanded that all parts of Marylhurst be held accountable for their actions. Concerns about new projects should lead to adaptation, not to prolonged consideration by many, and certainly not to a sapping monopolization of a president's time and energy. Dr. Wilgenbusch balanced leadership of a small college with concern for its faculty and community. For example, she built up pay and support for full-time and part-time Marylhurst employees. Her overall success gained far-reaching recognition. Marylhurst won several awards including the Best Practices award from the Council for Adult and Experiential Learning, as well as a Best Value award from *U.S. News and World Report*.

NICHOLS COLLEGE

Nichols College was not a pretty picture when Debra Townsley became president in 1998.[*†] She found 10 years of deficits, declining enrollments, and deteriorating infrastructure. As she said in a NACUBO *Business Officer* article in 2004, "When deficits are growing and investments are declining, the time available to manage a turnaround is short." If there is one truism in turnarounds, it is that statement. Turnarounds are not necessary if the college is on solid footing. However, turnarounds are necessary if everyone ignores the problem until events and reality force recognition. Then, it takes someone with the wit and wisdom to pull off the turnaround.

From 1989 to 1998, enrollment declined 28 percent and deficits averaged $1.5 million per year.[8] Yet tough decisions had not been made to cut staff as one tactic to control the downward spiral of the college. The college kept deficits from eating the entire budget by ignoring the deteriorating condition of its plant and grounds. However, there was a cost to pay because it no longer had the charm of a college located on a square in a quaint little village in central Massachusetts. The college and the town had become dreary, beat-up, and unsightly as a place to learn or to live. No wonder visiting high

*The information for this section comes from an article by Debra M. (Murphy) Townsley and Susan K. Tellier, "Financial About-Face," *Business Officer*, July 2004; a presentation made at the New England Association of Schools and Colleges (NEASC) annual meeting in December 2005; and discussions with Dr. Townsley and Ms. Tellier.

†Debra Townsley, as noted earlier, is married to the author. The turnaround and her success at maintaining its momentum occurred prior to meeting the author.

TABLE 12.2—TOWNSLEY STRATEGIC PLANKS

1. Develop a doable plan.
2. Look inward.
3. Reach outward.
4. Review your operations.
5. Manage your money.
6. Reassess your human assets.
7. Factor in further growth.

school seniors scurried out of town, choosing colleges that did not have a depressed appearance. Worse than the past was the future: the new president and vice president for finance discovered that the budget was based on an "alarmingly unrealistic enrollment projection."[9] When the enrollment estimates and budget were corrected, it turned out that the original $1.5 million deficit had jumped to a $3.6 million deficit, which represented 36 percent of the budgeted revenue. Clearly, this was no ordinary deficit; it was disaster staring in the face of the new president. She and her management team would not have the luxury of a honeymoon. They had to act immediately or watch the financial condition collapse in short order.

So, what was the strategy that Dr. Townsley used to address an impending catastrophe? Her approach was based on that rarest of attributes—common sense! The underlying strategic principles that led to the turnaround and laid the groundwork for long-term growth are listed in Table 12.2.

Here is how her strategic planks were used to build a successful turnaround. The first plank, "develop a doable plan," meant that they had to construct a five-year model to figure out where they needed to concentrate their effort to gin-up the turnaround. They estimated that it would take four years to start producing surpluses, but they got there two years early.[10] The budget strategy was realistically designed so that it did not overpromise and underdeliver; it worked the other way. Real performance meant that they exceeded their goals, which fostered their credibility with the board.

The second plank, "look inward," involved a careful review and revision of the mission so that it matched the possibilities available to the college. This plank included "paying attention to your curb appeal."[11] As the president noted, because students and parents lack an easy tool for assessing quality, they turn to the attractiveness of the plant as a proxy for quality.[12]

The features of the third plank, "reach outward," required "friend raising" and new market development. Friend raising is a necessary element in rebuilding alumni and donor trust. This must continue beyond the initial turnaround stage because it lays the groundwork for the future. Rebuilding the commitment of friends of the college is the most time-consuming task that the president will have. Trust relies on personal relationships; a phone call, e-mail, or newsletters are not enough. A turnaround needs more than a fund-raising strategy because initially no one will want to make the large commitments needed to sustain a college in dire financial straits. The president, according to Dr. Townsley, must be the catalyst for pursuing new markets that have a greater chance of generating the big money needed to restore financial stability.[13] In addition, the college needs to cut programs that are no longer financially viable. Some people will be upset by the cuts, but a weak college cannot afford to subsidize programs that cost more than they deliver. The last element in this plank is not to ignore student retention. There is often a ready pool of students who leave a weak college without finishing their degrees. Go after them and show them why it makes sense to complete their degree during the turnaround. Retention also involves seeing to it that the students who enroll stay until they get their degrees. It costs too much in new financial aid and admissions efforts to find replacements. Provide the services and the incentives to convince students that it makes sense to stay and graduate.

Dr. Townsley assiduously pursued both elements of friend-raising and new markets. This plank laid the basis for the big turnaround because Nichols added new programs in sports management and criminal justice management. As she notes, some initiatives will fizzle, but a president during a turnaround must remain upbeat, must press on, and must continue to be market savvy.

The fourth plank, "review your operations," is the flip side of looking for new revenue. The college must "right size" itself to its revenue and increase its operating efficiency. Cut administrative costs where they are redundant; eliminate services that do not directly benefit the students or the college; get rid of unused assets; and rent until you can afford to buy.[14] This is where leadership is salient if a president can be sympathetic to the pain, but realistically understand that he or she has to get the costs of operations down. It is not easy; people will fight to protect their jobs, their tradition, and their hopes, but none of this justifies driving the college over the cliff. The first loyalty of the college is to its students and its alumni so that a viable institution continues and provides them with valid degrees that will enhance their life.

The fifth plank, "manage your money," is intuitively obvious but not always carried out. Managing your money involves preserving investment capital, instituting departmental accountability for budgets, and using consortiums.[15] Turnarounds are always tempted to use long-term investment funds to cover the rough patches, which is a bad idea, regardless of whether it is a short-term panacea or a long-term strategy. Spending down investments removes any protective reserves. Also, replacing spent capital is very expensive. It will take $20 to $25 for every dollar of capital used for current expenses. The high cost is because of the prudent investor rule that limits investment draws in the future to this range. Avoid doing this at all costs. Making departments accountable is serious business because the president will be inundated with pleas, bargains, and sad stories. The purpose of accountability is to make people understand that they cannot ignore the money side of their responsibility or treat it as trivial. Keeping to the rules during the turnaround is tough, but necessary, and will prove valuable for all concerned. Consortiums are money savers if they are used correctly. There are information technology, library, purchasing, and other types of consortiums. A struggling college can join them to cut the cost of operations and yet still buy the supplies or services that are needed. Why own a multi-million-dollar IT system when the college can share the cost with a half dozen other institutions? It not only also reduces costs, but it cuts risk because weak colleges lack the resources to run a smoothly operating IT system on a 24-hour-per-day cycle.

The sixth plank, "reassign your human assets," is where the fur begins to fly.[16] A turnaround requires that the college employ the right number of faculty given its enrollment. Too many faculty and too few students is a luxury that is too rich for tuition-paying students. Operational efficiency requires that the president and senior administrators of the college evaluate the number of staff and their pay and find the best and least expensive organizational structure to do the work. There is one place where stinting on human talent is counterproductive and that is in skilled positions. Hire the best and pay them what they are worth. They will do the work of many but do it skillfully. Last, the hardest nut to keep cracked is fringe benefits because cost savings this year are often absorbed by big increases from third-party insurers the next year. The president has to see that the benefits do not swamp the college with huge costs. Yet it is only fair that employees have reasonable protection for health and retirement benefits.

The last plank, "factor in further growth," is based on the proposition that if you can get the turnaround moving, then do not simply hold the institution to the downward spiral. Work the plans so that they move upward to achieve big changes in the financial condition. What matters is upward momentum. Once that is achieved, go for the big change because by now the college has set in place the mechanisms to grow and prosper. If the president takes small steps on the way up, then the college may well be swept back into a shaky financial condition. Take reasonable risks in planning and make them happen. The college community wants the president's plans to succeed so that it can escape the dreary hand-to-mouth state in which it has existed.

Nichols represents a story that must be recognized because it came back from the brink to live again and grow into a credible institution recognized for its quality. Wilmington College is the next big story because it was not at the brink;* it was sliding into oblivion in 1981. A unique set of circumstances saved it and has propelled the institution into one of the great turnaround stories of the last two decades.

*Wilmington College in Delaware is now Wilmington University.

WILMINGTON COLLEGE (UNIVERSITY)

Wilmington could be the most interesting turnaround story in higher education.[*] In 1981, when the nascent pieces of the turnaround began to come together, the college had a negative net asset position with little cash.[†] The only thing going for it, which was not a minor advantage, was a chairman of the board who was willing to cover cash flow shortages. However, he had reached a point where the college had no forward momentum; his cash gifts simply disappeared into a rat hole. He asked the president to figure out in two years whether the college was worth preserving. If not, close it down.

Fortunately, Wilmington had by pure chance happened on a strategy of survival during the last two years of the late 1970s. The strategy was relatively simple: target adults who wanted to complete their degree and charge a common tuition rate for day or evening classes. This provided students with the chance to take only those classes that fit into their busy work schedules. The tuition strategy, combined with a payment plan similar to a credit card, opened the flood gates to new students. Within a short time, enrollment began to grow at a double-digit rate, and by 1992, the college no longer needed a cash gift from the chairman to subsidize operations.

The major refinements in the financial strategy have been to limit price increases, keep financial aid to the bare minimum (less than 5 percent of tuition), and add new programs or sites every year. This strategy turned Wilmington College into a nonprofit version of the University of Phoenix. By 2001, the college had grown to 7,000 students from a headcount of 700 students in 1981. In the fall of 2007, enrollment was about 11,000 students, and the strategy continued intact. The college has done this without selling out its academic quality, as evidenced by its high marks from the Middle States Association of Colleges and Universities. The strategy is not difficult to make work. What is difficult is breaking the mold that imprisons colleges in unworkable traditions.

---

[*]The information on Wilmington College comes from its XXV Anniversary publications and interviews with Dr. Jack Varsalona, the current president.
[†]Negative net assets mean that there were more liabilities than assets.

TABLE 12.3—WILMINGTON COLLEGE'S BIG PLAN

1. Add new programs or sites every year.
2. Do not increase tuition at a rate higher than the rate of inflation.
3. Do not use financial aid as a means of reducing price.
4. Aggressively go after colleges in the same geographic area.
5. Use adjunct faculty during the massive increases in enrollment.
6. Use full-time faculty to supervise adjunct faculty closely.
7. Quickly add new academic programs in response to the market.
8. Eliminate programs that no longer respond to the market.
9. Make the new programs work—leadership is everything!

Wilmington had a strategic troika: the president, Dr. Audrey Doberstein; the provost, Dr. Jack Varsalona;[*] and Dr. Michael Townsley,[†] the senior vice president. Table 12.3 lays out the basic strategic elements that got Wilmington College to the place where it is today (just be advised that this strategy is not a universal recipe for success).

Wilmington University is a special case among not-for-profit institutions because it aggressively pursues academic quality, continuously evaluates its academic programs, develops new markets, and sets reasonable tuition rates. Its success is illustrative of a higher education model that can successfully compete with for-profits and maintain its academic integrity. Any college can settle for mediocrity, but these colleges will be forced to respond constantly to competition. The Wilmington model is a strategy for pushing others to respond aggressively.

GWYNEDD-MERCY COLLEGE

In 1861, the Sisters of Mercy arrived in Philadelphia.[§] The nuns were called the "walking nuns" because their vows did not require them

---

[*] Dr. Jack Varsalona is the current president at Wilmington University (née College).

[†] This is the same person as the author.

[§] The information for Gwynedd-Mercy was taken from information provided by the president in addition to contact over several months with faculty and administrators during intensive strategic planning sessions.

to live a cloistered existence. They agreed to come to Philadelphia if they could immediately offer their works for the sick, poor, and uneducated, including immigrant women and children and the wounded of the then-ongoing Civil War.

The Sisters established Gwynedd-Mercy College (GMC) as a junior college for women. It was rechartered as a coeducational, baccalaureate-granting institution in 1965. In the early 1980s, the college offered its first graduate programs. In 2001, the board of trustees defined its expectations for a new president with strong support from the Sisters of Mercy to appoint the college's first lay president.

Kathleen Owens was appointed in 2002 as the current and first lay president. She offered strong presidential leadership and employed strategic thinking, planning, and good governance to enable the college to flourish and grow. She clearly understood "the vision thing" and recognized that the strategic plan would serve as the tool to actualize the vision. Through a year-long process, the president engaged the college community and the board in shaping the college's then-evolving strategic agenda. In June 2004, the board voiced unanimous support for the college's vision and its realistic guide to action.

Just as the board was open to the appointment of a lay president, the time was right to consider appointing a lay board chair. Throughout its history, the superior of the religious community automatically served as board chair. In collaboration with then-board chair Sister Christine McCann, and with an explicit hiring expectation for the president to guide and assist the board to become a more effective governing and leadership body, Owens initiated a process to gain trustee ownership of a new governing model. Over a many month period, the board introduced significant change, including election of its own chair (resulting in the appointment of the first lay chair), reduction of board seats allocated to the religious community, a new executive committee structure, a new committee on governance and trustees, new board evaluation protocols, and much more.

Dr. Owens, with the support of the board of trustees, introduced a new governance model that delineated responsibilities for each of the governing partners. The president sought to focus on faculty and academic excellence and to reintroduce tenure-track faculty appointments that had been suspended since the mid-1990s. In a collaborative process involving board members, faculty, and administrators, Owens appointed a task force to make recommendations that were consistent with best practices to promote academic excellence through recruiting, developing, and maintaining the highest-quality faculty while focusing and supporting faculty commitment to mission, students, other stakeholders, and one another. The faculty agreed to work with definitions of faculty excellence and academic excellence, more rigorous faculty evaluation processes, post-tenure review protocol, more rigorous criteria for awarding tenure, and new multiyear contract options. Subsequently, the similarly constituted Faculty Salary Plan Task Force led to implementation of a market and longevity-influenced salary structure. As a devotee of Jim Collins and his *Good to Great* mantra, Owens got the right people on and the wrong people off the bus and persistently used a hedgehog-like approach to focus the ongoing activities of the institution around the strategic plan.

After nearly 20 years with little or no changes to the curricula, the faculty approved a new general education/core curriculum and first-year experience program. The new curriculum includes faculty-inspired and -designed signature courses; a curricular and cocurricular sequence for all first-year students, including a required service learning experience; and a capstone experience for upper-class students. This new vision was designed to prepare "distinctive Mercy graduates."

Through the addition of new programs and facilities, all delineated in the strategic plan, college enrollment grew by 25 percent to more than 2,800 students in 2008. New residence halls helped transition Gwynedd-Mercy from a primarily commuter college to a more traditional residential campus. The most recent hall, a 205-bed facility, opened in 2006 and is now filled to capacity, bringing total residential enrollment to more than 600. More new housing is anticipated for 2009. New facilities also addressed the unique needs of working adults, such as a campus in Center City Philadelphia where working adults have easy access to evening classes, offered in an adult-friendly format, and in an environment supported by the appropriate and necessary resources.

A nearly completed athletic complex, including a state-of-the-art synthetic turf field surrounded by an eight-lane track and various related structures, has strengthened the college's commitment to NCAA Division III athletics, while simultaneously enabling the college to achieve its goals for growth in full-time undergraduate residential students and gender and geographic diversity among undergraduates.

"*To put students first*" and "*be wise stewards of our resources,*" the college established the Campbell Solution Center, a one-stop shop designed to answer questions and solve problems for students. To staff the center, already existing positions were morphed into student-support-specialist positions, and individuals were cross-trained in all areas. The right vice presidents got the center up and running in Fall 2008 with great support from key personnel.

The administrative team has introduced the use of key financial ratios, meaningful dashboard indicators, multiyear budget projections, multiyear revenue center data profiles, market force factors, and other tools into the yearly budget process. Moreover, the timing of yearly tuition adjustment decisions has been separated from annual compensation discussions. Owens's ability to use data wisely to illustrate issues and make meaningful comparisons has proven to be a powerful leadership tool.

The president has used fund-raising to complement the tuition strategies of the college. Fund raising has three priorities: (1) a much-needed (and planned) academic building to house the School of Education, (2) growth of the college's endowment, and (3) special projects to enhance the student-life experience for the college's growing residential population.

As Gwynedd-Mercy College continues to grow and evolve in relation to its Catholic and Mercy identity, it is clear that the leadership provided by its first lay president and now second lay board chair is proportional to the vision and spirit of the college's founders, the Sisters of Mercy. What once was a junior college is now a master's-level institution with a strong foundation in the liberal arts. GMC's academic distinction lies in the intersection of excellent programs in health care, education, and business administration, which prepare students to become leaders in the region's powerful and growing life-sciences industry. Gwynedd-Mercy is an excellent example of the importance of presidential leadership in generating change and making the change work. Dr. Owens brought a finely tuned ability to recognize the strengths and needs of her institution, while being aware of what needed to happen to convince faculty, administrators, and staff to accept major governance and strategic changes to the institution.

FLOURISHING TURNAROUNDS: BASIC PRINCIPLES

A turnaround is possible and it will flourish when the board, president, and alumni recognize that the president must construct a vibrant relationship from mission, to services, to markets, to price. Why is this relationship of any importance? It is important because mission defines what the college can do and do successfully. The mission leads to services that the market demands at a price that students are willing to pay. When this relationship is recognized, the college has significantly improved its chance of devising a successful turnaround.

A TURNAROUND STRATEGY

The specifics of the turnaround plan ought to be well defined and tested against established financial principles. From Georgetown to Marylhurst to Wesley to Nichols to Wilmington College to Gwynedd-Mercy, all the presidents in our stories spoke to the rigor of a successful financial strategy. Dr. Crouch of Georgetown and Dr. Wilgenbusch of Marylhurst exemplify the savvy financial mentor, both coming to their colleges with clear plans to embolden slackened financial structures. Crouch also clearly shows that once the turnaround is achieved, the competitive position of the college is not to be ignored. He, like other presidents who successfully make a turnaround, recognized that private colleges must continually press for change and quickly respond to threats in the marketplace. Anything less can push the college back to a state of financial instability where it exists at the brink of its demise.

First, a president must ensure that he or she can rebuild working assets and donor goodwill as the college transitions from penury to prestige. Without enough capital to get the ball rolling, a financial strategy will amount to no more than good intentions and perhaps a merger or a closure. Second, a president must identify a viable market (see Nichols College). An isolated campus without an enrollment pool won't make much of a turnaround. Third, and not least important, is community or market perception of the college. Some colleges die an image death, with community members mistaking a campus for a quaint collection of old buildings, soon to be knocked down and replaced with a Target and a great big parking lot.

Like Marylhurst College and Nichols presidents Dr. Wilgenbusch and Dr. Townsley, respectively, the turnaround president must engage every willing ear in the community. From service to professional organizations, and from churches to college-sponsored luncheons to catered parties, the message must be broadcast that this college is undergoing a transformation and that employees, applicants, and the larger public can look forward to a viable provider of educational services. Recall how the *News Journal* took Wesley College under its wing by spreading word of its transformation, which at the very least helped boost appearances and may just have tapped unexpected revenue resources for the college.

If there is one other constant besides a financial strategy, it is leadership. A turnaround strategy does not take place just because everyone recognizes that the college is facing a major problem and that they must be willing to put differences aside and voluntarily forgo their interests to produce and initiate a new strategy. Turnarounds require strong leaders like Miller at Wesley, Crouch at Georgetown, Wilgenbusch at Marylhurst, Townsley at Nichols, Varsalona and Doberstein at Wilmington, and Owens at Gwynedd-Mercy. These presidents are not shrinking violets. They recognized that managing a turnaround requires a president who is willing to get his or her hands dirty, get into the mix, and make something happen. As strong leaders, they did not just run around yelling to march forward; they had the wit, wisdom, and personal skills to convince others to follow and to work together to achieve significant changes at their colleges.

Beyond the laying of the foundation for a turnaround, these six college presidents made nine points about conducting and maintaining a successful turnaround strategy. The points listed in Table 12.4 follow directly from the discussion on financial strategy in an earlier chapter.

Before putting the turnaround plan to bed, the cycle of the turnaround must be considered. Many colleges in the past decade have gone through a financial resurrection. They reach a point of decline, find a new leader, and grow enrollments—eventually outgrowing financial distress but then reaching an enrollment plateau. For many small colleges, enrollment plateaus translate into higher costs and subsequent tuition increases, leading ultimately to an ironic constraint of enrollments caused by market inability to bear the tuition increase. Plateaus may tilt downward because graduations and attrition may shrink the base.

TABLE 12.4—TURNAROUND STRATEGY

1. Reenforce strengths.
2. Rebuild the strongest financial source.
3. Find new sources of income.
4. Manage debt.
5. Run a disciplined budget and business office.
6. Work the problem. If the college can regain financial stability, then go for it; if not, find a college that can take on the academic responsibilities.
7. Compete aggressively. Go after markets of competitors.
8. Make sure that the college builds its plans to support the relationship of mission to services to markets to price.
9. Leadership is everything!

From 1988 to 1997, only 15 private colleges were not constrained by enrollment plateaus—their annually compounded growth rates were above 10 percent.[17] It is difficult to say precisely what accounted for sustained growth in each case, but evidence in a number of cases suggests that some of their presidents maintained relationships with faculties such that the college did not slip backward into collegial governance. Recall Dr. James Fisher's contention that small colleges cannot afford contentious collegial decision making. Faculty and administrators must be responsible and accountable *partners*.[18] It is the small college tied to a system of serving multiple interests that depletes its own time, energy, and resources, thereby reducing its ability to respond to market shifts in a timely fashion.

Whether because of chaos or inertia, stalemates and lead feet are anathema to college turnarounds. Department heads must work in conjunction with the president and board in the name of progress. For the college in financial distress, change is all that separates an open door from a closed one. Change must be heralded on all fronts with enthusiasm, participation, determination, and accountability. Progress... change... transformation... mere euphemisms for the uncomfortable yet continuous process whereby a leadership tests a small college's most cherished beliefs and clichés.[19,20]

ENDNOTES

1.   Keller, G. *Academic Strategy* (Baltimore: Johns Hopkins University Press, 1983), p. 3.
2.   Cowan, R. B. (1993). "Prescription for Small-College Turnaround," *Change, 1*, 38.
3.   National Science Foundation. (2001). Sheet 15565881.wk1: Opening fall enrollment: 1967–1997. *WebCASPAR Database System*. Retrieved August 5, 2001, from http://caspar/nsf.gov/.
4.   Ibid.
5.   Keller, G. *Academic Strategy* (Baltimore: Johns Hopkins University Press, 1983), p. 3.
6.   Feemster, R. (2000). "Faith in Financials," *University Business*, 3(3), 39.
7.   Cohen, M. D., & March, J. G. *Leadership and Ambiguity: The American College President*. (New York: McGraw-Hill, 1974).

8.   Murphy, D. M., & Tellier, S. K. (July 2004). "Financial About-Face," *Business Officer*, 20.

9.   Ibid.

10.   Ibid.

11.   Ibid.

12.   Ibid.

13.   Ibid.

14.   Ibid.

15.   Ibid.

16.   Ibid.

17.   National Science Foundation. (2001). Sheet 15565881.wk1: Opening fall enrollment: 1967–1997. *WebCASPAR Database System*. Retrieved August 5, 2001, from http://caspar/nsf.gov/.

18.   Fisher, J. L., personal interview, Baltimore, Maryland, September 5, 2001.

19.   Ibid.

20.   Fisher, J. L. *Power of the Presidency*. American Council on Education. (New York: MacMillan, 1984).

CHAPTER 13

FINANCIAL SUCCESSES AND FAILURES: LESSONS

Turnarounds are the flip side of decline and failure, especially decline leading to failure. Turnarounds reverse the slide toward oblivion, while year after year deterioration in financial position seems to have a momentum that appears irreversible. Yet, turnarounds indicate that the momentum is stoppable, and that it takes a lot of bad decisions to push a college over the cliff. Between 2005 and 2007, only nine not-for-profit four-year institutions closed.[1] This was less than 1 percent of all the private institutions in existence in this period.[2] This reflects the resiliency of the business model in higher education. However, the data do not count the institutions that merged or were bought by other institutions because of their financial problems.

This chapter answers two questions on financial turnarounds or failures: first, how to start and maintain a turnaround; and second, how to recognize financial decline. It addresses the first question by focusing on these factors: leadership, strategy, market responsiveness, operational management, financial discipline, easing internal conflict, and the Composite Financial Index (CFI). The second question is addressed by showing how to diagnose financial decline.

HOW TO MANAGE A SUCCESSFUL TURNAROUND

A turnaround is not to be confused with having a positive net income for one year. A strong turnaround definition should fit the following conditions. Net income is consistently positive over a five-year period; net income and cash increase annually; enrollment increases; and the college does not slip into multiyear deficits after several years. The greatest challenge for presidents managing a turnaround is that after several years the college hits an enrollment and net income plateau, and the college can no longer improve its financial position. The main reason that this happens is that improved financial condition implies that the risk of closing is eliminated. Under these circumstances, leadership may become complacent, faculty may make greater demands to improve their situation, or the college may increase spending on buildings and grounds improvements. The pressure to minimize expenditures or find new markets is lessened as the board, president, and faculty turn their attention from saving the college to other more pressing matters. The result is that the turnaround stalls, and in some unfortunate cases, the college returns to a pattern of decline. Although turnarounds are tough and require constant vigilance during the turnaround and long after the college has attained its turnaround goals, the perspective is based on an optimistic assumption that colleges and boards can turn around even the sorriest college if they put in the effort and build a rational plan for change. What follows is a discussion of the factors that are critical to a turnaround's success.

Leadership

A turnaround must have a president and board that lead from the front. Straight talk, not cute, political, two-step dancing around the problem, is the foundation of leadership during a turnaround. The college community is usually aware of the general condition of the institution, so they will not be flummoxed by news that the college is in bad shape and needs to take dramatic, long-term action to reverse its decline. So, mincing words is not needed, but precise information should be given to everyone on what has happened and what is needed to make the turnaround.

Board support for the president is another necessary ingredient. There is nothing more debilitating to a president than a board that half-heartedly supports change. Even more destructive is a board that allows its members to use innuendo or openly criticize the action of the president. It undermines everything that the president tries to do. If board members cannot support the president, they must either leave or find a new president.

Presidential leadership is a must. The president must be everywhere, be seen by everyone, be optimistic, be the chief mediator, and make the right decisions. Anything less and risk increases that the turnaround will fail. Leadership skills are not suddenly acquired by a bolt from the sky. Presidents who are good leaders are known by their reputation. It is difficult to turn a reclusive, self-effacing person into a cheerleader for change. Leadership is not something that is learned from a book or at a weekend retreat. How does someone learn the skills? People learn leadership skills throughout their careers as they practice leadership and refine their techniques. They become comfortable in front of others, taking public hits about their decisions, and carrying out plans without irritation, antagonism, or reticence.

Strategic Plans

Turnarounds must be driven by strategic plans because they involve long-term changes in the outcomes of the institution. There are two levels to strategic plans for a turnaround. The method of moving the college through the turnaround is the first level. The second level is the strategic plan that sets the goals, objectives, and plans for taking the college out of decline and into a new level of financial stability.

The first level has to be conceived quickly; excessive delay will eat away at the implicit authority that comes with being new. This is also the time when tough action can take place because everyone is expecting major changes in jobs and direction. They may not like what will happen, but most will understand the need. The first-level strategy requires the following: working with good data,* identifying

---

*Good data include these sources: finance, audit management letters, enrollment, academic, plant, accreditation reports, and anything else that influences the current condition of the college.

the major players, locating sources of cash to support the turnaround, and knowing which conditions will limit change.* Additionally, there must be a method for developing the strategic plan, that is, who is involved, how problems are identified, how goals are set, and how plans are made to carry out the strategy.

The second-level strategy is developing the strategic plan for turning around the college. The turnaround strategy should include goals, a statement relating the goals to the mission, measurable objectives, action plans, outcomes assessment, and contingency plans. There is nothing unusual about what makes up the strategic plan. The main condition of the process is that it should not take years to design and implement the plan. It has to be completed expeditiously. The board and faculty senate should have major roles in developing the plan and should give their assent to the strategy when the plan is concluded. There is nothing more forlorn than a strategic plan that lacks legitimization granted by the board and faculty.

Turnaround strategies have to be grounded in reality; that is, plans that set unrealistic expectations for change will frustrate everyone, accomplish nothing, and may even accelerate the decline. What does it mean to ground strategy in reality? Reality means that the strategy has to recognize the financial, market, operational, and capital (buildings and equipment) conditions of the college. The financial condition, if it is severe (i.e., very little cash and a long string of deficits), will limit actions that are solely based on using internal cash. Moreover, banks will be reluctant to provide loans because the college's credit rating will categorize it as high risk for default. The action plan will have to figure out how to get loyal supporters of the institution to provide start-up cash for the turnaround. The college needs to understand whether its student market has the potential to pull the college out of the doldrums. If the market is small and shrinking, then a marketing strategy will have to consider other markets, which may also involve adding or revising instructional programs to attract new students. The operational condition of the college may warrant immediate action if it is a major cause of the problem. For

---

*Limits on change could include conditions imposed by incorporation papers, state departments of education, regional accrediting agencies, local laws, and/or federal regulations.

instance, the college will have to make quick and major changes to operational management if the following types of conditions prevail: managers continually overspend budgets, the finance office is unable to control spending or produce reliable and valid reports of its financial condition, admissions has low yield rates, or administrators are unskilled. One of the first things that many turnaround presidents do is find money to immediately spruce up the campus. A campus that looks run down will not attract students.

Market Action

Strategic planning in higher education cannot ignore the marketplace. Strategy should be market driven. In other words, what does the market want from a degree today and in the near future? This is particularly true of turnarounds at tuition-dependent colleges. Because turnarounds need to deliver fund-raising dollars, fund raising or development strategies should be a major component of a turnaround strategy. Development also has to be market driven. Fund-raising drives that ignore the demands of the donor market waste money. Strategy, for enrollment or development, that ignores the marketplace is doomed to failure. The following are types of strategic market plans:

- *Enrollment-driven market plans:* These are based on a solid understanding of the student marketplace.[3] Market-driven plans are based on a keen understanding of the college, its competitors, its student market, and the market potential for existing or new academic programs.[4] Presidents and admissions administrators with an intuitive understanding of the potential for the market are more than useful; they are necessary during a turnaround. Nevertheless, intuition must be supported by data about the market, the competition, and what degrees are viable. To get good market data, a turnaround president needs to find a few dollars. The fundamental elements of a market-driven plan include:

  - *Market segments:* Who the college serves, the scale of the segment, and any projected changes in demographics;

- *Market segment geography:* Where potential students are located;

- *Market share:* What share of the market the college currently has;

- *Competitors:* Who the major competitors are and why students enroll at the competitor schools;

- *New student preferences:* Why students choose the college and how they choose it (parents, friends, counselors, or achievement test scores);

- *Sources of new students:* What data are needed to locate potential students within the market segment;

- *Admitted students who reject the college:* Why admitted students choose another college; and

- *Message:* What message the college will use to sell itself to potential students.

- *Major capital development strategies:* Development strategies have to establish who is willing to give to the college and why they will give. Altruistic donors provide gifts and do not expect a building or a plaque to recognize their beneficence. But most donors want some sort of recognition for their generosity. The work of the development team is to know their potential donors so well that they understand what motivates the gift. A campaign plan embraces these elements: the message for the campaign, the dollars needed, how the dollars will be spent, a schedule of action, lists of donors and potential gifts, and the method used to solicit gifts.* A development strategy is not a short-term event. It requires hard and persistent work to convince big or small givers to contribute. If the head of development does not have a history of success, a professional firm may be needed to design and set up annual and major campaigns. Campaigns may be for a specific project (a capital campaign) or may

---

*There are many ways of soliciting gifts—letters, phone calls, team solicitors, friends soliciting friends, or highly renowned alumni seeking gifts for the campaign.

be comprehensive (projects plus annual funds). The staff of the development office must be personable and have a record of closing the sale, that is, getting the gift! Timing is everything in a major campaign. Going to the alumni or major donors before the college has successfully ended its slide and is climbing back to respectability will result in a failure. The old rule applies: no one wants to give money to a loser. Also, general economic conditions must be strong. When the economy is weak, most donors, even rich donors, will look to their own situation before they give money to someone else.

Operational Management

Strategy that does not have an operational component is just whistling in the wind. Operations must deliver the turnaround, and they can do this only if steps are taken to ensure that there is a strong management plan in place. A significant aspect of having strong management in place is to hire the best and most skilled person for the job, as noted in Chapter 7, "Operations: Management for Success." The president must get the right people in the right places so that the turnaround has a chance of success.

Financial Discipline

Financial discipline is more than the chief financial officer (CFO) crying, "No, no, and no" in the wilderness. *The first rule of a turnaround is to stop the hemorrhaging of cash!* This requires all the authority and support of the president and the board. They have to make the case that the college has to change its financial ways. This means that the president with the board's authority must inform the college community that current financial practices will change immediately and that those who will not change will be answerable to the president. It goes without saying that change includes the financial department. If it does not have the people or the procedures to manage financial operations carefully, then its people have to be trained or changed. Time is everything in a turnaround and delays in taking financial action mean that the college will probably slip deeper into financial decline.

Once the first steps are taken, the college can then work on establishing plans to create the basis for long-term financial discipline. Financial discipline simply means that the finance department has policies and procedures to guide financial management and that these are enforced by the CFO with the support of the president. Long-term financial discipline depends on five ingredients: skills, systems, reports, controls and policies, and fiscal restraint.

Skills are an imperative. The CFO must be proficient with generally accepted accounting principles (GAAP) and have considerable experience with managing financial operations. The preferred qualification for a CFO is a CPA (certified public accountant); and if the CFO is not so qualified, then the controller or someone else in the financial office should be a CPA. The other major positions—bursar, payables, payroll, and bookkeeper—should also have the experience and training to each do their job well. Skills count for everything in an efficient and competent financial or business office.

Systems are a critical adjunct to skills and refer to the accounting system that holds and processes records, payables, payroll, tax reports, purchasing, reports, and all the other things that a business office does. By now, systems at even the smallest college should be automated, reliable* and valid.† If the college does not have a system that meets these basic requirements, it quickly needs to find the money to buy an accounting system. Without a good system, delays will occur and reports will not be trusted. Even though installing a new system requires time, it must be done. Often the auditing firm can assist in buying and installing the new system.

Reports should provide the full range of information that is needed to make informed decisions. Financial reports include all the familiar reports, such as departmental budgets and monthly, quarterly, semester, and annual reports to the board, president, and chief management officers. The nondepartmental budget reports should include data on the institutional factors that drive the financial condition of the college. Therefore, a good financial report includes

---

*Reliable means that given the same information at different times, the same result is produced.
†Valid means that (1) the reports reflect the information that is input, and (2) the underlying processes are based on generally accepted accounting principles.

budget and actual and year-to-date performance comparisons for these areas: admissions, enrollment, personnel, utilities, dorm residents, the major functions in the budget, and income statements for all income centers. Reporting is the pin on which controls and policy hinge.

Controls and policy are interlinked. Controls track performance and decisions, and policies limit financial action and state sanctions to be taken in response to noncompliant financial decisions. Controls are based on budget plans, goals, or accounting processes. The only way controls and policies work is when the president and board support enforcement of policies and procedures. Obviously, policies should not be so rigid as to preclude good sense. Nevertheless, members of the college who fail or refuse to follow reasonable procedures need to be held accountable for their actions. Turnarounds rest on the solid work of a financial office, presidential leadership in supporting the policies and actions of the office, and fiscal restraint.

Fiscal restraint is the final piece of the financial puzzle. Colleges can lose turnaround momentum when new money is spent without planning or diverges from the strategic plan. New money is like finding 50 bucks when you are broke. Colleges coming out of a long period of financial decline will find that new money is very alluring and sidetracks strategic plans. If the money is spent on big pay raises for employees, everyone is happy; however, the college has just made the turnaround more difficult because it has raised its long-term breakeven points for enrollment, revenue, and gifts. Prudent spending and spending to goal should be the watchwords of a turnaround.

Internal Conflict

Too often internal conflict comes with financial decline. The unfortunate aspect of internal conflict is that it may prevent action that could moderate or even forestall continuing decline. A typical conflict bottleneck is the juncture at which the faculty senate has to approve curriculum changes. The administration needs to terminate financially weak academic programs whose markets have evaporated or add new programs to attract more students to the college. If the senate and the academic administration are at each other's throats, decisions are stalled, frustration builds, and each side will counterattack. The only result is that the college is unable to stop its decline.

Another conflict juncture is between the chief financial officer, department administrators, and the president regarding purchases. Department administrators may have learned that they can ignore the business office rules because the president may tell the administrator to ignore the business office. This happens when the president feels that the CFO instigates conflict and does not provide solutions. Given these circumstances CFOs soon find that they are outsiders who have no impact on controlling financial decline.

Presidents must deal with the conflict within their institution that curtails action that will stop the decline and improve the financial condition of the college. Presidents need people skills to convince faculty and administrators to do what needs to be done. Charles Dwyer, in his book *Managing People*, describes theses skills as serving the needs of others so that they serve the needs of the organization.[5] It sounds simple, but presidents need practice, reflection, and experience to become effective managers of people. Presidents who do not possess these skills are not good choices for a turnaround.

Composite Financial Index (CFI) and Financial Forecasts

CFI as a Strategic Testing Instrument

CFI provides a handy instrument to design and test the financial components of turnaround strategies. This measure has been used extensively by private colleges seeking a commonly accepted measure of their financial condition. The index was designed by KPMG and Prager, McCarthy & Sealy based on their experience in analyzing the financial condition of clients.[6] The methodology is similar to the approach that the U.S. Department of Education uses to measure whether a private institution has the financial wherewithal to receive the authority to grant federal financial aid awards.

The measure uses the sum of the values from four core ratios modified for strength and weight to estimate financial condition. The core ratios are primary reserve ratio, which measures whether there are adequate funds to cover emergencies; net income ratio, which measures short-term results; return on net assets, which measures the ability to increase wealth; and the viability ratio, which measures the capacity to support long-term debt.*

Index scores can fall in a wide range, but healthy institutions usually have scores of 3 or better. The CFI can play a role in testing financial initiatives by following the steps outlined in Table 13.1. (See the CFI Strategic Initiative Testing Instrument on CD.)

Financial Forecasts

A financial forecast (typically five years) is an important method for testing strategic initiatives and planning major budget changes. The base year for the forecast is the last audited fiscal year. The data for the base year should come from the last budget report after it was adjusted to reconcile with the audit. A forecast should produce statements of

---

TABLE 13.1—USING CFI TO TEST STRATEGIC INITIATIVES

Step 1: Compute the financial value of the strategic initiatives.

Step 2: Set "3" as the goal for the CFI score.

Step 3: Using the CFI instrument, test each initiative separately (no single initiative may achieve the goal score).

Step 4: Test the initiatives together.

Step 5: Test the initiatives together in a *five-year financial forecast* to determine whether it interacts with other financial factors.

Step 6: Use the CFI instrument to test the forecasts. The forecasts will have to generate statements of activities and financial position for each year to provide meaningful data for the test.

---

*See Appendix G, Composite Financial Index, for an in-depth discussion.

activities, position, and cash. The forecast template for each institution will be different, but it should include these components:

- *Growth rate:* In this section, growth rates for each of the five years can be entered for enrollment, tuition rates, fees, financial aid, compensation, investment principal, and other major variables in the financial structure.

- *Revenue:* This should test tuition, fees, financial aid, investment income and draws, auxiliaries, and other revenue sources that are part of the audit.

- *Expenses:* This section tests compensation and other expenses for each major department. The departments are organized around the expense functions in the audit.

- *New departments:* Any new income-producing or purely expense department needs to be tested. This is one place that initiatives are tested.

- *Capital finance projects:* Projects should test the impact of interest and principal payments.

- *Depreciation:* The effect of depreciation expenses must be tested.

- *Other components:* Nonoperating activities, statements of financial position, and cash should be included.

The forecast should be designed so that various scenarios in addition to strategic initiatives can be tested. However, it is best during a strategic analysis to treat every change as a strategic change. So, if strategic plans exist to increase enrollment, then the growth rates should reflect the initiative and any known factors that may have positive or adverse impacts on enrollments. The same is true for other revenue sources and expense departments.

Forecasts have to be checked for reality and error. If there are huge jumps in net income after an initiative, ask whether this is realistic, or is the jump the result of an error in one of the cells? A typical forecast may contain several thousand cells, so it is not unexpected that cell formulas may contain errors. Although forecasts are tedious to develop, they are necessary instruments for testing plans and serve as an adjunct to the CFI strategic initiative test.

RECOGNIZING FINANCIAL DECLINE

It is usually intuitively obvious that a college is in financial decline. There are a string of deficits, lousy creditor ratings, unpaid bills, shrinking enrollments, or pages of audit management comments. Yet, it is useful to identify the major issues that are driving the decline. This involves a thorough diagnosis of every part of the institution.

Any worthwhile strategy must rest on a reliable assessment of the institution's financial condition and market position. The data phase of strategic planning involves the collection of common sense financial and market information, such as budget reports, financial statements, cash flow reports, trend analyses, cost reports, admissions reports, and competitor performance. The president reviews all data with a financial task force as the process of strategic planning begins. To determine the best way of presenting collected information to both the president and the board, the chief financial officer ought to test several reporting formats. Most accounting software can be configured to convey basic financial information, downloadable to a spreadsheet. Custom reports can then be created to fit the monitoring requirements of the institution. The monitoring system should track and report the performance of the institution relative to its financial strategy and to a set of external benchmarks.

The gathering of financial data may prove especially difficult for small colleges; many have no reporting system in place for the analysis and monitoring of operations. The president may recruit auditors to help the chief financial officer not only with the data collection process but also with the establishment of a formal monitoring system (and with any software and spreadsheet operations necessary to those ends). The work of data analysis and the development of a prudent strategy could be hamstrung by failure to establish a reliable way to track operations and financial progress.

The first phase of data collection establishes a general picture of the college's financial condition. This is a crucial process because such information will inform the leadership's actions during the construction of the financial strategy. Strategic questions help draw out the basic financial condition of the institution, and many answers do not require an exhaustive or expensive effort to collect. Most of the questions, in fact, can be answered simply "yes" or "no." The chief financial officer and the auditors should prepare a joint report on the general financial condition of the college for the president and board to review. Without the knowledge afforded by the general diagnostic process, the president will be ill equipped to perform the more detailed financial diagnostics to come.

The more specific phase of data collection involves four components of the financial system: revenue and expenses, cash, working capital, and permanent assets. Dollars, ratios, and financial trends will coagulate into a detailed picture of the current and historical condition of the college, and this information will generate benchmarks for the monitoring system. Trend and ratio analysis may be the most significant part of the financial analysis because the two can show whether finances are deviating from published norms or from internal expectations. The chief financial officer should track trends to spot major and undesirable changes. Trend analysis after the disaster has happened only raises the question about who was keeping watch.

The president may want the assistance of the auditors to help pull the data together and interpret it. Their involvement is well worth the investment. Appendix B, Financial, Marketing, and Management Diagnostics, contains lists of questions and issues that can help in diagnosing the financial and marketing condition of the institution. These forms are also in customizable format on CD.

Diagnostic Step 1

Before the board and president delve into the details of the college's financial condition, they need a snapshot of the college's operations, which should include views of the mission, audits, licensing, deficits, basic business practices, and the basic financial position of the college.

Answers to these questions, many of them obvious yet obscured in the daily fog of operations, form the baseline of the diagnostic endeavor. You want to know what the college is doing, and whether it is operating effectively.

- *Mission and strategic goals:* Do they accurately depict the college's present or future purpose? Will the strategic goals permit the college to achieve its given mission? If the mission and goals conflict, or are out of sync with the board's intentions, college operations will be anything but orderly. If synchronization drastically alters the college's mission, bylaws may have to be revised to comply with state licensing or corporate regulations. The college cannot operate without state licensure, which grants the authority necessary to offer educational programs and award degrees based on the college's mission, as stated in its corporate bylaws.

- *Accrediting agencies:* Agencies verify that college degree programs are legitimate and substantive; together with licensing agencies, they control the institution's crown jewels. To win authority and secure accreditation, many colleges find themselves increasing investment in educational programs or in student or academic services. Whatever the requirement, the board and president ought to acknowledge any conflicts with these agencies and endeavor to accommodate their demands. Resistance would be futile.

- *Audits:* Audits ensure the reliability of financial statements and the integrity of financial practices. If the college has not conducted annual audits, it must begin doing so. To clarify board oversight of the audit and to reduce the likelihood of audit information being filtered by staff or administrative self-interest, the contract for the audit should be between the board of trustees and the auditor.

- *Deficits and growth rates:* After assessing the college's present condition, the president and board must get a feel for the college's recent financial tendencies. Has the college run a deficit for two or more years? Have deficits recurred over five-year periods? If the college has been running regular deficits, it is probably ricocheting from one financial crisis to another. Is the growth rate for revenue less than the growth rate for expenses, and is the gap increasing? If the college does not run deficits, but revenue and expense growth rates are out of balance and the gap is increasing, deficits will eventually appear. Sound financial strategy rests on the proposition that deficits rarely occur and that revenue and expense growth rates are either in balance or favoring revenue growth.

- *Instructional and auxiliary programs:* Eliminating deficits goes hand in hand with adapting instructional and auxiliary programs to the realities of a sound financial strategy. Instructional programs are the financial drivers of the institution. If they produce a significant loss, they threaten the survival of the college. The same holds true for auxiliaries. If they lose money, they drain core services. Are these programs losing money? If no one knows, someone had better find out.

- *Liquidity:* Like a balanced operational budget, cash is essential to a college's solvency. The president and board need answers to several simple questions. Does the college have sufficient cash to pay its bills and cover its payroll for the next several months? Will it have enough cash without having to borrow for the rest of the year? Frequent borrowing to make payrolls and bill payments may indicate a serious liquidity problem. There are several possible causes for a liquidity problem. Many colleges fail to bill students regularly and/or fail to collect unpaid student balances. Many colleges have not drawn down financial aid allotments from the government. Many colleges' operations do not produce excess cash.

  Cash problems may be evident in payroll and accounts payable offices. Are payroll taxes and benefit deductions deposited on time, and are bills paid on time? Are bills held because of insufficient cash? A Dunn & Bradstreet report will show whether the college is slow paying its bills.

Late payments on taxes and benefit deductions must be corrected immediately. Failure to do so could lead to dire consequences.

- *Debt:* Excess debt places the destiny of colleges in the hands of a third party, bankers, who can quickly become the dictators of college policies and operating conditions. College leaders must ascertain the amount of outstanding debt and establish a policy that delineates the circumstances in which debt may be reasonably incurred. Note that off-balance-sheet financing can obscure the true extent of debt obligations, but it must nevertheless be included in the total amount of outstanding debt.

- *State and federal financial aid funds:* These funds are critical in the revenue mix of every college. The leadership should scan the latest financial aid audits for any irregularities or management problems. Major problems with federal financial aid could lead to the loss of those funds or to onerous conditions imposed by the U.S. Department of Education. Prior to the transfer of funds, the Department could require that the college have a letter of credit equal to 50 percent or more of the financial aid amount. This is a devastating stipulation for a financially weak college. Any loss of financial aid could spell a college's demise.

- *Incentives:* Like all organizations, colleges use incentives to encourage members to subordinate their personal interests to the goals of the organization. Decentralization of authority, ambiguity of goals, and collegial decision making can subvert incentive systems in larger colleges. By virtue of their size, small colleges are less likely to have autonomous departments that act outside the institutional goals. Some colleges use incentives in an inconsistent fashion or they are distorted by self-interest. Incentives lose their power under these conditions. The president, chief financial officer, chief academic officer, and other key institutional leaders should examine the consequences, intended or unintended, of the existing incentive system. Incentives that work at cross purposes with the goals of the college should be redesigned or abandoned.

- *Accounting and budget systems:* Some colleges, to the surprise of their presidents and boards, fail to post monthly accounting records. (Problems with accounting records are usually evident in audit management letters.) Many budget systems are rudimentary at best and nonexistent at worst. Accounting systems and the crucial functions they perform must be in place before a college can expect to implement financial strategy. They record financial transactions, track cash flow, delineate policies and procedures, and report on the financial condition of the college. Budget systems transform strategy into action by matching forecasts to plans, establishing performance benchmarks, and identifying responsibility areas relevant to the implementation of budget plans. Accounting and budget systems must work symbiotically.

  Because financial strategy would be worthless without the coordinated accounting and budget systems, the president should ask auditors and the chief financial officer to report on both systems before planning begins in earnest. The report should cover all aspects of the finance office—payables, payroll, billing, accounting records, and software. It should identify report formats, procedures, policies, responsibilities, and deficiencies. Where deficiencies are reported, relevant solutions should be proposed. The president should meet independently with the auditors to evaluate the capabilities of the chief financial officer and his or her staff. Whoever among them cannot perform effectively must be replaced. Financial duties are too important to leave in the hands of ill-prepared employees.

Diagnostic Step 2: Financial Condition

To understand the college's historical financial direction, the president and board must consider trends in revenue, expenses, cash, working capital, permanent assets, and broad measures of financial performance. Beyond serving as a historical backdrop, a look at trends can indicate which changes in financial structure were intended and which were not. Leaders must understand what has been driving their institution's financial performance to make coherent, well-founded adjustments to it.

Audits represent a third party's report on a college's financial structure and should provide most of the necessary historical financial data. Because audits usually reflect financial data found in Independent Postsecondary Education Data System (IPEDS) reports, cross-referencing of information from both sources enables comparisons of one college's financial performance to that of its competitors and enables benchmarking of one college's financial performance against that of a "best-practices" college. In addition to the financial reports, three years of registration, billing, and human resources data round out the trend analysis.

The CFO should prepare the reports for review by the president and other institutional leaders. Given the labor and time involved in collecting data, and given the urgency of the cause, a CFO at a struggling college may indeed need the help of auditors. Any changes made during the collection and analysis of revenue and expenses, working capital and cash, and permanent capital data ought to be incorporated in the final financial strategy:

Revenue and expenses

- *Core services:* To analyze revenue and expenses generated from operations, the college's core services must first be determined, be they instruction, research, or community service. If allocation decisions have not benefited core services, the leadership must assess the sensibility of its decisions. The budget process, without the discipline of a strategic plan, may haphazardly redirect allocations from core services to those noncore services whose leaders do the best job of bargaining for increases. Core services allocation data should ultimately tease out two pieces of information: (1) current allocations of revenue and expenses, which will be compared to allocations several years earlier, and (2) historical allocation shifts, to include rates of change by revenue or expense category, and where new dollars went.

- *Tuition dependency rate:* Unless an institution has intentionally done something to change it, tuition dependency will remain stable. The college should be concerned if the rate has increased substantially in the absence of any effort by the college to foster such an increase. Whatever has occurred to change the tuition dependency rate, whether in the market or within the institution, must be discovered, for any increase in dependence on tuition thrusts the college into a risky position based on sudden changes in the student market.

- *Unfunded financial aid:* This is a critical variable because it represents market decisions and reduction to cash generated by tuition revenue. Audits present the impact of unfunded financial aid on tuition as follows: Tuition and Fee Revenue – Financial Aid = Net Tuition Revenue. When unfunded aid increases and net tuition falls, the net operating condition deteriorates over time. This condition also suggests that increasing unfunded aid is not resulting in increased enrollments.

- *Auxiliaries:* These provide important services to the institution and generate additional income to support core operations. Though auxiliary services need not generate huge amounts of income, their operating expenses should at least break even with their depreciated capital investment. Otherwise, they drain resources from the core operations of the institution. If auxiliaries perform poorly, the college must conduct a separate study of their management and financial operations to determine how they can be improved. No college can tolerate auxiliary services that deplete resources.

- *Student flow:* College leaders must consider the flow of students into and out of the college. Student flow at most colleges is critical to their financial condition and market position. Trend data should be analyzed with an eye to how numbers of incoming students, quitting students, and graduating students have changed over time by level (undergraduate or graduate), by instructional major, and by instructional program. Student flow ultimately drives operations, and relevant data highlight those programs with strong and weak enrollment levels, those programs with high rates of attrition, and those programs associated with high or low graduation rates. The net income each program generates should indicate which level, programs, or majors have been most or least productive.

Well-defined data not only indicate changes in student flow, but also suggest their causes as well as their historical impact on revenue and expenses. Resource allocation will show whether enrollment flows have been supported and exactly how new dollars have been spent. Numbers of faculty and staff members, student-faculty ratios, student-employee ratios, class size, number of classrooms, square footage of classrooms, and capital assets show how the college allocates resources by level, major, or program. (The college must eventually take this information one step further and lay out the revenue, expenses, price discounts, and net income produced by level, major, and program.)

- *Noncore services:* Colleges must get a handle on resource allocations to noncore services, to include academic support and business or auxiliary services. Data highlight expense allocations, number of employees, student-employee ratio, square footage of office space, and capital assets for noncore services and should show changes in allocation amounts to noncore services, as well as how new dollars were spent. Trends in resource allocations (expenses, employees, square footage, and capital assets) between core and noncore activities ought to be compared. If the college is directing its largest increases to noncore activities, leaders must begin asking some hard questions.

- *Net income:* Net income is generated by operations and must be evaluated on two levels: (1) Is net income positive? (2) Is revenue growth balanced with expense growth? If net income is not positive or if it spikes up or down, the college must control either the flow of revenue to support expenditures or the rate of change in expenditures. Net income should be positive over time, and growth in revenue and expenses should be balanced. Colleges with meager resources may bob from deficits to positive net income, which prevents them from building adequate reserves. As a result, the institution is more vulnerable to economic shocks. A college in this precarious financial position must develop goals for enrollment flows, resource allocations, and net pricing for tuition, all with the intent to achieve positive net income and a balance between revenue and expenses.

- *Cash and working capital:* Cash will shrink or increase working capital (current assets minus current liabilities) depending on the scale and direction of net income. Working capital takes cash from operations and from payments on receivables, which is then available to pay bills and cover the payroll. Data on working capital can be found in the current assets and liability section of the statement of financial position (balance sheet) of the audit. The cash flow section of the audit provides information on the sources and uses of cash during the fiscal year. Presidents must know whether operations are generating cash and how cash is used for financing operations and investments. It is imperative that the president and chief management officers recognize that net income and net cash are not the same. When working capital is inadequate, the college will have to turn to short-term loans to finance the payment of bills and cover payroll.

Cash analysis should set forth (1) the rates of change for cash, short-term investments, and net cash flow, and (2) the cash and short-term investments to total expenses ratio. The trends and the rates of change will indicate the magnitude and direction of the changes in cash. Cash and short-term investments should represent at least three months of expenses to ensure adequate reserves.

Beyond simple trend analysis, the source of changes in cash should be identified. Were they caused by increases in net income, changes in accounts payables or accruals, changes in receivables, or changes in short- or long-term debt? An association between cash and short-term investments *and* increasing payables or accruals suggests that bills are going unpaid. The college should carefully analyze the flow of funds into cash, as well as the trend in cash following short- or long-term borrowing. What would the cash position be if debt had not increased?

The college should also go beyond the net cash flow from operations and examine changes in total net cash flow. The audit statement on cash will help to answer several questions. Were increases or decreases to net cash flow caused by changes in cash flowing from operations, from financing activities (contributions or changes in debt), or from investing activities (investments or purchases of assets)? What is the trend for these changes?

Receivables are problematic for any colleges that allow students to abuse payment plans. When students fail to make payments, the balance rolls to the next billing period. Over time, the college sees eroding cash levels, and the student sees that the college is not serious about bill collections. Many colleges face a dilemma; payment plans may entice students to enroll, but enforcing those payment plans may cause students to leave. Worse yet, late-paying students may gossip to potential students that the college aggressively collects overdue bills. Presidents should understand that once they implement a reliable collection system, only a small core of delinquent payers will remain.

A classic measure for tracking adequacy of working capital is the *quick* ratio [(Current Assets − Inventory) ÷ Current Liabilities], the data for which can be found in the audit. Current assets typically include cash and receivables, and current liabilities refers to payables and receivables. The ratio depicts the amount of cash that could be generated from cash and receivables to cover payables and accruals. If it is declining or less than 1, the college needs to figure out the problem. Has cash declined, or have receivables, uncollectible receivables, or payables increased beyond the rate of change in expenses or tuition revenue? The ratio factors should be continuously monitored for problems.

- *Assets and liabilities:* Presidents must have a passing knowledge of the institution's assets and liabilities because they are needed to provide debt capacity to finance strategic initiatives. A trend table ought to track property, plant, equipment, investments, debt, other major assets or liabilities, and net assets by category (unrestricted, temporarily restricted, etc.). The table should also include the debt leverage ratio, return on net assets ratio, capitalization ratio, composition of net assets ratio, and the rates of change for each category of permanent capital. Information on payout rates for the endowment, rates of return on investments, and a long-term debt list should complement the trend table.

- *Debt:* Colleges should have a list of all outstanding debt including the lender, maturity, principal, debt service, interest rates, any conditions to the debt, and purpose of the debt. The list should include *all* forms of debt, including off-balance sheet financing, which seems to act as an expense, but in reality establishes future payment obligations much like debt. Such a list, if kept current and reported regularly to the board, will help a college keep track of its obligations. If debt increases to cover cash flow problems, the list will point out that change and facilitate the leadership's informed review and action. The college can also use the list to determine whether debt should be refinanced when market interest rates are favorable.

- *Investments:* Colleges must ask the following questions about their investments and endowment: What is the rate of return on investments? How does the rate of return compare to a market benchmark, the S&P 500, for example?

Investment benchmarks should be constructed to reflect the mix of investments held in the portfolio. For instance, if the portfolio is 40 percent equity stock and 60 percent bonds, the benchmark should reflect that mix. What is the payout rate on the endowment fund? Does the rate reflect a prudent course, such as 5 percent on a moving three-year average? What proportion of total revenue is produced by the endowment payout? Is the rate of return sufficient to maintain the proportion or increase it? More detail may become necessary as the college struggles to ascertain specific causes of the weaknesses. Once again, auditors can be of assistance here.

Financial condition summative indicators

- *Moody's:* John Nelson, senior vice president of Moody's, has found that the strongest indicators of a small college's financial ability to handle debt are its operating margin and expendable resources to debt ratios.[7] Colleges should be alarmed if they have more than two years of operating margin deficits greater than 5 percent or free expendable resources to debt ratio* less than 10 percent. In his experience, the values for the preceding ratios indicate a significant potential for financial trouble.[8]

- *Composite Financial Index:* CFI can play both sides of the fence in estimating financial strength or weakness. An index score less than or equal to three is problematic, and a score greater than three suggests that the institution is in a strong financial position, according to the *Ratio Analysis in Higher Education* scoring system.[9] A score in the range of one to three suggests that the board and president need to redesign the institution; simple tweaks will not be good enough to preserve the college.[10] When the score drops to one or less, then the viability of the institution is called into question.

*Free expendable resources to debt ratio is: (Unrestricted Net Assets + Restricted Net Assets − Net Plant) / Direct Debt.

Scores greater than three indicate that the institution is in the fortunate position of being able to use its resources to transform itself and improve its competitive position.

Diagnostic Step 3: Market Diagnostics

Because the financial strategy and market strategy must fit hand-in-glove, the college needs to understand its place in the market. Why do some applicants prefer to enroll in another college? Why do students drop out after a semester, a year, or shortly before earning their degrees? The chief academic officer, financial aid director, and the chief enrollment officer are the key members of the market diagnostic team. They should conduct an exhaustive study of demographics, enrollment, attrition, and competitors. The following suggests ways of looking at these four key components of market analysis:

- *Demographics:* The market diagnostic team should profile the current enrollment pool by program and level (graduate or undergraduate), compiling demographics for each. Is the current student mix desirable with its present combination of student characteristics, home versus campus residency, full-time versus part-time status, prior schooling, and test scores? If not, the market scheme should be adjusted or reconstructed to target the desired student pool.

- *Enrollments:* What attracts students? Is it tuition discounts, the campus, amenities, streamlined application processes, faculty, or renowned graduate and undergraduate programs? Each program at every level should generate a clear profile of participants. The market diagnostic team should question students and staff to determine which factors encourage registration. Though the happy student is the least likely to offer opinions, both current and former satisfied students should be interviewed when possible. Former students will share their experiences with friends and family and potential enrollees, so it behooves the alma mater to get the alumni dirt on the good old days. Even employers of alumni can offer valuable insights into the strengths of the college, given their take on the pertinent academic qualifications of their new or veteran hires.

- *Probability of graduation and attrition:* National studies suggest that the probability of graduating with a bachelor's degree from a private institution in six years (the standard measure used by most studies) is 80 percent.[11] Thus, the attrition rate is 20 percent. So, if the attrition rate at your institution is substantially higher than the average, it is probably too high to provide a stable enrollment base for the institution. Retention is costly for a college because more money is spent finding replacements for the attrited class. Plus, the college ends up absorbing a tremendous amount of time and expense dealing with students who are not doing well in class.

  The marketing and student service teams must interview dropouts and develop a marketing plan (up to and including tuition discounts) to bring them back. Is the graduation rate less than 15 percent? Why? Maybe academic policy does not allow for courses to be offered frequently enough. Problems must be identified and remedied before new enrollments are dissuaded.

  The admissions department should follow up by phone (no one reads letters) with all inquiries, admitted students, and enrolled students for a year. It should also keep close watch of potential dropouts, arranging personal meetings when practical to encourage continued enrollment. Remember, graduates are a college's best references.

- *Competition:* The president and finance team should meet with relevant offices (admissions and development) and faculty to identify and classify the competition. Have new not-for-profit or national for-profit institutions entered the market? Not-for-profits might be thrown by an aggressive campaign including direct mail, phone counseling, improved services, new advertisements, and/or new channels for advertisements, but for-profits won't be foiled so easily. For-profits build market share quickly. Strategic planning is a must to combat for-profits. A joint venture may be the only way to keep them from stealing the college's student pool.

Every competitor should be classified according to its marketing strategies, themes, and campaigns, and then compared with the college on the same counts. How do competitors rank in terms of their programs, services, and amenities? Obviously, students who forsook the college for a competitor would have much insight to offer regarding the competitor's strengths. But interviews with the college's current *dissatisfied* students may be just as useful. From the application process to the course selection process to the matriculation process to the graduation process, unhappy students will not withhold their opinions where conveniences are concerned; they will be the first to let the college know where its services and programs are weak.

What about the competition's tuition, net price, revenue, gifts, endowment return, fund raising, and debt trends? (Sources of financial and enrollment data include John Minter and Associates; Guidestar; IPEDS;* and data are also available from state postsecondary agencies.) Such information can provide yield rates for each level of student matriculation, which will be useful later in the establishment of benchmarks in the college's competitive financial strategy.

As the college filters market goals from its research, it must remain amenable to various approaches to strengthening market position. Colleges often stick with the first potentially fruitful market approach they find, thereby closing the door on a host of alternatives. To help identify and evaluate alternatives, Robert Lenington suggests that colleges employ consultants who can perform careful market and cost-benefit analyses of each new approach.[12]

---

*IPEDS is the Independent Postsecondary Education Data System run by the U.S. Department of Education.

If the college can determine why some students enrolled and graduated, and why some students left, it has a chance of maintaining or rebuilding its market share. Building on strengths is a given. Enticing traitors or dropouts back with tuition discounts may be wise. But certainly, the financially troubled college would do well to tend its flock, however small it may still be, especially in the presence of new and existing predators.

- *Market realities:* No college can survive if it ignores the marketplace. A market is not simply a store where you go to sell products to students. Even the best endowed private institutions have to be cognizant of their place in the market. If they ignore their donor market, or their research market, or their student markets, they will have a Potemkin village where the board and president spend money to sanctify their sense of virtue, but only the most faithful will come. Private colleges are as market driven as any business. They must respond to the marketplace if they expect to have students, research grants, or donors. Otherwise, the place is doomed!

WHAT IF A TURNAROUND IS NOT FEASIBLE? END GAMES

For some colleges the odds are too overwhelming. Deficits, cash shortages, shrinking enrollment, and the use of debt to fund ongoing operations push the college to the brink. If the CFI score is low to negative and their Moody's ratios are well below the median, then the college lacks the financial resources to carry out its mission. It must look at its options with a critical eye because it is unfair to students to offer an inadequate education or to run them out the door when the college suddenly closes its doors. Boards that are contemplating exit strategies should look at three options: mergers, sales, or closing the doors of the college.

Mergers or Sales

If the college has residual value (e.g., property, a student market, licensing and accreditation of programs), it may be attractive to another college. However, it cannot wait until it is desperate before it considers a merger or sale. Other not-for-profit institutions will be reluctant to merge with an institution that has no residual value. They will see the offer as a losing proposition in which they use scarce resources to rebuild market and academic integrity of the troubled institution. Robert Lenington says that mergers can be a viable option:

> Assuming an institution has an appropriate mission, a good program, and a service that is in demand. And all of the constituencies associated with an institution in financial difficulty are best served by merger if the alternative is the eventual financial collapse and demise of the institution. Allowing an institution to fail financially[,] and then have society pay for the start-up and development of similar operations elsewhere is wasteful.[13]

The same problem exists when offering the college for sale. The college must have residual value, which minimally includes a viable market and accreditation. Otherwise, the potential purchaser may believe that it can get a better deal by waiting for liquidation. If a sale is made, the issue is what happens with any funds in excess of outstanding liabilities. There is a low probability that this would happen. If it could happen, the board needs to consult with a good tax attorney. As a not-for-profit entity, the college was granted a waiver on income taxes. The sale and ending of the mission of the college may have state and federal tax implications.

Closing the Doors

If the college has little or no residual value, it may have no choice but to close its doors. This calls for more than merely locking the doors and handing the keys to the banker. As a board confronts the demise of the college, they have a duty to look after the welfare of the students and the employees. The board should observe the guidelines listed in Table 13.2.

TABLE 13.2—STEPS TO CLOSING A COLLEGE

1. Do not close the doors part way through a semester.
2. Find another college that will take the student records.
3. Notify students so that they can make their own plans.
4. Help students transfer to another college.
5. If funds are available, arrange for outplacement for the faculty and staff.
6. Transfer financial records and archives to storage for safekeeping.
7. Give copies of tax records to the auditors.
8. Determine what is to be done with personnel records.
9. Hire counsel to handle relationships with creditors.
9. Sell remaining assets; use funds for outstanding liabilities.

Forestalling foreclosure is only possible if a college takes steps before distress becomes a crisis. If the college waits until foreclosure is threatened, it is too late to take remedial action. Small colleges must act as soon as they detect serious problems with their financial or market conditions. This means that the college must continually track its financial and market conditions to avoid the sad end of the college. Strategic planning, leadership, management, and good business practices must have time to take effect.

SUMMARY

Table 13.3 on the next page provides a simple summary of the steps that a board can take when trying to determine what they should do with long-term decline. These steps may provide the basis for a reasonable decision.

TABLE 13.3—DIAGNOSTIC AND TURNAROUND SUMMARY

1. Get good financial, marketing, and academic program data.

2. Conduct standard financial analysis using trends, ratios, and benchmarks.

3. Build a five-year financial forecast model.

4. Use Moody's and CFI summative analyses to estimate the current financial condition.

5. Use current conditions in the financial forecast model to estimate financial condition in five years.

6. With chief management officers, board representatives, and other key institutional leaders, identify internal strengths and weaknesses, and external opportunities and threats (this should be based on data and analysis collected in the previous steps).

7. Based on preceding steps, determine whether a turnaround is feasible or whether the college needs to look at transition alternatives, such as merger, sale, or closing down the institution.

8. If turnaround is recommended, identify strategic initiatives and prepare action plans with budgets.

9. Test strategic initiatives with the CFI and the forecast model.

10. Prepare the final list of recommended strategies and plans.

11. Review the plan with the faculty for their input subject to the condition of not being bogged down in process.

12. Submit recommendations to the board of trustees for approval.

13. Initiate action!

ENDNOTES

1. U.S. Department of Education. (2008). Table 257: Degree-grant-
    ing institutions that have closed their doors, by control and type
    of institution: 1969–70 through 2006–07. National Center for
    Education Statistics. Retrieved August 31, 2008, from http://nces.
    ed.gov/programs/digest/d07/tables/dt07_257.asp?referrer=list.
2. U.S. Department of Education. (1999). Table 256: Degree-grant-
    ing institutions and branches by type and control of institution
    and state of jurisdiction 2006–07. National Center for Education
    Statistics. Retrieved August 31, 2008, from http://nces.ed.gov/
    programs/digest/d07/tables/dt07_256.asp?referrer=list.
3. Lenington, R. *Colleges are a Business!* (Phoenix, AZ: Oryx Press,
    1996), p. 34.
4. Dehne, G. C. *Student Recruitment: A Marketing Primer for Presidents.*
    (Old Saybrook, CT: GDA Integrated Services, 2001).
5. Dwyer, C. *Managing People* (2nd ed.). (Dubuque, IA: Kendall/
    Hunt, 1996).
6. Salluzzo, R. E., Tahey, P., Prager, F. J., & Cowen, C. J. *Ratio Analysis
    in Higher Education* (4th ed.). (Washington, DC: KPMG & Prager,
    McCarthy & Sealy, 1999).
7. Nelson, John (Senior Vice President, Moody's Investors Service),
    E-mail interview, New York, November 8, 2001.
8. Ibid.
9. Salluzzo, R. E., Tahey, P., Prager, F. J., & Cowen, C. J. *Ratio Analysis
    in Higher Education* (4th ed.). (Washington, DC: KPMG & Prager,
    McCarthy & Sealy, 1999), p. 24.
10. Ibid.
11. Higher Education Research Institute. *How "Good" is Your Retention
    Rate?* (Los Angeles: Higher Education Research Institute, Univer-
    sity of California, 2003) Retrieved July 17, 2008, from http://
    www.gseis.ucla.edu/~heri/PDFs/DARCU_RB.PDF.
12. Lenington, R. *Colleges are a Business!* (Phoenix, AZ: Oryx Press,
    1996), p. 36.
13. Ibid, p. 41.

CHAPTER 14

MAINTAINING FORWARD MOMENTUM

Once a private college or university has built a strong and viable financial base, it needs to nourish that base carefully so that changes in student markets, the economy, or leadership do not significantly erode its financial condition. There is ample evidence that tuition-dependent private institutions* face continuing challenges in retaining their financial viability. There is little margin for error for these institutions because the surplus from revenue and expenses is so narrow (see Figure 14.1 on the next page). This suggests that colleges or universities with small endowments will face greater stress as higher education responds to changes in the number of high school graduates, and this stress could be amplified during periods of economic turmoil.

Some independent institutions will also be pressured by changes in demographics as student markets shrink in the Northeast and Midwest and by tougher competition from public institutions in the South and Southwest where markets continue to expand. Public institutions in these regions have become savvier at marketing and keeping their students from moving out of state to regions where the markets are shrinking. Private institutions from the cold climates and weakened economies of the Midwest and Northeast will have a hard time convincing prospective students from the South to move north.

***

*Tuition-dependent is defined as a ratio of tuition and fees to total revenue equal to or greater than 60 percent.

FIGURE 14.1—REVENUE AND EXPENSES FOR TUITION-DEPENDENT PRIVATE COLLEGES AND UNIVERSITIES, 1998–2002

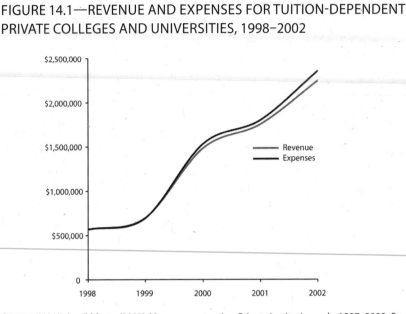

Source: JMA Higher Ed Stats. (2002). Management ratios: Private institutions, xls: 1997–2000. Boulder, CO: John Minter and Associates.

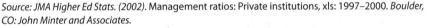

So, what do financially stable institutions (or those going through a turnaround) need to do to maintain their forward momentum? It is imperative that everyone understand that the financial condition is dependent on everything that happens in the college. This calls for a comprehensive strategic plan integrating finances, academic programs, student services, marketing, administrative services, and capital investment. Chief academic and financial officers must work as a team with a president who motivates everyone to "perform beyond the ordinary."[1]

An effective strategic plan is not just a set of documents saying what will be done; it has to incorporate a monitoring system that evaluates all sectors in the strategy. The strategic plan needs measurable objectives that become the references for the monitoring system. Moreover, each year, the president and chief administrative officers need to review and revise the plan in response to economic conditions, the student market, and other salient factors that drive the financial condition of the institution.

In the end, astute and rational leaders will attend to details and work very, very hard to ensure more than the mere *survival* of their colleges in this next decade. To *prosper* involves acquiring the resources necessary to provide quality education while responding to intensifying competition, student demands, and various impending economic federal regulations and tax challenges. Doing this requires that leaders in private colleges and universities become well acquainted with the ingredients of financial strength and market savvy (regardless of how distasteful they may be at first).

PERFORMANCE MEASURES FOR MONITORING STRATEGIC PERFORMANCE

Even the most charismatic president will find the coming challenges difficult to surmount, especially when scarce resources limit responses to the marketplace. Nevertheless, as they gear up for the next challenge, leaders can take knowledge and inspiration from the observations, experiences, and suggestions of learned consultants, financial analysts, and presidents, which is distilled in the following subsections.

Financial Performance

There are a few simple rules to follow when it comes to managing financial performance. Simplicity in higher education is always fraught with controversy and laden with complexity. Table 14.1 on the next page provides a ready guide to help in decision making and in designing a device to monitor financial performance.

Marketing Performance

Marketing boils down to this simple formula: prospective students must know about the college, the college must meet their academic and social needs, and the cost must fit within their financial means. Currently, the marketing literature suggests that colleges need to develop a recognizable brand name known to prospective students. Also, the marketing plan must reach the right target market for the college, the pool of prospective students must be large enough to

TABLE 14.1—GUIDELINES: FINANCIAL PERFORMANCE MEASURES

General Financial Objectives

- Is the Composite Financial Index (CFI) score greater than 3?
- What is the trend for net tuition; is it growing or falling?
- Are auxiliaries producing positive net income after depreciation?
- Does the development office produce gifts or indirect costs[a] from grants in excess of its operational costs?
- Are revenue and expense growth rates balanced or in favor of revenue?
- How is net income used; is it simply placed in a cash account?
- Are cash reserves equal to or greater than 16 percent of expenses?
- Are uncollectible receivables growing faster than receivables?
- Do the athletic programs generate revenues that offset the rate of growth in their expenditures?
- Do the financial reports tie back to audited financial statements—activities, financial position, and cash flow?

Operations

- Are operational costs per student for academic programs growing at the same rate when compared to benchmark institutions or to tuition revenue per student?
- Are classes approaching the size that only covers the direct cost of instruction?
- Are operational costs per student for administrative and student service departments growing at the same rate in comparison to benchmark institutions or to inflation?
- Has the athletic department set reasonable operational costs per athlete based on institutional, conference, or peer benchmarks?
- Is the attrition rate declining?
- Is the graduation rate increasing?
- Are graduation skills commensurate with objectives and with the cost of producing those skills?
- Does the college have operational productivity benchmarks, are they monitored, and are administrative reviews conducted on operational performance?

TABLE 14.1—GUIDELINES: FINANCIAL PERFORMANCE MEASURES

Capital Investments

- Are the investments in the endowment fund growing at a rate equal to or greater than a basket of similar investments in the financial market?
- When investing in a capital project that will generate revenue, is the net present value[b] of the investment greater than zero?
- When investing in a capital project that does not generate revenue, how will the institution cover operational, depreciation, and capital expenses?
- When a capital construction project is awarded, does the contract include bonding requirements for the contractor and penalty clauses for failure to perform?

[a] *Indirect costs from grants are administrative and capital expenses that granting agencies (usually the government) permit an institution to recover by including these expenses in the total funds authorized by the grant.*
[b] *See Appendix C, Financial Measures, for the computation of the net present value. This benchmark is typically used to evaluate investments by computing the present value of future cash flows and netting them against the original cost of the investment.*

produce sufficient revenue to support the operational costs of running the college, and academic programs should respond to changes in the student and job markets. The guidelines in Table 14.2 suggest questions that need to be asked to determine whether the marketing strategy works.

TABLE 14.2—GUIDELINES: MARKETING PERFORMANCE MEASURES

- Is there a tuition discount plan that allocates institutional aid based on the characteristics of the students that the institution prefers to enroll?
- Are yields (not rates) adequate to support enrollment and to enroll students with preferred characteristics?
- Are new programs attracting sufficient net tuition to cover expenses?
- Are new full-time-equivalent students enrolling in sufficient numbers to provide robust classes given the attrition rate and the cost of operating the institution?

GENERAL ADMINISTRATIVE RULES

Strategic plans are the framework to building and continuing the financial viability of a private institution. Undergirding any strategy must be a set of administrative or management rules that provide the policies and procedures to carry out the strategic plan. The set of rules are not arcane, but leaders who intend to apply basic management rules to point the institution in the right direction must expect to support the rules and act as role models. There is nothing more destructive to leadership than leaders who flaunt the rules but expect others to follow the same rules or leaders who turn a blind eye to others in the organization (often seen as friends or toadies) who ignore the rules.

Although policies and procedures are meant to provide a consistent, coherent, and cogent framework for decisions, they should not become hidebound or negate the need to improve the productivity of the institution. Policies and procedures should follow the proposition that workflows should be constantly reviewed to eliminate bottlenecks, to simplify workflow, to reduce labor-intensive tasks, and to provide a straightforward process that students can easily understand. Table 14.3 on the next page lists several basic guidelines that others have found to be effective in supporting the strategic aims of the organization.

POSSIBLE EVENTS FORCING RESTRUCTURING OF THE MARKETPLACE

Given the events of the first years of this century, it is not unreasonable to assume that the market for higher education will be upset by ongoing trends and by unexpected events. However, there is clear evidence that certain trends are going to have a dramatic impact on higher education in general and private institutions in particular. Several trends already evident may force a major restructuring of the market for private institutions. The greatest impact could be on the weakest sectors of the private market for higher education—tuition-dependent and small colleges with modest endowments.

TABLE 14.3—GUIDELINES: GENERAL ADMINISTRATIVE RULES

- The business office should have policies and procedures that govern its work and that are derived from standard practices in the profession.
- The rules should be kept simple and be published (the intranet site is the best place).
- Administrative procedures for students should be simple and for their benefit.
- Administrative software should be used to manage student flow[a] through the institution.
- Accountability should be matched with the distribution of authority. Do not assign responsibilities without authority.
- Formal evaluations of all employees prior to assigning pay increases need to be done.
- Adequate cash and purchasing controls must be in place to ensure that unauthorized purchases are eliminated.
- Monitoring of class scheduling will maximize classroom use, minimize self-dealing among instructors, and achieve reasonable class size for all programs.

[a] *Student flows are the set of processes and policies that take a student from admissions through course enrollment, instruction, and graduation.*

Some possible events may force restructuring of the weakest sector of the private market for higher education, including those discussed in the following subsections.

Competition

Competition from online programs and shifting demographics could force colleges and universities to make large reductions in net price. This will place the weakest sectors of the private market at risk because they cannot meet cash needs or debt obligations. Additionally, competition from online programs could strip the easy cash flowing from continuing education programs that often offsets the deficits produced in the traditional day programs.

The Higher Education Act (HEA)

The new federal rules in the Higher Education Act (HEA) will see private institutions posted on a "wall of shame" when they increase their tuition by an above-average rate. Parents or prospective students may use the wall of shame as a way of identifying private colleges to avoid. This could be catastrophic to financially vulnerable colleges because they may need above-average tuition increases to balance their budgets and to keep from sliding into a financial morass.

New federal unfunded mandates represent a desire to achieve a good end, but they also carry heavy costs. Over the years, governmental mandates have added to the cost of education either directly by requiring new expenditures or indirectly by not providing support unless the institution complies with unrelated federal regulations. A quick sampling of federal mandated compliance includes the disabilities act, education services for students who are challenged by the requirements of higher education, publication of crime statistics, and federal standards on financial aid. The recent reauthorization of the HEA requires that colleges produce information on textbooks, fire safety, graduation rates, drug safety, alumni activity, and foreign gift reporting, just to name a few new items. Some of these items will have a minor effect on most colleges, such as foreign gift reporting, while others, such as the regulations on textbooks, fire safety, graduation rates, or alumni activity, could add a considerable amount of work to financially stressed colleges already inundated with meeting other unfunded mandates. If new personnel and information technology systems are needed to track and report data, then there is a real cost that must eventually be borne by the student through higher tuition. Of course, this unintended consequence of the HEA reauthorization reporting requirements could push the institution to the wall of shame, thereby adding to the problem of finding enough students to fund the cost of education. Ironically, the new mandates have the real effect of increasing the financial fragility of some private colleges.

The Credit Crunch

The credit crunch may have the greatest impact on private institutions. News that Commonfund had to close down two money funds with a delayed payout has sent many colleges scrambling for credit lines. The crunch has also clamped down funding for major capital projects. Boston University, in the midst of the credit crises, put all new capital projects on hold and froze hiring.[2] This is a university with a sterling financial reputation that was forced to confront the threat posed by the collapse of the credit markets.

The credit crunch also undermines the student market because many of the private lenders have abandoned this market, and the role that federal support of student loans will have is not yet clear. The most vulnerable colleges or universities are those that draw a significant number of students who do not have the personal or family funds to support their own education.

The *Chronicle of Higher Education* provides a tidy summary of which colleges would be the winners and losers from the credit crunch:

"Winners:

- Colleges with big endowments, low debt, and strong name brands... colleges that can handle... distance-education programs

- Deep-pocket institutions that can expand programs, poach faculty members, or buy up stocks on the cheap

- Colleges that focus on doing a few things well rather than being everything to everyone

- Institutions with diverse donor pools or donors who can make money in this market.

Losers:

- Middle-class families

- Colleges that rely on donor money for student aid

- High-priced, tuition-dependent private colleges

- Colleges that are behind schedule on projects and maintenance

- Fund-raising programs heavily dependent on Wall Street

- States slammed by the housing slump—Arizona, California, Florida, Nevada."[3]

As is evident from this list, there are two types of winners: institutions that have a strong financial base, wealthy alumni, and a historical reputation for quality and prestige that is attractive to donors, or colleges offering quality distance education programs that allows them to jump outside the geographic bounds of their on-campus markets. Winners are strategically focused institutions. The losers include any institution that is directly or indirectly dependent on the credit market to generate enrollment and to finance capital projects.

The credit crunch has the potential of being the *black swan event*** that could threaten the financial viability of many private colleges. Whether this is a black swan or not will depend on the speed with which the credit markets respond to federal initiatives to stabilize them. Even if these initiatives swiftly take hold, easy credit for students and colleges may not return for many years.

Demographics

Demographic declines in high school graduates in the Northeast and Midwest take significant chunks out of the enrollment of the financially vulnerable sector, which could force institutions to merge, sell out, or close. Demographic transition to a student pool mix heavily weighted with Hispanic students, who prefer to remain in their locality and who need additional support to strengthen their academic skills, could further erode private institutions that are not prepared for the change. Private institutions in the Northeast and Midwest will have the most difficult time convincing these students to move a long distance from home. In addition, financially fragile institutions lack the capability to provide the academic support that these students may need.

---

*A black swan event is the billion-to-one circumstance that everyone knows about but no one expects to happen. They assume that even though a black swan could wreak havoc, it is so unlikely that there is no reason to prepare for it.

SUMMARY

Why do so many financially weak private colleges persist? The answer is multifaceted, but the best reason for explaining their persistence was given by Moody's Investors Service. A common reason that students and parents are willing to pay a high price for a degree from a private college or university is that they either trust that students are not lost in the gigantism of public institutions or they believe that graduates do better in the job market.[4]

Another idiosyncratic reason, according to Christopher Jencks and David Riesman is that private institutions can cater to homogeneous student populations, and public institutions are not politically mandated to build smaller institutions needed to serve niche markets.[5] Though most small independent colleges don't face an imminent danger of being swept away, their missions and financial integrity will face powerful challenges in the years to come.

After competitive and market pressures push colleges (or whole sectors) into decline, cash shortages could force them to close. Loan calls, loss of confidence among donors, enrollments that fail to generate sufficient cash, student neglect of bills, and government denial of college access to financial aid funds constitute just a few of the sudden causes of cash shortages. In most cases, however, evidence of decline has been readily apparent for some time; and following a college closure, many lament that "someone" should have done "something" to stop it.

Alternatives to closure, such as mergers, partnerships, or new leadership, are vulnerable to loyalties and location restrictions. Mergers and partnerships are especially hard to realize because no concentrated ownership remains to make profit-maximizing decisions. Urban or suburban colleges may be the best candidates for mergers or partnerships, provided that they offer valuable services and that their leaders are poised to act quickly. Colleges isolated in rural regions with declining student markets and no way to fund emergencies through donors may find closing their only option.

Private colleges waiting for a federal bailout shouldn't hold their breath. The federal government, which awards nearly $600 million in Pell grants alone, excluding college work-study funds, supplemental educational opportunity grants, and subsidized loans (Stafford and Perkins loans, and nonsubsidized Plus loans), is not likely to tolerate arguments that college closures will constrain student choice or limit access to education. First, the government would argue that it already supports choice through awarding money that students can use at any college; a particular college's (or an entire sector's) inability to entice students falls far outside the government's rescue scope. Second, though small private colleges answer a need for accessible centers of higher education in geographically isolated areas, the lack of such access simply doesn't carry enough weight to spur the government's notice. Besides, states have answered the accessibility problem themselves by investing heavily in conveniently located community colleges and public universities; why should the government interfere? All told, small colleges present neither a large nor a united constituency capable of rousing the government's protection.

Whether a precipitating event will force massive changes in the small college market is not immediately evident. Nevertheless, there appear to be powerful forces such as the collapse of credit markets that could precipitate massive changes in the private college and university market. These forces could be accelerated if auditors take aggressive action against shaky private institutions, as they did with small hospitals in the 1980s and 1990s, and if credit rating agencies tighten credit requirements on fragile institutions. Then, financially distressed colleges may find themselves in the same unenviable position of being trapped between the Scylla of shrinking markets and the Charybdis imposed by government pressure to limit tuition price increases.

Financially fragile private colleges can save themselves, but they cannot wait until they are in the middle of a full-blown financial crisis. Leaders must diagnose current financial, market, and academic conditions; construct a viable and integrative strategy; inspire the college from its board members to the community at large; press for action; make the tough decisions; and finally, build and put a strategic plan into operation. Some strategies come with risk. Unnecessary risk is ever present when colleges enter into debt to finance revenue projects with fuzzy financial forecasts, recruit international students from politically volatile regions of the world, offer tuition discounts that negate cash flow increases, approve student payment plans *sans* effective collection policies, or condone off-sheet financing that hides true credit position at their peril.

So, how will private colleges fare as competition surges, costs remain intransigent to control, credit markets remain inaccessible, and demographics work against their academic strategy? Data suggest that many colleges will continue to bumble from one crisis to the next, surviving on small gifts from caring alumni. Mere survival may no longer be a realistic strategy given all that is befalling higher education.

Answers to the questions of who will or will not prosper or fade into the mists may be clearer if private colleges and universities are divided into three categories: those that are rich, those that are financially distressed and whose leaders recognize them as such, and those that suffer financial distress under a clueless leadership. The rich college will fare well because it has the means and the resource capacity to absorb unexpected crises. Financially distressed colleges, however, will need to forgo luck and turn to a sharp leader who can avert it from the brink. In the absence of shrewd leadership, old ways will persist in the face of new pressures that have high likelihood of forcing small, hard-pressed colleges into mergers or out of existence. Nevertheless, short of bankruptcy, there is not enough market, financial, or government pressures to force troubled colleges to make dramatic changes. Absent the demands of creditors or patrons, these colleges will stumble along on their own path satisfied with taking the scraps left over in the market.

How will private colleges and universities that do not have their backs against the wall flourish? There is no single answer to this question. To flourish, private colleges and universities must do the following:

- Move from administration* of the college's resources and operations to management of the same. Managers work from the premise that work is defined in terms of mission, strategy,

*Administrators make sure that records are kept; authority, policies, procedures, and regulations are enforced; and personnel work within institutional rules and governmental regulations.

goals, and performance. Managers vigorously pursue work in the best and most cost-effective way to meet the needs of the market.

- Become mindful that the viability of the institution depends on how well the college's mission defines its services or products that fulfill the needs of a target market and the willingness of the market to pay the college's price for those services. This means that the board, president, chief financial officers, and other faculty must understand the college's market.

- Remain vigilant that strategic plans meet the needs of the college and measure whether or not performance is achieving strategic goals.

- Produce financial reports that meet these criteria:

  - The data on factors that determine the scale of major revenue and expenditure accounts are reported;

  - Financial reports are tied to audited financial statements for activities, financial position, and cash;

  - Productivity measures are included in financial reports; and

  - Financial performance is compared to benchmarks.

- The financial position of the college will improve when:

  - Cash increases relative to operational expenses;

  - Net income is positive and growing faster than expenses;

  - Excess cash is converted into long-term investments;

  - Debt is mainly used for projects that produce net revenue or improve operational efficiency; and

  - The score for the Composite Financial Index[*] is greater than three, and it continues to improve over time.

---

[*]Appendix G: Composite Financial Index and the CFI Worksheet on CD explain the purpose, reasoning, and methodology behind the index.

A well-managed college is readily apparent to students, parents, visitors, and employees because it looks well run, instruction and services are delivered effectively and efficiently, all employees are acknowledged for their contribution to the success of the institution, and the college is always seeking new services, markets, and improvements in the operation of the institution. None of this is easy, but it will ensure that the college will do more than survive, by providing an important service to its students, donors, and grantors, and to the country.

ENDNOTES

1. Keller, G. *Academic Strategy* (Baltimore: Johns Hopkins University Press, 1983), p. 125.

2. Jan, T. (2008). "BU Head Calls for Hiring Freeze," *Boston Globe, City & Region*, B1.

3. Chronicle of Higher Education. (2008). *Winners and Losers in the Shake-Up*. Retrieved October 3, 2008, from http://chronicle.com/daily/2008/10/4850n.htm.

4. Moody's Investors Service. *U.S. Higher Education Outlook*. (New York: Moody's Investors Service, 2008).

5. Jencks, Christopher., & Riesman, David. *The Academic Revolution* (Garden City, NJ: Anchor Books, Doubleday and Company, 1969), p. 288.

CHAPTER 15

PRIVATE INSTITUTIONS: FUTURE PROBLEMS OR OPPORTUNITIES

The fall of 2008 was not an auspicious period for higher education or, for that matter, for any other organizations dependent on the vagaries of the economy for their survival. Has the world turned upside down, leaving private colleges and universities to the mercies of a merciless economy? Or have new opportunities presented themselves to those colleges with the prescience and fortitude to turn economic misery into newfound opportunities? More than likely, the fate of most institutions is not a swift fall from financial stability into the dismal swamp of failure and bankruptcy as has been the case with banks, investment houses, retail outlets, and major manufacturers. Private colleges and universities are somewhat like graduates standing with families, diplomas in hand, smiling and wondering if they can make sense of the world and their futures.

What has happened during this first decade of the third millennium? The tech bubble burst, the 9/11 crisis occurred, Congress pushed higher education to hold down costs, and the credit crunch, the market crash, and the end of many fortunes that were generous to higher education all followed. Revenues of colleges were cruising well above expenses between 1998 and 2000 during the fat years caused by the technology boom. There was a huge investment in new computers and software as everyone tried to avoid the prophesized horrors of Y2K. The run-up in the financial markets spilled over to colleges

FIGURE 15.1—REVENUE AND EXPENSES, 1998–2002

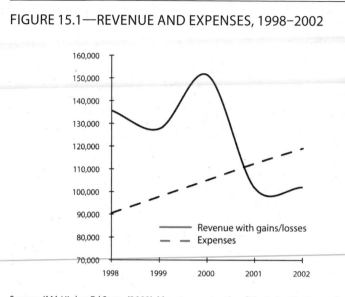

Source: JMA Higher Ed Stats. (2002). Management ratios: Private institutions, xls: 1997–2000. Boulder, CO: John Minter and Associates.

as endowments grew almost exponentially and gifts flowed as if every day was Christmas. Revenue first nosedived below expenses in 2002 as colleges felt the full brunt of the bursting tech bubble, when demand for new computers dried up because the fears of Y2K were either under control or were merely a chimera. Then, just as the economy and financial markets were poised to recover, 9/11 took the wind out of the economy. A week without airliners in the sky, the East Coast frozen in fear, everyone avoiding planes like a plague, and the start of the Afghanistan and Iraq wars just sucked the economy dry. Colleges saw endowment values plunge, meaning endowment draws sunk and gifts also shrunk. The impact of world events on higher education is chronicled in Figure 15.1, which shows what happened between 1998 and 2002 as the economy boomed and crashed.

The real estate market boom followed the same boom and bust cycle, and it was followed by the credit crunch of 2008. Private colleges and universities can expect to see the same impact on their endowments, gifts, and bottom lines during this period. This cycle, however, is different, as is evident from the failure of the market to make a quick return to stability. In fact, it is evident that this economic downturn could be the worst since the Great Depression.

What does this latest financial crisis, given the factors creating it, signify for private institutions? Is it just another period of hunkering down and waiting for the economy to right itself, or will the upheaval in credit markets push some independent institutions to merge or close, leading to major changes in the market structure for private institutions of higher education? Time will tell. Nevertheless, this is not a standard recession when the president of Harvard feels it is imperative to tell the university community that even with its multibillion endowment it must tighten its belt and prepare for an extended period of economic uncertainty.[1]

Previous chapters have cited the most significant threats: student loans, demographics, price controls, cost pressures, and sharpened competition. This economic upheaval has caught private colleges at the end of their options of what to do to solidify their financial situation. Private colleges and universities, both the poor and the well-to-do, have expanded markets, increased financial aid, built Taj Mahals for their students, added star research faculty, created new academic programs, enlarged student support services, and dumped large sums on reducing attrition and increasing graduation rates. Now they are told that they must do more and must do it better if they expect to survive. This is bitter medicine to swallow after most private colleges and their presidents had thought they had made significant strategic strides in turning their college into top-flight institutions of higher education. This new economic threat boils down to a set of immediate and pressing strategic issues that private institutions must address if they want to avoid slipping into financial instability:

- *Issue 1:* Will the credit crunch do away with private loans for many high school students, thereby shrinking the pool of high school graduates who can afford a private college or university?

- *Issue 2:* Will the sharp decline in home values eliminate home equity loans, and will tougher rules on private loans push prospective students into public institutions?

- *Issue 3:* Will demanding credit rules force currently enrolled students to switch to less expensive private institutions or finish at a public institution?

- *Issue 4:* Will banks call in variable rate debt, compelling private colleges onto an unforgiving credit market and raising cost of debt or draining cash resources to pay the balance due?

- *Issue 5:* Will colleges that live on credit lines find that banks are reluctant to increase the line or to continue to provide the line, throwing the college into a cash crisis?

- *Issue 6:* Will colleges that depend on annual funds and draws from small endowments to break even find that big gifts dry up, driving them into deficit?

- *Issue 7:* Will the decline in endowment values lead to two years of deficits as it did in 2001 and 2002?

- *Issue 8:* Will economic growth slow to a snail's pace, reducing endowment growth to a small portion of the double-digit rates experienced previously and turning nontuition-dependent private colleges into tuition-dependent colleges for which they are unprepared strategically or tactically?

- *Issue 9:* Will the combination of depressed endowment values, tight credit markets, and the precipitous fall in home values conspire to drive many students out of the market, leaving colleges on the verge of financial crisis?

The answer to these questions will have to come on a college-by-college basis. Yet, as was noted in earlier sections, several basic rules can guide colleges as they respond to this sharp and painful blow from this dispirited economy. The rules are based on the presumption that the president, board, and the key leaders of the institution are amenable to responding to the crisis and not just doing a white-knuckle ride out. If management chooses the latter, they better hope that the government throws tons of money at the student loan problem and that the market makes a quick recovery. If management wants more than the white-knuckle ride, then they should consider the following rules:

- *Rule 1:* Immediately rework your strategy.

- *Rule 2:* Expand your markets with new programs, new geographic regions, and/or new delivery systems.

- *Rule 3:* Clearly define your niche; give students a valid reason to enroll; be more than another liberal arts college.

- *Rule 4:* Sharpen your competitive skills; find your market and go after it like a college coach goes after a top prospect for next year's team.

- *Rule 5:* Form administrative partnerships to cut operational costs.

- *Rule 6:* Redesign your administrative systems; simplify and cut costs; stop wasting money.

- *Rule 7:* Find academic partners to run synergistic instructional programs.

- *Rule 8:* See whether it makes sense to join with another college to create an administrative umbrella or even a quasi-university.

As noted earlier, these rules force the college's leadership to come to terms with the fact that what they did in the past is now in the past and that they must again work to push the Sisyphean rock up the mountain. These rules are just starting points; you will have to figure out how they apply to your college and to its situation.

Presidents who do the hard work, use the tools in this book, and are sensitive to their student market and to the economy will be rewarded in the long term with an institution that rests on a strong and secure financial foundation.

ENDNOTES

1.   Jan, T. (2008). "Harvard Looks to Tighten its Belt," *Boston Globe, Metro Edition*, B1, B4.

APPENDIX A

STRATEGIC PLANNING COMPONENTS

This appendix provides institutions with a scheme for preparing a strategic plan.

LOGIC OF THE STRATEGIC PLAN

This document assumes that the institution is mission, market, and student driven. This strategic mission logic also assumes that the mission indicates the service offered for purchase by prospective students is desired by prospective students and that the aggregate set of student purchasers is large enough to cover the costs of producing and managing the services offered.

COMPONENTS OF A STRATEGIC PLAN

A strategic plan works as a feedback system in which new information on conditions in the marketplace and measurement of performance are used to review, modify, and improve the probability of achieving the institution's strategic goals. The strategic plan links together the following set of components that are designed to guide action to a specific outcome, to present what has to be done to achieve the outcome, and to measure the success or lack of success in reaching that outcome:

- Mission statement
- Goals
- Objectives
- Action plan
- Performance assessment plan

Mission Statement

The mission statement defines the service or products that respond to a buyer's needs, identifies the target market that contains the set of buyers, and establishes the resources and technologies that will be deployed to satisfy the customer.[1]

Goals

A goal sets out the expectations for the institution and for each major sector of the institution. For instance, goals should be stated for the institutions and for each academic program, major research programs, academic administration, student services, marketing, financial operations, institutional administration, information technology, plant and grounds operations, capital investments, and auxiliaries. The goal statement should clearly identify the long-term (three to five years) expectations for the preceding sectors. Expectations would indicate that the sector would expect to achieve a major accomplishment by the end of the goal period.

Objectives

Objectives indicate how to achieve goals.[2] Objectives convert goals into measurable performance targets to be accomplished by a specific deadline. The strategic plan usually includes short- and long-term objectives with the short term to be completed within a year and the long term to be accomplished in more than a year.

Action Plan

A plan is prepared for each objective that shows who, what, and when major decisions or actions have to be completed to attain the performance target set for the objective.

Performance Assessment Plan

Assessment determines whether the goals and objectives of the strategy have or have not been achieved. If the objectives logically follow from the goals, and if the objectives include measurable targets with specific deadlines, then it is possible to measure whether actual performance met, exceeded, or fell below expectations.

A SAMPLE STRATEGIC PLAN

Mission

The mission of Resolute College is to offer career-focused bachelor's degrees to high school graduates with grades of C or better or to students transferring from community colleges.

Goals and Objectives

- *Institutional Goal:* Students at Resolute College will earn sufficient credits for a career-focused degree.
- *Academic Affairs Goal:* Academic Affairs will add two new majors to its business degree—major in nonprofit financial accounting and retail management.
  - *Academic Affairs Objective 1:* Ninety-five percent of graduates will be placed within six months in employment suitable for their career ambitions.
  - *Institutional Objective 2:* Eighty percent of graduates will have a cumulative GPA of 3.0 or better in their major courses.

Action and Assessment Plan
INSTITUTIONAL GOAL—OBJECTIVE 1

Responsibility	Action	Deadline	Date Completed
Chief Academic Officer	Assign faculty to new major planning committee	Complete by [date]	
New Major Planning Committee	Review programs by competitors and identify their strengths and weaknesses	Complete by [date]	
New Major Planning Committee	Write description, goal, objectives, and curriculum sequence for the new majors	Complete by [date]	
New Major Planning Committee	Design assessment plan for the new majors	Complete by [date]	

ENDNOTES

1.   Thompson, A., Gamble, J., & Strickland, A. J. *Strategy: Core Concepts, Analytical Tools, Readings* (New York: McGraw-Hill, 2006), pp. 17–18.

2.   Ibid.

APPENDIX B

FINANCIAL, MARKETING, AND MANAGEMENT DIAGNOTICS

I. Financial Diagnostics

A. Operations

	Check off
1. Is the operating net or total net increasing or decreasing; if it is decreasing, why?	
2. Are revenue and expense growth rates in balance?	
3. If revenue is falling, why?	
4. What is the trend for net tuition price relative to expense growth—rising, falling, or stagnant?	
5. What is the trend for net tuition revenue relative to expense growth—rising, falling, or stagnant?	
6. What proportion of revenue is gifts?	
7. Do auxiliaries produce a positive net income?	
8. If the expenses are growing faster than revenue, why?	
9. Is the growth rate for core expenses less than for noncore expenses; if so, why?	
10. What is the trend in total compensation?	
11. What is the tuition dependency rate?	
12. How does operational performance compare to the competition?	

B. Operations—Drivers

	Check off
1. What is the enrollment—by level and by program?	
2. What is the attrition rate—by level and by program?	
3. What is the graduation rate—by level and by program?	
4. How many employees—faculty, staff, and administration?	
5. What is the cost of employees—faculty, staff, and administration?	
6. How are employees allocated between core and noncore services?	
7. What is the student–faculty ratio?	
8. What is the average class size?	
9. How many classrooms are there?	
10. How is space allocated between core and noncore services?	
11. How many parking spaces are there?	

C. Working Capital

	Check off
1. Are cash and short-term investments increasing over time?	
2. Are cash and short-term investments growing as fast as expenses?	
3. What is the source of the increase in cash—operations, increases in payables and accruals, reduction in receivables, increase in short- or long-term debt?	
4. Are cash and short-term investments greater than 16% of expenses? (This is a rough measure of one month of cash disbursements from expenditures.)	
5. Are receivables as a proportion of tuition increasing; if so, why?	

	Check off
6. Are uncollectible accounts as a proportion of receivables increasing; if so, why?	
7. Are students billed monthly?	
8. What is being done to collect outstanding bills?	
9. Is inventory as a proportion of auxiliary sales increasing; if so, why?	
10. Are payables and accruals as a proportion of expenses increasing; if so, why?	
11. Are vendors, taxes, and benefits paid on time?	
12. Is short-term debt increasing; if so, why?	
13. Prepare a short-term debt list—terms, lender, payment schedule, and reasons for borrowing.	
14. Is the available funds ratio (cash and short-term investments to current liabilities) declining; if so, why?	

D. Permanent Capital

	Check off
1. Is long-term debt increasing?	
2. List for long-term debt—terms, conditions, payment schedules, and uses? (Include all forms—on and off-balance sheet borrowing.)	
3. Is the debt leverage ratio less than 2:1? If so, debt may be excessive.	
4. Does the college have a debt policy?	
5. Is the return on net assets declining; if so, why?	
6. Is the capitalization rate less than 50%? If so, it may limit future borrowing.	
7. How does the return on investments (endowment) compare to a benchmark (ex. S&P 500)?	
8. What is the investment policy of the college?	
9. What is the payout ratio for the endowment fund?	

	Check off
10. How is the payout ratio computed?	
11. Is there deferred maintenance? If so, how much is it and list the major categories.	
12. Is there a long-term strategy for space utilization for the campus?	
13. Does the college have sufficient parking?	
14. Are new facilities designed and located to permit sale?	

E. Financial Performance (place all reports in a three-year trend table)

	Check off
1. Have weights and growth rates for revenue and expenses been computed?	
2. Have growth rates been computed for working capital?	

3. Have these ratios been computed?
  a. Tuition dependency
  b. Net tuition after unfunded institutional aid
  c. Operating margin
  d. Cash income
  e. Cash expense
  f. Current ratio
  g. Available funds ratio
  h. Receivables
  i. Uncollectible receivables
  j. Inventory ratio
  k. Payables and accruals
  l. Viability
  m. Debt service
  n. Interest expense
  o. Composition
  p. Capitalization
  q. Age of facility
  r. Free expendable resources to operations
  s. Total financial resources per student
  t. Endowment payout	

	Check off
4. Compute the preceding ratios for the previous five years and compare trends.	
5. Is the primary ratio less than .40? (A ratio less than .40 means that the college may not have the capacity to transform itself or to cover five months of expenses.)[1]	
6. Is net income with depreciation less than 2% of total revenue? (If so, this suggests that the college is living beyond its means and may not be building adequate reserves.)[2]	
7. Is the viability ratio less than 1:1? (When this ratio falls below 1:1, a college's ability to respond to adverse conditions from internal resources is jeopardized; the ratio should fall in the range of 1.25 to 2.0.)[3]	
8. Compute the CFI score for the college.	

F. Financial Distress—CFI Score < 3

	Check off
1. Conduct strategic analysis of the college.	
2. Is the current market viable? Why do students choose or not choose the college?	
3. Can the institution produce new revenue or cut expenses to survive? a. Are there new sources of revenue? b. Can costs be cut through reorganization? c. Can the college run a fund-raising campaign? Who are the benefactors? d. What is the condition of the plant? e. Can debt be refinanced or reduced through gifts?	
4. What is the college's strategic turnaround plan?	

F. Major Financial Distress

	Check off
1. Is the CFI score < 1?	
2. Has the state warned that licensing will be withdrawn?	
3. Has the U.S. Department of Education imposed financial conditions before student aid can be received?	
4. Has an accrediting agency warned that accreditation will be withdrawn?	
5. Does the college have sufficient cash or other investments to pay its bills?	
6. Can the college meet its payroll?	
7. Are payroll tax payments delinquent?	
8. Are payroll benefits delinquent?	
9. Is the college delinquent on debt payments?	
10. Has the college considered a merger?	
11. Does it have a survival or turnaround plan? Is it feasible?	
12. Has the college declared financial exigency?	
13. Is there a viable plan to close in an orderly fashion?	

II. Marketing Diagnostics

A. Competition

	Check off
1. Who are the major competitors?	
2. What is their enrollment?	
3. What is the market share for each competitor and the college?	

	Check off
4. How does the enrollment growth rate of the college compare to competitors?	
5. How does the college's net price compare to competitors?	
6. What services do competitors provide students that the college does not?	
7. Why do students choose a competitor?	
8. What would the college have to change to compete with its competitors?	
9. Are new competitors entering the market?	

B. Market Analysis

	Check off

1. What do you know about your students?
   a. Why do they choose the college?
   b. Why do some students not leave the college?
   c. Can you give a description of the student market for the college?
   d. Can you give a description of the student market for each program?	

2. What are the yield rates for:
   a. Admissions (students applying/inquiries)?
   b. Admitted students (admitted/applications)?
   c. Matriculated students (matriculated/admitted students)?	

3. Have students been surveyed to see what they would change or improve?	
4. What is the attrition rate for first-year students?	
5. What is the graduation rate?	
6. How effective is the alumni office in building enrollment?	
7. What are the components of the marketing campaign and are they effective?	

	Check off

8. Is the student market viable?
    a. Is the population shrinking?
    b. Is the college in an isolated rural area?
    c. Does the college offer programs that other colleges offer?	

9. Does the pricing policy bring in the students that the college wants?	
10. Does the pricing policy respond to the competition?	
11. What is the college's image to visiting prospective students?	
12. Does the college have an effective public relations program?	
13. Develop a marketing program attuned to the reasons students would choose the college per George Dehne's themes—reduce risk of the choice, inform the prospective students on how the college fits them, reach the students through a variety of sources, and make sure *product*, *price*, and *place* are attuned to the promotion campaign.[4]	

III. Management and Oversight

	Check off
1. Does the college have an annual audit?	
2. Does the board meet privately with the auditors to review financial management and performance?	
3. Does the board review the financial aid audit?	
4. Does the college conduct compensation and benefit tests to ensure conformity with federal regulations?	
5. Are personnel practices reviewed to ensure conformity with regulations?	
6. Does the college have unrelated business income that must be reported?	
7. Are there policies on providing services by board members and by businesses owned by key administrators?	

	Check off
8. Are there policies on review of expense reimbursements and purchases by key administrators?	
9. Does the college have a business policies and practices manual?	
10. Is there a formal review and evaluation process for all levels of the college including the key administrators?	
11. What is the college's Dunn & Bradstreet rating?	
12. What is the strategic plan for the college—education, finance, and marketing?	
13. Is the college on target—is it healthy and will it be around another five years?	

ENDNOTES

1. Salluzzo, R. E., Tahey, P., Prager, F. J., & Cowen, C. J. *Ratio Analysis in Higher Education,* 4th ed. (KPMG and Prager, McCarthy & Sealy. Washington DC, 1999), p. 13.
2. Ibid, p. 15.
3. Ibid, p. 22.
4. Dehne, G. C. *Student Recruitment: A Marketing Primer for Presidents* (Old Saybrook, CT: GDA Integrated Services, 2001), pp. 10–15.

APPENDIX C

FINANCIAL MEASURES

NET PRESENT VALUE

Net present value (NPV) is used to compute the current value of future cash flows that are discounted at a capital cost rate (not really applicable to not-for-profit institutions) or the investment rate of return or risk-free rate, for example, a Treasury Note rate.[1] NPV is used to evaluate the income generated by a project to see whether it produces a positive net present value. If there are multiple projects, the decision to select one or more projects depends on the order of the net present value for each project. NPV is calculated by using the following equation:

$$NPV = \sum_{t=0}^{N} \frac{C_t}{(1 + r)^t}$$

t = time;
N = total number of time periods;
C = net cash flow; and
r = the discount rate.

Note on discount rate: Use either a risk-free rate (for example, 10-year notes) or the average rate of return for institutional investments.

BREAKEVEN MEASURES

Breakeven measures estimate the number of units or price needed to achieve the point where revenue equals expenses. In higher education, units may be full-time-equivalent students, headcount, seats, or credit hours; price may be tuition or the price charged for dormitory rooms, meals, or other services.

Breakeven Units = f / (p – vc)

f = fixed costs of the project;

p = price; and

vc = variable costs of the project—unfunded financial aid, adjunct faculty with their taxes and benefits.

Note on breakeven units: The purpose is to estimate the number of units—headcount, seats, credit hours, or full-time-equivalent students to achieve breakeven. The issue is whether the college believes that the units are attainable.

Breakeven Price = (f + vc) / u

f = fixed costs of the project;

p = price;

vc = variable costs of the project—unfunded financial aid, adjunct faculty with their taxes and benefits; and

u = units (headcount, seats, credit hours, or full-time-equivalent students).

Note on breakeven price: The purpose is to estimate the price needed to reach breakeven given the units, fixed costs, and variable costs. Higher education would find this computation difficult to carry out because colleges usually charge a standard rate by level rather than by program.

SIMPLE PRODUCTIVITY MEASURES

Productivity measures the relationship of output to input. The problem in higher education is defining output (graduates, credit hours, headcount, employed students, grant dollars, or employed graduates) and input (faculty time, student academic skill measure, class size, or cost). The purpose here is to suggest several simple measures for productivity that can then be benchmarked with other institutions. Undergraduate colleges that do not offer certificates or associate's degrees are the easiest to measure. Other types of institutions—graduate programs, associate's degrees programs, research—are more complex and the data are difficult to disaggregate for the productivity measures.

Total Productivity: Output/Input

Productivity of the institution
Output = student credit hours; and
Input = total cost of operations.

Segmented Productivity: Segment Output/ Segment Input

Productivity of a segment or sector of an institution; for example, the productivity of the undergraduate instructional programs

Segment Examples
Instructional Example 1: Student Credit Hours/ Total Cost of Segment;
Instructional Example 2: Student Credit Hours/ Instructional Hours;
Instructional Example 3: Cohort Credit Hours/ Total Cost of Cohort;
Student Services: Students Served/Total Cost of Segment;
Residence Hall: Students in Hall/Total Cost of Segment;
Food Service: Revenue from Student Meals/Total Cost of Segment;
Bookstore Net Income/Bookstore Revenue
Grounds: Acres/Compensation;
Maintenance: Maintenance Cost/Square Footage of Campus Buildings

ECONOMIC MODEL

The economic maximization model for private institutions can be generalized through the following relationships[2]:

Maximize $V(X, S, P)$ subject to the following constraints:
$$F^k(X, S) = 0 \quad (k = 1, 2 \ldots m)$$
$$D^k(X, S, P) = 0 \quad (k = 1, 2 \ldots n)$$
$$R(X, S, P) - C(X, S, P) = 0$$

Where

V = values to be maximized;

X = activities (tangible and intangible);

S = stocks;

P = price;

F = production function; $F = 0$, the elements stand in relation to each other;

D = demand function; $D = 0$, the elements stand in relation to each other;

R = revenue;

C = cost;

$R - C = 0$; revenue minus costs over the long-term equal zero; and

k = there are k production and demand functions.

Long-run financial equilibrium, subject to
$$[R_g(X_{gw}, S_{gw}, P_{gw})]_t = [C_g(X_{gw}, S_{gw}, P_{gw})]_t$$

Where

R_g = rate of growth for revenue;

C_g = rate of growth for expenses;

X_{gw}, S_{gw}, P_{gw} = rate of growth and weighted value for X, S, and $P1$; and

t = time period $(1, 2, \ldots n)$.

RESPONSIBILITY-CENTERED MODEL

Responsibility-centered models (RCMs) attempt to measure the ability of revenue-generating programs to cover their direct and indirect costs of operation. Indirect costs refer to academic support, student services, institutional support, plant and maintenance, depreciation, and debt interest. This model provides one way of determining where the strategic effort and resources of the college should be placed. So, if a program is generating net after costs, then it would make sense to strategically support strength. If the program is not covering cost and is serving a declining market, the college needs to ask whether it is worth the strategic effort and resources of the college to support weakness.

- **Data needed**
  - Final fiscal year budget report that was reconciled to the audited statement of activity report;
  - Credit hours by major and by school that is reconciled to the audit; and
  - Depreciation allocations by major and schools.
- **Steps**
  - **Prepare the credit hour matrix (see the Credit Hour Matrix Excel Worksheet on CD).**
    - "Selling center" is an instructional center that provides course instruction to another college;
    - "Purchasing center" is an instructional center that purchases course instruction from another instituton;
    - Total instructional expenses are divided by total credit hours;
    - This is the average cost per credit hour;
    - The proportion of the dollar value retained by the selling center must be determined because it incurred the expense of enrolling, advising, and permitting

the course purchases by its students. Usually, this is in some range between 30 percent and 35 percent of the credit hour fee.

- **Prepare the RCM matrix (see the RCM Matrix Excel Worksheet on CD).**
  - Allocate direct revenue and direct expenses to the RCM revenue centers (includes instructional, auxiliaries, development, other income centers, and athletics—if they produce revenue).
  - Allocate the dollar value of credit hours sold or purchased among the instructional centers.
  - Allocate net grant revenue.
  - Allocate plant and depreciation expenses by revenue center.
  - Allocate general administrative expenses (institutional) to the revenue centers (instructional and noninstructional).
  - Allocate academic and student services expenses to the instructional revenue programs.
  - Allocate other revenue and expenses.
  - Net the results and compare to the audit; it should be the same.

ENDNOTES

1. Wikipedia. (2009). Net Present Value. Retrieved February 24, 2009, from http://en.wikipedia.org/wiki/Net_present_value.
2. Hopkins, D. S. P., & Massy, W. F. *Planning Models for Colleges and Universities*. (Stanford, CA: Stanford University Press, 1981).

APPENDIX D

FINANCIAL MANAGEMENT RATIOS

Ratios	General Form	Ratio Formulae
Primary Reserve	Expendable Net Assets/ Total Expenses	(Unrestricted Net Assets + Temporarily Restricted Net Assets − Net Property, Plant, and Equipment + Long-Term Debt)/ Total Expenses
Secondary Reserve	Nonexpendable Net Assets/Total Expenses	(Permanently Restricted Net Assets)/ Total Expenses
Capitalization Ratio	Modified Net Assets[a]/ Total Assets	(Total Net Assets − Goodwill − Interentity Receivables + Patents + Royalties)/ (Total Assets − Goodwill − Interentity Receivables + Patents + Royalties)
Viability Ratio	Expendable Net Assets/ Long-Term Debt	(Unrestricted Net Assets + Temporarily Restricted Net Assets − Net Property, Plant, and Equipment + Long-Term Debt)/ Long-Term Debt
Debt Burden Ratio	Debt Services Adjusted Expenses	(Interest Expenses + Principal Expenses)/ (Total Expenses − Depreciation + Principal Payments)
Leverage Ratio	Available Net Assets/ Long-Term Debt	(Unrestricted Net Assets + Temporarily Restricted Net Assets)/ Long-Term Debt
Return on Net Assets Ratio	Change in Net Assets/ Total Net Assets	(Net Assets End of Year − Net Assets Beginning of Year)/ Total Net Assets (beginning of year)
Financial Net Assets Ratio	Total Net Assets - Plant Net Assets / Total Net Assets	(Total Net Assets − Net Property, Plant, and Equipment + Long-Term Debt)/Total Net Assets

Ratios	General Form	Ratio Formulae
Physical Net Assets Ratio	Net Investment in Plant Net Assets/Total Net Assets	(Net Property, Plant, and Equipment – Long-Term Debt)/ Total Net Assets
Physical Asset Reinvestment Ratio	Capital Expenditures + Capital Asset Gifts / Depreciation Expenses	(Capital Expenditures + Capital Asset Gifts)/ Depreciation Expenses
Age of Facility	Accumulated Depreciation/ Depreciation Expenses	(Accumulated Depreciation)/ Depreciation Expenses
Net Operating Revenues Ratio Form [1]	Excess (deficiency) of Unrestricted Operating Revenues Over Unrestricted Operating Expenses / Total Unrestricted Operating Revenue	(Excess (deficiency) of Unrestricted Operating Revenues – Unrestricted Operating Expenses)/ (Total Unrestricted Revenue and Gains + Net Assets Released from Restrictions)
Net Operating Revenues Ratio Form [2]	Change in unrestricted net assets / total unrestricted revenue	Change in Unrestricted Net Assets/ (Total Unrestricted Revenue and Gains + Net Assets Released from Restrictions + Unrestricted Investment Return in Excess of Spending Rate)
Cash Income Ratio	Net Cash from Operating Activities / Total Unrestricted Income Excluding Gains or Loses	Net Cash from Operating Activities/ (Total Unrestricted Revenue and Gains + Investment Return in Excess of Spending Rate + Net Assets Released from Restriction – Net (Unrestricted) Realized Gains – Net Unrestricted Unrealized Appreciation)
Net Tuition and Fees Contribution Ratio	Net Tuition and Fees/ Total Expenses	Net Tuition and Fees/ Total Expenses
Net Tuition Dependency Ratio	Net Tuition and Fees/ Total Revenue	Net Tuition and Fees/(Total Unrestricted Revenue and Gains + Net Assets Released from Restrictions)

[a] *Modified Net Assets excludes intangible assets such as goodwill and interentity receivables, but includes income-producing intangible assets, such as patents and royalties.*
Source: National Association of Colleges and Business Officers. (2005). Strategic financial analysis for higher education (6th ed., pp. 56–60, 63–67, 69, 73–78, 85–88, 90). Washington, DC: NACUBO.

APPENDIX E

FINANCIAL BENCHMARKS

Ratios	Total Ratios			
	$0–$100M	$100M–$400M	$400M–$1,000M	$1,000M+
Primary Reserve	0.57	1.35	2.45	2.41
Secondary Reserve	48.9%	93.7%	114.3%	81.4%
Capitalization Ratio	66.0%	74.0%	76.0%	78.0%
Viability Ratio	0.87	1.75	2.83	4.67
Debt Burden Ratio	4.1%	4.5%	4.3%	2.5%
Leverage Ratio	3.17	4.22	4.68	8.01
Interest Burden Ratio	2.23%	2.64%	2.67%	1.87%
Return on Net Assets Ratio	7.89%	10.31%	96.80%	11.10%
Financial Net Assets Ratio	194%	308%	409%	665%
Physical Net Assets Ratio	36%	22%	18%	11%
Physical Asset Reinvestment Ratio	1.18	1.81	1.78	2.01
Age of Facility	11.38	10.71	10.6	9.58

Ratios	Total Ratios			
	$0–$100M	$100M–$400M	$400M–$1,000M	$1,000M+
Net Operating Revenues Ratio Form [1]	3.39%	3.07%	2.20%	2.18%
Net Operating Revenues Ratio Form [2]	7.9%	15.2%	18.3%	2.2%
Cash Income Ratio	7.00%	5.40%	2.20%	1.70%
Net Tuition and Fees Contribution Ratio	0.648	0.567	0.418	0.192
Net Tuition Dependency Ratio	0.611	0.547	0.416	0.188

COMPOSITE FINANCIAL INDEX ESTIMATE BY CATEGORY

Ratios	Values			
Prime Ratio	0.57	1.35	2.45	2.41
Net Income Ratio	3.39%	3.07%	2.20%	2.18%
Return on Net Assets Ratio	7.89%	10.31%	96.80%	11.10%
Viability Ratio	0.87	1.75	2.83	4.67

CFI Score	Scores			
Prime Ratio	1.50	3.55	6.45	6.34
Net Income Ratio	0.48	0.44	0.31	0.31
Return on Net Assets Ratio	0.79	1.03	9.68	1.11
Viability Ratio	0.73	1.47	2.38	3.92
Total Score	3.50	6.49	18.82	11.68

Source: Salluzzo, Ronald and Frederick Prager; Bearing Point, Prager, Sealy and KPMG. (2005). Strategic Financial Analysis for Higher Education *(6th ed.). Washington, DC.*

FINANCIAL AID: NET TUITION RATES AND NET TUITION REVENUE

TUITION RATE NET OF FINANCIAL AID DISCOUNT (IF TUITION RATE IS $25,000)

High School Rank	Top 10%	11% to 20%	21% to 30%	31% to 40%	41% to 50%	51% to 70%	Totals
Awards							
70% of tuition	$7,500						$7,500
60% of tuition		$10,000					$10,000
50% of tuition			$12,500				$12,500
40% of tuition				$15,000			$15,000
30% of tuition					$17,500		$17,500
25% of tuition						$18,750	$18,750
Totals	$7,500	$10,000	$12,500	$15,000	$17,500	$18,750	$81,250

NET TUITION REVENUE (IF THE TUITION RATE IS $25,000)

High School Rank	Top 10%	11% to 20%	21% to 30%	31% to 40%	41% to 50%	51% to 70%	Totals
Awards							
70% of tuition	$375,000	$0	$0	$0	$0	$0	$ 375,000
60% of tuition	$0	$750,000	$0	$0	$0	$0	$ 750,000
50% of tuition	$0	$0	$1,875,000	$0	$0	$0	$ 1,875,000
40% of tuition	$0	$0	$0	$3,000,000	$0	$0	$ 3,000,000
30% of tuition	$0	$0	$0	$0	$7,000,000	$0	$ 7,000,000
25% of tuition	$0	$0	$0	$0	$0	$9,375,000	$ 9,375,000
Total Net Tuition	$375,000	$750,000	$1,875,000	$3,000,000	$7,000,000	$9,375,000	$22,375,000

APPENDIX G

COMPOSITE FINANCIAL INDEX

FINANCIAL RATIO SCORING SYSTEM

The *Composite Financial Index* *(CFI)* is a modified credit rating system that evolved from a U.S. Department of Education project designed to determine the eligibility of colleges to receive student aid funds. The CFI scoring system focuses on a set of "core ratios... represent[ing] key components in relation to financial risk that must be monitored consistently [by a college]."[1]

The core ratios are as follows: the primary reserve ratio measures whether there are adequate funds to cover emergencies; the net income ratio measures short-term results; the return on net assets measures the ability to increase wealth; and the viability ratio measures the capacity to support long-term debt. The core ratios are listed in Table G.1.

TABLE G.1—CFI RATIOS

Primary Ratio	Total expendable net assets divided by total operating expenses
Net Income Ratio	Operating surplus (deficit) divided by operating income
Return on Assets	Change in net assets divided by net assets beginning of the year
Viability Ratio	Total expendable net assets divided by total long-term debt

Source: Salluzzo, R. E., Tahey, P., Prager, F. J., & Cowen, C. J. (1999). Ratio Analysis in Higher Education (4th ed., pp. 11, 14–15, 20). KPMG and Prager, McCarthy & Sealy. Washington DC.

Primary reserve ratio measures the financial strength of an institution, indicating the surplus resources an institution could use for debt without recourse to additional net income (net asset) support from operations.[2] Preferably, the ratio increases at the same rate as growth in expenses.[3] If it grows at a slower rate than expenses, expendable net assets will represent a shrinking margin of protection during adversity.[4] A declining primary reserve ratio indicates a weakening financial condition.[5] A ratio of .4 indicates that the institution has five months of reserves (40 percent of 12 months) for short-term cash needs, reasonable levels of cash for facilities maintenance, and reserves for unanticipated events.[6] When the ratio is below .15, the institution probably uses short-term borrowing for cash and struggles to find reserves for reinvestment.[7]

Net income ratio indicates whether operations produced a surplus or a deficit, the outcome of which has a direct bearing on the other three ratios (primary reserve, return on net assets, and viability).[8] Given the impact of depreciation, net income ratio should fall within or above the 2 percent to 4 percent range.[9] Large deficits over a period of years are a "warning signal that management and the governing board should focus on restructuring the institution's income and expense streams."[10] A deficit in any one year is not cause for alarm "if the institution is financially strong, is aware of the causes…, and has… a plan to… cure the deficit."[11] There are two computational forms of this ratio. The first, *excess (deficiency) of unrestricted operating revenue over operating expenses*, is used when operating activities are separated from nonoperating activities.[12] The second form, *change in unrestricted net assets*, is used when operating activities are not disaggregated.

Return on net assets ratio shows whether the institution is increasing its wealth, its trend being the best indicator of long-term changes in wealth.[13] Owing to the volatility of the underlying asset returns (e.g., endowment funds), a *real* (discounted for inflation) rate of return should be in the range of 3 percent to 4 percent.[14] The degree of volatility in the underlying assets depends on the mix of endowment-to-plant assets. When liquid assets are turned into plant assets, the presumption is that the institution is adding to its productive capacity. Changes in plant assets may temporarily depress returns until either production expands to offset the loss of investable wealth, or donations are received to offset the investment in plant. The return on net assets ratio may be calculated by removing permanently restricted net assets from the numerator and denominator, leaving assets that are under the direct control of the institution.[15] Those are the assets that the board can redeploy toward investments or production.

Viability ratio is "one of the most basic determinants of clear financial health: the availability of expendable net assets to cover debt should the institution need to settle its obligations as of the balance sheet date."[16] The preferable range for this ratio is between "1.25 and 2.00 and higher, which is based on reviews of financial statements."[17] The viability ratio is an institution's safety net in the event of extraordinarily adverse conditions. When the ratio falls below 1:1 (expendable net assets match long-term debt), external agencies may see the institution as a credit risk and deny it capital.[18] Institutions may survive for long periods with a high level of debt leverage, but they lose their flexibility to raise capital, putting severe pressure on them to borrow for short-term cash needs to respond to changes in the market.[19]

Computation of the CFI score follows a four-step process. Refer to the CFI Excel Worksheet on CD for computation methodology. In short, here are the steps:

1.   Compute the value of each ratio.

2.   Convert the ratio to a strength factor.

3.   The strength factor is then weighted for the relative importance of that factor in the final CFI score.

4.   CFI is a sum of the weighted strength values of these four financial ratios.

TABLE G.2—CONSOLIDATED FINANCIAL INDEX SCORING SCALE

Scale Level	CFI Scoring Range	Action
One	–1 to 1	Assess viability of institution's survival.
Two	0 to 2	Reengineer the institution.
Three	1 to 3	
Four	2 to 4	Direct resources toward transformation.
Five	3 to 5	
Six	4 to 6	Focus resources to compete.
Seven	5 to 7	
Eight	6 to 8	Experiment with new initiatives.
Nine	7 to 9	Experiment with new initiatives. Achieve a robust mission.
Ten	> 9	Deploy resources to achieve a robust mission.

Source: Salluzzo, R. E., Tahey, P., Prager, F. J., & Cowen, C. J. (1999). Ratio Analysis in Higher Education (4th ed., p. 24). KPMG and Prager, McCarthy & Sealy. Washington DC.

Note: The CFI can then be assigned to one of 10 levels of progressively stronger financial conditions (see Table G.2).

For instance, a low CFI score indicates a high level of financial distress, whereas a high CFI score indicates a financially strong and flexible college. CFI, like the Moody's ratios, provides colleges with powerful tools for financial strategy because the components of the ratios suggest where colleges need to focus their attention.

The financial health of a private college is ascertained by comparing the CFI score to the CFI performance chart in Table G.3. The scores overlap because CFI is not intended to represent financial health as a precise point on a chart, but rather a range for a particular level of health. Given the CFI score, the range also suggests action the institution ought to consider. For example, if primary reserve

TABLE G.3—CFI PERFORMANCE BOUNDARIES

1. Is the *primary ratio* (Expendable Net Assets ÷ Total Expenses) greater than .40? Evidence suggests that with a score greater than .40 an institution has the flexibility to change with market conditions. A ratio less than .15 suggests that the institution needs to cover expenses through short-term loans.
2. Is the *net income ratio* [(Operating Revenue − Operating Expenses) ÷ Total Unrestricted Operating Income] greater than 2%? In this case, the college lives within its means and builds financial reserves. The conditions related to net return on assets are covered in the previous section.
3. Is the *viability ratio* (Expendable Net Assets ÷ Long-Term Debt) less than 1? If so, the college may not be able to respond to adverse conditions because it will have devoted its reserves to debt service. This ratio should fall with a range of 1.25 to 2.0 for a college to have sufficient flexibility under adverse conditions.

Source: Salluzzo, R. E., Tahey, P., Prager, F. J., & Cowen, C. J. (1999). Ratio Analysis in Higher Education (4th ed., pp. 16, 17, 21). KPMG and Prager, McCarthy & Sealy. Washington DC.

= 1.32, net income is .05, return on net assets is .60, and viability ratio is 1.20, then the CFI score = 3.17. The scoring scale in Table G.2 suggests that the institution, given a score of 3, should seriously consider reengineering itself. Severe financial distress under the CFI scoring system is defined as any institution whose score, averaged over a three-year period, is less than 1. Institutions meeting that criterion barely have working capital to cover short-term cash needs and may be surviving on borrowed funds. Moderate financial distress under CFI is defined here as any institution with a score greater than 1 but less than 3.

Performance ranges provide colleges with financial targets for improving their CFI scores.

ENDNOTES

1. Salluzzo, R. E., Tahey, P., Prager, F. J., & Cowen, C. J. *Ratio Analysis in Higher Education,* 4th ed. (Washington DC: KPMG and Prager, McCarthy & Sealy, 1999), p. 10.
2. Ibid, p. 11.

3. Ibid.
4. Ibid.
5. Ibid.
6. Ibid, p. 14.
7. Ibid.
8. Ibid.
9. Ibid, p. 15
10. Ibid.
11. Ibid, p. 14.
12. Ibid, pp. 14–15.
13. Ibid, p. 17.
14. Ibid.
15. Ibid, p. 20.
16. Ibid, p. 21.
17. Ibid, p. 22.
18. Ibid.
19. Ibid.

APPENDIX H
DATA SOURCES

Association of Governing Boards (AGB)

http://www.agb.org/wmspage.cfm?parm1=1531

The Association of Governing Boards (AGB) offers comprehensive databases for higher education, tracking and comparison tools for institutions and peer institutions, graphic formats, customized reports, and templates.

Bureau of Economic Analysis (BEA)

http://www.bea.gov/about/index.htm

The Bureau of Economic Analysis (BEA) produces economic accounts statistics that enable government and business decision makers, researchers, and the American public to follow and understand the performance of the nation's economy. To do this, BEA collects source data, conducts research and analysis, develops and implements estimation methodologies, and disseminates statistics to the public.

Bureau of Labor Statistics (BLS)

http://www.bls.gov/bls/demographics.htm

The Bureau of Labor Statistics (BLS) makes significant amounts of data available for specific demographic categories. Demographic categories used by BLS include sex, age, race, and ethnic origin. BLS also has data on inflation, employment, pay and benefits, productivity, and other related labor issues.

Chronicle of Higher Education

http://chronicle.com/

The *Chronicle of Higher Education* is an excellent source of data and articles on the current state of higher education. You must register for this service. If your office or library receives the *Chronicle*, you may be able to link into the online service through it.

Digest of Education Statistics

http://nces.ed.gov/programs/digest/

The primary purpose of the *Digest of Education Statistics* is to provide a compilation of statistical information covering the broad field of American education from prekindergarten through graduate school. The *Digest* includes a selection of data from many sources, both governmental and private, and draws especially on the results of surveys and activities carried out by the National Center for Education Statistics (NCES).

GuideStar

http://www.guidestar.org/

GuideStar offers compensation benchmarking, research, oversight, and market analysis; its primary service is access to 1990 tax reports for private colleges and universities.

Independent Postsecondary Education Data Systems (IPEDS)

http://nces.ed.gov/IPEDS/about/

Independent Postsecondary Education Data Systems (IPEDS) is the core postsecondary education data collection program for National Center for Education Statistics (NCES). Data in areas including enrollments, program completions, graduation rates, faculty, staff, finances, institutional prices, and student financial aid are collected from all primary providers of postsecondary education in the country.

John Minter Associates

http://www.jmahestats.com/AboutJMAInc.cfm

John Minter Associates (JMA) has prepared financial and finance-related data for college and university administrators since 1974 following the Bowen-Minter studies of financial trends in independent higher education and public higher education in the late 1960s and early 1970s.

Moody's Investors Service

http://www.moodys.com/cust/default.asp

Moody's Investors Service has developed a set of useful data on the financial condition of private colleges and universities. This service is also one of the main credit rating agencies for bonds. You must register for this service.

National Association of College and University Business Officers (NACUBO)

http://www.nacubo.org/

NACUBO is an excellent source of information on the current and near-term condition of higher education. You must register to access selected area of the service.

Regional Accrediting Agencies

Regional accrediting agencies are the bodies that accredit colleges and universities. Accreditation is required to receive Title IV financial aid funds from the U.S. Department of Education.

Regional accrediting agencies:

New England Association of Colleges and Universities: http://www.neasc.org/

Middle States Association of Colleges and Universities: http://www.msche.org/

North Central Association of Colleges and Universities: http://www.ncahigherlearningcommission.org/

North West Commission on Colleges and Universities: http://www.nwccu.org/

Southern Association of Colleges and Universities: http://www.sacscoc.org/

Western Association of Colleges and Universities: http://www.wascweb.org/

State Departments of Education

If you are looking for state regulatory information, go to the Department of Education website for that state. (Departments may also be called Commissions on Higher Education.)

Western Interstate Commission for Higher Education (WICHE)

http://wiche.edu/

Western Interstate Commission for Higher Education (WICHE) provides a wide range of initiatives and information to support western states' concerns about higher education public policy issues and informed decision making. WICHE also collects national data if they may have an impact on western states. It is an excellent source of research on major issues in higher education.

Yahoo College Directory

http://dir.yahoo.com/Education/Higher_Education/Colleges_and_Universities/United_States/Private/

The Yahoo College Directory provides a quick list and access to private colleges and universities.

APPENDIX I

MASSEY AND HOPKIN'S ECONOMIC MODEL

Maximize V(X, S, P) subject to the following constraints:

$$F^k (X, S) = 0 \quad (k = 1, 2, \ldots m)$$
$$D^k (X, S, P) = 0 \quad (k = 1, 2, \ldots n)$$
$$R(X, S, P) - C(X, S, P) = 0$$

Where

V = values to maximize

X = activities (tangible and intangible)

S = stocks

P = price

F = production function; F = 0, the elements stand in relation to each other

D = demand function; D = 0, the elements stand in relation to each other

R = revenue

C = cost

$R - C = 0$; revenue minus costs over the long term equal zero

k = there are k production and demand functions

Long-run financial equilibrium, subject to:

$$[R_g (X_{gw}, S_{gw}, P_{gw})]_t = [C_g (X_{gw}, S_{gw}, P_{gw})]_t$$

Where

R_g = rate of growth for revenue

C_g = rate of growth for expenses

X_{gw}, S_{gw}, P_{gw} = rate of growth and weighted value for X, S, and P

t = time period (1, 2, ... n)

Source: Hopkins, D. S. P., & Massey, W. F. (1981). Planning Models for Colleges and Universities. Stanford, CA: Stanford University Press.

BIBLIOGRAPHY

Adelman, C. *The Toolbox Revisited: Paths to Degree Completion From High School to College.* Washington, DC: U.S. Department of Education, 2006.

Astin, A. *What Matters in College?* San Francisco: Jossey-Bass, 1993.

Balderston, F. E. *Managing Today's University.* San Francisco: Jossey-Bass, 1975.

Baldridge, V. J., Curtis, D. V., Ecker, G., & Riley, G. L. *Policy Making and Effective Leadership.* San Francisco: Jossey-Bass, 1983.

Baurn, S., & Ma, J. *Trends in College Pricing.* Washington, DC: College Board, 2007.

Blumenstyk, G. (2008). "Lessons From For Profit Institutions About Cutting College Costs," *Chronicle of Higher Education.* Retrieved August 21, 2008, from http://chronicle.com/daily/2008/06/3116n.htm.

Bowen, H. R. *The Costs of Higher Education.* San Francisco: Jossey-Bass, 1981.

Bowen, H. R. "What Determines the Costs of Higher Education?" In L. L. Leslie & R. E. Anderson (Eds.), *ASHE Reader on Finance in Higher Education.* Needham Heights, MA: Ginn Press, 1990.

Bugeja, M. (2008). "How to Fight the High Cost of Curricular Glut," *Chronicle of Higher Education.* Retrieved September 19, 2008, from http://chronicle.com/weekly/v54/i21/21a03301.htm.

Carlson, S. (2008). "As Campuses Crumble, Budgets Are Crunched," *Chronicle of Higher Education.* Retrieved September 19, 2008, from http://chronicle.com/weekly/v54/i37/37a00101.htm.

Carnegie Commission on Higher Education. *Governance of Higher Education.* New York: McGraw-Hill, 1973.

Chronicle of Higher Education. (1991). "Board Votes to Shut Down Nazareth College," *Chronicle of Higher Education.* Retrieved November 14, 2008, from http://chronicle.com/che-data/articles- 37.dir/issue-29. dir/29a00302.htm.

Chronicle of Higher Education. (1992). "Spring Garden College Fails to Meet Payroll," *Chronicle of Higher Education.* Retrieved September 19, 2008, from http://chronicle.com/che-data/articles.dir/articles-36.dir/ issue-38.dir/38a00203.htm.

Chronicle of Higher Education (2008). "Winners and Losers in the Shake-up," *Chronicle of Higher Education.* Retrieved October 3, 2008, from http:// chronicle.com/daily/2008/10/4850n.htm.

Clotfelter, C. T. (1999). The amiliar but curious economics of higher education: Introduction to a symposium. *Journal of Economic Perspectives, 13-1,* 3–12.

Cohen, D. (2007). Australian universities cull overseas programs. *Chronicle of Higher Education.* Retrieved September 19, 2008, from http://chronicle. com/weekly/v53/i46/46a03201.htm.

Cohen, M. D., & March, J. G. (1974). *Leadership and ambiguity: The American college president.* New York: McGraw-Hill.

College Board. (2008). Graph 4: Ten year trend in critical reading, mathematics, and writing mean scores. Retrieved October 15, 2008, from http://professionals.collegeboard.com/data-reports-research/sat/cb-seniors-2008/tables.

College Board. (2008). Slide 17: Higher education landscape, update 078. ppt. Retrieved September 24, 2008, from http://professionals.collegeboard.com/date-reports-research/sat/cb-seniors-2008/tables.

Commodity Systems. (2001). NASDAQ: May 1999–May 2001. Retrieved June 12, 2008, from http://finance.yahoo.com/.

Commodity Systems. (2001). S&P 500 Index: May 1999–May 2001. Retrieved June 12, 2008, from http://finance.yahoo.com/.

Cowan, R. B. (1993). Prescription for small-college turnaround. *Change, 1,* 38.

Dehne, G. C. (2001). *Student recruitment: A marketing primer for presidents.* Old Saybrook, CT: GDA Integrated Services.

Drucker, P. (1974). *Management: Tasks, responsibilities, practices.* New York: Harper & Row.

Drucker, P. F. (1954). *The practice of management.* New York: Harper & Row.

Dwyer, C. (1996). *Managing people* (2nd ed.). Dubuque, IA: Kendall/Hunt.

Fain, P. (2007). Antioch's closing signals end of an era. *Chronicle of Higher Education.* Retrieved September 19, 2008, from http://chronicle.com/weekly/v53/i42/42a00101.htm.

Fain, P. (2008). Antioch announces it will close its doors. *Chronicle of Higher Education.* Retrieved September 12, 2008, from http://chronicle.com/weekly/v54/i27/27a01502.htm.

Farrell, E. F. (2007). Is bigger better? *Chronicle of Higher Education.* Retrieved September 12, 2008, from http://chronicle.com/weekly/v54/i13/13a02301.htm.

Feemster, R. (2000). Faith in financials. *University Business, 3*(3), 39.

Feldman, K. A., & Newcomb, T. M. (1976). *The impact of college on students* (Vol. 1). San Francisco: Jossey-Bass.

Field, K. (2008). Bank freeze leaves hundreds of colleges cut off from short term funds. *Chronicle of Higher Education.* Retrieved October 10, 2008, from http://chroncile.com/weekly/v55/i07/07a02001.htm.

Field, K. (2008). Congress' cost cure may have side effects. *Chronicle of Higher Education*. Retrieved September 5, 2008, from http://chronicle.com/weekly/v54/i22/22a00101.htm.

Field, K. (2008). Pending bill would double colleges' reporting burden, critics say. *Chronicle of Higher Education*. Retrieved September 5, 2008, from http://chronicle.com/temp/email2.php?ed=83n8MMcD5sdbfmjRz2cPzykpSV85xy4w.

Financial Accounting Standards Board. (2007). *Statements of financial accounting concepts*. Norwalk, CT: Author.

Fischer, K. (2007). Small Alaska college suspends operations. *Chronicle of Higher Education*. Retrieved September 12, 2008, from http://chronicle.com/weekly/v53/i45/45a02403.htm.

Fisher, J. L. (1984). *Power of the presidency*. American Council on Education. New York: MacMillan.

Fisher, J. L. (2001, September 5). Personal interview. Baltimore, Maryland.

Fitzgerald, S. (2007). *Private college and university medians 2007*. Moody's Investors Service. Retrieved October 22, 2008, from http://www.nacubo.org/Images/Moody's%20HE%20priv%20medians%20May07.pdf.

Getz, M., & Siegfried, J. J. (1991). Costs and productivity in American colleges and universities. In C. T. Clotfelter, R. G. Ehrenberg, M. Getz, & J. J. Siegfried (Eds.), *Economic challenges in higher education*. Chicago: University of Chicago Press.

Goodman, R. (2008). Even substantial declines FY 2008 and FY 2009 unlikely to erase all gains of last 5 years. In *Moody's global U.S. public finance: Impact of the credit crisis and a weaker economy on U.S. higher education*. New York: Moody's Investors Service.

Goodman, R. (2008). *Moody's global U.S. public finance: Impact of the credit crisis and a weaker economy on U.S. higher education*. New York: Moody's Investors Service.

Goodman, R., & Nelson, J. (2008). *Moody's Investors Service: 2008 U.S. higher education outlook.* New York: Moody's Investors Service.

Gravois, J. (2004). William Tyndale College to close its doors. *Chronicle of Higher Education.* Retrieved September 12, 2008, from http://chronicle.com/weekly/v51/i15/15a02702.htm.

Greene, B. (2003). *Remedial education at degree granting post secondary institutions in fall 2000.* Washington, DC: National Center for Education Statistics.

Higher Education Research Institute. (2003). *How "good" is your retention rate?* University of California: Graduate School of Education and Information Studies. Retrieved July 17, 2008, from http://www.gseis.ucla.edu/~heri/PDFs/DARCU_RB.PDF.

Hopkins, D. S. P., & Massy, W. F. (1981). *Planning models for colleges and universities.* Stanford, CA: Stanford University Press.

Hussar, W., & Bailey, T. (2008). Table 26: Actual and projected percentage changes in public high school graduates, by region and state: Selected years, 1999–2000 through 2017–2018. In National Center for Education Statistics, *Projections of Education Statistics to 2017* (36th ed.). Washington, DC: U.S. Department of Education.

Ip, G. (2008). The declining value of your college degree. *Wall Street Journal.* Retrieved September 15, 2008, from http://online.wsj.com/public/article_print/SB121623686919059307.html.

Irwin, H., & Thompson, R. (2008). Making it as a multinational university. *Business Officer, 20.*

Jan, T. (2008). BU head calls for hiring freeze. *Boston Globe, City & Region,* B1.

Jan, T. (2008). Harvard looks to tighten its belt. *Boston Globe, Metro Edition,* B1, B4.

Jashik, S. (1991). Ivy league agrees to end collaboration on financial aid. *Chronicle of Higher Education.* Retrieved July 17, 2008, from http://chronicle.com/.

Jencks, C., & Riesman, D. (1969). *The academic revolution.* Garden City, NJ: Anchor Books, Doubleday and Company.

JMA Higher Ed Stats. (2002). *Management ratios: Private institutions, xls: 1997–2000.* Boulder, CO: John Minter and Associates.

JMA Higher Ed Stats. (2003). *Management ratios 2002 private colleges, universities, catalog #3690103.* Boulder, CO: John Minter and Associates.

JMA Higher Ed Stats. (2008). *Strategic higher education trends at a glance: F2 2002.csv and F2 2007.csv financial data.* Boulder, CO: John Minter and Associates.

Keller, G. (1983). *Academic strategy.* Baltimore: Johns Hopkins University Press.

Kimberly, A. M. (1999). *The response of small private colleges to financial distress in the nineties.* Ann Arbor: University of Michigan.

Lapovsky, L., & Hubbel, L. L. (2001). An uncertain future. *Business Officer,* 29.

Lenington, R. (1996). *Colleges are a business!* Phoenix, AZ: Oryx Press.

Lesick, L. (2008). Deliberate redesign improves processes. *Business Officer,* 10.

Lindbloom, C. (1968). *The policy making process.* Cambridge, MA: Harvard University Press.

Machiavelli, N. (2004). *The prince.* New York: Simon & Schuster.

MacTaggart, T. (2007). The realities of rescuing colleges in distress. *Chronicle of Higher Education.* Retrieved July 17, 2008, from http://chronicle.com/weekly/v54/i07/07b01101.htm.

Massey, W. F. (1990). A new look at the academic department. *Distillations. The Pew Higher Education Research Program*, 1.

Massey, W. F. (1998). Remarks on restructuring higher education. In *Straight talk about college costs and prices: Report of the National Commission on the cost of higher education*. Phoenix, AZ: Oryx Press.

McKay, P. A., & Curran, R. (2009, January 18–19). Smart Money takes a dive
on alternative assets. *Wall Street Journal*, B1.

McPherson, M. (1978). The demand for higher education. In D. Breneman & C. Finn Jr. (Eds.), *Public policy and private higher education*. Washington, DC: Brookings Institution.

Mehrling, P., Goldstein, P., & Sedlacek, V. (2005). Endowment spending: Goals, rates and rules. In M. Devlin (Ed.), *Forum futures 2005*. Educause. Retrieved February 26, 2009, from http://net.educause.edu/ir/library/pdf/ffp0516s.pdf.

Mercer, J. (1995). Death throes at Upsala. *Chronicle of Higher Education*. Retrieved September 12, 2008, from http://chronicle.com/.

Minter, J. (2001, January 15). E-mail interview. John Minter and Associates.

Moody's Investors Service. (2001). *Private colleges and universities outlook 2001/02 and medians*. New York: Author.

Moody's Investors Service. (2008). *Higher education outlook*. New York: Author.

Moser, K. (2008). Worsening economy could cause trouble for smaller colleges. *Chronicle of Higher Education*. Retrieved September 5, 2008, from http://chronicle.com/weekly/v54/i45/45a01502.htm.

Mundel, D. (1973). Whose education should society support? In L. C. Solmon & P. J. Taubman (Eds.), *Does college matter?* New York: Academic Press.

Murphy, D. M., & Tellier, S. K. (2004). Financial about-face. *Business Officer,* 20–26.

National Science Foundation. (2001). Sheet 08180820: Unrestricted and restricted fund types 1987-1996. *WebCASPAR Database System.* Retrieved August 5, 2001, from http://caspar/nsf.gov/.

National Science Foundation. (2001). Sheet 10463025.wk1: Enrollment level: 1988–1997. *WebCASPAR Database System.* Retrieved August 5, 2001, from http://caspar/nsf.gov/.

National Science Foundation. (2001). Sheet 15565881.wk1: Opening fall enrollment: 1967-1997. *WebCASPAR Database System.* Retrieved August 5, 2001, from http://caspar/nsf.gov/.

Nelson, J. (2008, August 25). Personal interview.

Pulley, J. L., & Borrego, A. (2001). Wealthiest colleges lost billions in endowment value in last year. *Chronicle of Higher Education,* A-24.

Reed, W. S. (2001). *Financial responsibilities of governing boards.* Washington, DC: Association of Governing Boards and NACUBO.

Riesman, D. R. (1998). *On higher education.* New Brunswick, NJ: Transaction Publishers.

Salem, D. A. (2000). Endowment management. In C. M. Grills (Ed.), *College and university business administration* (6th ed.). Washington, DC: National Association of College and University Business Official.

Salluzzo, R. E., Tahey, P., Prager, F. J., & Cowen, C. J. (1999). *Ratio analysis in higher education* (4th ed.). KPMG & Prager, McCarthy & Sealy.

Simon, H. (1967). The job of a college president. *Educational Record,* 69.

Strong American Schools. (2008). *Diploma to nowhere.* Washington, DC: Author.

Supiano, B. (2008). Student aid is up, but college costs outpace family incomes. *Chronicle of Higher Education*. Retrieved October 29, 2008, from http://chronicle.com/free/2008/10/6171.n.htm?utm_source=at&utm_medium=en.

Thompson, A. A. Jr., Gamble, J. E., & Strickland, A. J., III. (2006). *Strategy core concepts, analytical tools, readings*. Boston: McGraw-Hill Irwin.

Townsley, M. K. (1991). Brinkmanship, planning, smoke, and mirrors. *Planning for Higher Education, 19,* 19.

Townsley, M. K. (2002). *The small college guide to financial health*. Washington, DC: NACUBO.

Townsley, M. K. (2005). Recognizing the unrealized. *Business Officer,* 19–26.

Townsley, M.K. (2007). *Leveraging facilities for competitive advantage*. In Fennell, M. & Miller, S.D. (Eds.). *Presidential perspectives*. Philadelphia: Aramark Higher Education.

U.S. Department of Education. (1994). *In the matter of Upsala College*. Student financial assistance proceeding. Compliance and Enforcement Division of the Office of Postsecondary Education.

U.S. Department of Education. (1999). Table 256: Degree-granting institutions and branches by type and control of institution and state of jurisdiction 2006–07. In *National Center for Education Statistics*. Retrieved August 31, 2008, from http://nces.ed.gov/programs/digest/d07/tables/dt07_256.asp?referrer=list.

U.S. Department of Education. (1999). Table 334: Current fund revenue of private nonprofit institutions of higher education by source: 1980–81 through 1995–96. In *Digest of Education Statistics*. Washington, DC: National Center for Education Statistics.

U.S. Department of Education. (2007). Table 19: College enrollment and enrollment rates of recent high school completers, by race/ethnicity: 1960 through 2006. In *Digest of Education Statistics*. Washington, DC: National Center for Education Statistics.

U.S. Department of Education. (2008). Table 257: Degree-granting institutions that have closed their doors, by control and type of institution: 1969–70 through 2006–07. *National Center for Education Statistics*. Retrieved August 31, 2008, from http://nces.ed.gov/programs/digest/d07/tables/dt07_257.asp?referrer=list.

U.S. Department of Labor. (2008). *Consumer Price Index*. Bureau of Labor Statistics. Retrieved August 31, 2008, from http://ftp.bls.gov/pub/special.requests/cpi/cpiai.txt.

van der Werf, M. (2002). The death of a small college. *Chronicle of Higher Education*. Retrieved September 17, 2008, from http://chronicle.com/weekly/v48/i36/36a03502.htm.

van der Werf, M. (2002). Marycrest International University will shut down at the end of spring semester. *Chronicle of Higher Education*. Retrieved September 16, 2008, from http://chronicle.com/weekly/v48/i18/18a03601.htm.

van der Werf, M. (2002). Mount Senario College will close. *Chronicle of Higher Education*. Retrieved September 16, 2008, from http://chronicle.com/weekly/v48/i36/36a03502.htm.

van der Werf, M. (2002). Mount Senario's final act. *Chronicle of Higher Education*. Retrieved September 16, 2008, from http://chronicle.com/weekly/v48/i40/40a02401.htm.

van der Werf, M. (2006). The end for a private college—with big assets. *Chronicle of Higher Education*. Retrieved September 29, 2006, from http://chronicle.com/weekly/v53/i06/06a03301.htm.

Weber, M. (1947). *The theory of social and economic organization*. New York: Oxford University Press.

Wikipedia. Generally accepted accounting principles (United States). Retrieved September 19, 2008, from http://en.wikipedia.org/wiki/Generally_Accepted_Accounting_Principles_%28USA%29.

Wildavsky, A. (1986). *Budgeting* (2nd rev. ed.). New Brunswick, NJ: Transaction Books.

Williams, A. V. (2001). Notre Dame College of New Hampshire will shut down. *Chronicle of Higher Education*. Retrieved September 17, 2008, from http://chronicle.com/weekly/v48/i16/16a02801.htm.

Williamson, O. E. (1975). *Markets and hierarchies*. New York: The Free Press.

Wilson, R. (2006). As credit crisis freezes colleges, worries mount. *Chronicle of Higher Education*. Retrieved August 31, 2008, from http://chronicle.com/.

Winston, G. C. (1999). Subsidies, hierarchy and peers: The awkward economics of higher education. *Journal of Economic Perspectives, 13*(1), 13–16.

Wirth, G. (Vice President and Director of Admissions, Goldey-Beacom College). (2001, October 11). Personal interview. Wilmington, Delaware.

Zemsky, R. (1990). The lattice and the ratchet. *Policy Perspectives*. The Pew Higher Education Research Program, *2*(4), 1–8.

Zemsky, R., Wenger, G. R., & Massey, W. F. (2006). *Remaking the American university*. Piscataway, NJ: Rutgers University Press.

INDEX

B

Cowan, Ruth
  presidential leadership, 199–200
  suggestions for presidents of small colleges, 204
Credit crisis of 2008. *See* Stock market fluctuations
Crouch, Dr. Bill
  Georgetown College's successful turnaround and, 246–248
  leadership characteristics, 246, 248, 262–263
Crouch, George
  monitoring of strategic goals, 185

D

Debt
  basic rule for, 104–105
  capital budgets and, 92–93
  cash hoards and, 30–31
  covenants imposed by lenders for capital projects, 60, 92–93
  effects of stock market declines on, 3
  financial distress and, 283
  financial health and, 30–31
  future problems and opportunities and, 320
  liabilities to assets ratio by size of institution, 2002 and 2007, *31*
  lists of outstanding debt, 290
  management of, 104–105, 108
  multinational business model and, 141
  payback plan for, 108
Deficits. *See* Net income and deficits
Dehne, George
  market-driven strategic planning, 170
Demographics
  component of market analysis, 292
  definition, 11
  high school graduates, 11–14
  high school graduates, enrollments in college, and participation rates,
      2000–2006, *14*
  market-driven strategic planning and, 171, 310
  minority students, 13
  percentage change in public high school graduates by region for
      selected years 2004–2005 through 2017–2018, *11*
  pressure on independent institutions from, 301
Development. *See* Gifts

F

I

O

P

Z